The Good Place
and Philosophy

Popular Culture and Philosophy®   Series Editor: George A. Reisch

For full details of all Popular Culture and Philosophy® books, visit www.opencourtbooks.com.

Popular Culture and Philosophy®

The Good Place and Philosophy

Get an Afterlife

Edited by

STEVEN A. BENKO AND
ANDREW PAVELICH

OPEN COURT
Chicago

Volume 130 in the series, Popular Culture and Philosophy®, edited by George A. Reisch

To find out more about Open Court books, visit our website at www.opencourtbooks.com.

Open Court Publishing Company is a division of Carus Publishing Company, dba Cricket Media.

Copyright © 2020 by Carus Publishing Company, dba Cricket Media

First printing 2020

All rights reserved. No part of this publication may be reproduced, stored in a retrieval system, or transmitted, in any form or by any means, electronic, mechanical, photocopying, recording, or otherwise, without the prior written permission of the publisher, Open Court Publishing Company, 70 East Lake Street, Suite 800, Chicago, Illinois 60601.

Printed and bound in the United States of America.

The Good Place and Philosophy: Get an Afterlife

ISBN: 978-0-8126-9476-5

Library of Congress Control Number: 2019942021

This book is also available as an e-book (ISBN 978-0-8126-9480-2).

For Lisa
and
For Michael

Contents

Welcome. Everything Is Great!

STEVEN A. BENKO AND ANDREW PAVELICH

The Good Place is a hilarious show about what it means to be a good person. It begins with thirty-something Eleanor Shellstrop waking up in a nondescript office where she meets Michael, who tells her that she is dead and is in the Good Place.

Michael is an 'architect': he designed the neighborhood where Eleanor will spend eternity. Filled with frozen yogurt shops and restaurants (one of which is called 'The Good Plates') all of Eleanor's needs will be met (we know this to be true because there is a store called 'Your Anticipated Needs').

Assisting Michael, Eleanor, and the rest of the residents of Neighborhood 12358W, is Janet. Janet is best described by what she is not: she is not a woman and not a robot. She is Siri or Alexa come to life. Janet possesses all the knowledge in the universe and can manifest any object Michael or the residents request from her.

Eleanor's dilemma, evident from the beginning of the show, is that she does not belong in the Good Place. She is, in her own words, a trash bag from Arizona. But she's not the only misfit. There is Chidi Anagonye, the surprisingly jacked philosophy professor. In "The Good Place," residents are paired with their soul mates. While Chidi is paired with Eleanor, her neighbor, British socialite, philanthropist, and serial name-dropper Tahani Al-Jamil is paired with a Buddhist monk, Jianyu Li, who frustrates his soul mate with his vow of silence.

In many ways the show harkens back to other comedies about class, education, and mistaken identity. *The Good Place* is *Pygmalion* or *My Fair Lady* if they were set in the afterlife. But all of this is just where the show begins. What makes *The Good Place* such a joy to watch is that the show constantly reinvents itself and goes in directions the audience doesn't see coming.

It's a great show. But what many people might not truly understand is how great it was to see if you were a philosophy student, or even more, a philosophy professor. You know the way you feel when you see a picture of two otters holding hands? That's how philosophers and cultural theorists felt when they first saw *The Good Place*. Here was a network TV show where one of the main characters was a professor of ethics and moral philosophy (focusing on deontology, no less!). While the golden age of television has seen a great expansion of representation—there have been characters from diverse genders, races, ethnicities, and sexual orientations—there is one group that has remained under represented: philosophy professors. But with *The Good Place*, we finally had a seat at the television table.

Doctors, lawyers, police officers, spies, and gangsters all have had their share of television representation, while our people were left out in the cold. This may seem natural: how interesting does a college professor's life seem? At some point in their life, everyone has seen a doctor or nurse, and we know that they encounter the extremes of the human condition. Lawyers too are in the thick of human drama. However, there are more college professors in the United States (1.6 million) than there are lawyers (1.3 million). Chances are good that you do know at least one college professor: 62 percent of US citizens have attended college and 40 percent have a college degree. You might even remember us: we were the weird people in the front of the room. Sometimes we wrote stuff on the board.

And if you're a professor of moral philosophy, there's a good chance that no one likes you.[1] So, while every other occupation has gotten a chance to be on TV (really, now, there have been multiple shows about serial killers, bus drivers, comedians, vampire slayers, elementary and high school teachers, and more than one about space cowboys) there have only been a few college professors represented. Ross Geller, Ted Mosby, and Jed Bartlette come to mind, but (a) they are not philosophy professors, and (b) they're not really shown doing the work of professoring. It turns out that most of television's college professor characters set have been scientists (does Bruce Banner count?),

---

[1] Fun fact: one of the editors of this book is a professor of moral philosophy. No one likes him.

probably because "science" sounds most college-y to TV producers. And so our people watched the shows, and told ourselves that we were lucky to see college on television at all, and we slowly gave up hope of seeing real philosophy on the small screen.

Our excitement about a show featuring a philosophy professor actually philosophizing was tempered by several concerns: would he be played for the fool? Would he be so philosophical that he would come across as obtuse? It would be so easy for a philosophy professor to be the punchline. Ever since Socrates, our people have been ridiculed for having our heads in the clouds ("The Clouds" was actually the name of a play that ridiculed Socrates during his lifetime).

Would they get the philosophy right? How would the writers address the inevitable conflict between character, plot, and philosophy? And probably most concerning: would the philosophy be so bland as to be pointless? What we weren't quite allowing ourselves to even hope for was that philosophy—real, actual philosophy—would be right there on the show. Not played for a joke, but taken seriously both by the show and the characters on the show.

We bring up the point about college professors not out of a sense of personal pride, and not just because William Jackson Harper, the actor who plays Chidi, has done a fantastic job capturing the passion and curiosity—as well as the insecurities and neuroses—that define the academic life. We bring it up to note something really special about *The Good Place,* and why we were excited to extend the philosophical conversations depicted in the show with this book.

The Good Place is a show about experts and expertise at a time when contemporary American culture is not exactly expert-friendly. Those of us with expertise in the humanities are used to hearing that our professions are in decline, that our years of study were useless, that analysis leads to paralysis, that we should climb out of our ivory towers, and that what expertise we have is too narrow and does not have practical applications.

But on *The Good Place*, philosophy really matters. Each show was a mini–ethics lesson that never became pedantic or trite. Chidi's ethics lessons were sophisticated and practical. He made connections between theoretical behavior and lived experiences. Most satisfying, the audience watched Eleanor come to a deeper understanding of herself, her motivations, and her behavior. Romantic entanglements, family, jobs, pressing social issues: all of them were played for jokes on *The*

Good Place. However, one constant throughout the show was Chidi's unwavering belief in the worth and usefulness of his knowledge.

Sure, he was teased: Eleanor called him 'Cheeto' and 'sweater vest'. He got picked on for his neurotic behaviors (but who among us doesn't have a favorite bookmark?). And, yes, he was called 'basic' (an insult that leaves its target devastated). But Chidi's knowledge of ethics grounded the show. Philosophy became the place that the characters returned to again and again to make sense of their predicaments and solve their problems. Philosophy became the vocabulary they spoke to make sense of themselves, each other, and the world around them.

The Good Place, along with the Popular Culture and Philosophy series itself, takes the intersection of philosophy and culture seriously. They both recognize the continued importance of philosophy for illuminating the contours of contemporary life. The show and the book series recognize that mass media continues to be a place where important philosophical ideas are explored. A book about this show is a natural. But this one is somewhat unlike other books in the series, because other books have to tease out the philosophy. Jerry Seinfeld never talked about moral philosophy. Deadpool, the merc with a mouth, may be immortal, but he spends more time thinking about the nature of chimichangas than the nature of reality.

So, the writers and editors of this volume had their work cut out for them: we had to bring something philosophically interesting to the table to talk about a show that has already done a great job of bringing philosophy to a wide audience. And while we're used to philosophy being a serious enterprise, we had to maintain Michael Schur's, the actor's and the writer's enthusiasm for philosophy. It is clear that the writers and actors are enthusiastic about ideas.

Animated by something that they thought was interesting and fun, the writers for this volume brought that same enthusiasm to this project. For the contributors to this volume, writing about philosophy and sharing their knowledge with a larger audience is their good place. Writing about a show that takes that knowledge seriously and brings it to a broader audience, well, that's even better. Still, the writers need to finish that rap about Kierkegaard.

Spoiler alert! This book assumes some familiarity with the show and the plot twists and surprises that have made it so much fun to watch. If you haven't seen the show before picking up this book, the book is going to spoil many of the show's biggest reveals. You have been warned!

Writing about this show presented us with a terminological challenge, since the name of the show, the name of the place the characters think they're in, and the name of the place they want to be in are all the same. Here's how we handle all that: *The Good Place* (in italics) refers to the show itself. "The Good Place" (capitalized, in quotation marks) refers to the place that the characters inhabit in Season One (also sometimes called the Fake Good Place, or Neighborhood 12358W). The Good Place (capitalized, but not in quotes) refers to the place that they think they're in in Season One, and that they're trying to get into in Seasons Two and Three.

So, the following sentence makes perfect sense and is true: "The Good Place" on *The Good Place* is not The Good Place.

Thanks

Nothing comes into being by itself, and so the editors would like to take the time to thank the publishers at Open Court for this opportunity, the contributors for their enthusiasm and efforts, and our colleagues, friends, and families who probably heard more about *The Good Place* than they wanted to.

Steven would like to thank the people who nurtured his enthusiasm for this show and his research. First, my family who jumped on this train (that is not a trolley) with me. To me, you're all Maximum Derek. A special debt is owed to Shannon Grimes for supporting the modification of my ethics course to follow the show (even though Season Two had not yet finished airing) and to the students in Religious Ethics and Social Issues: your enthusiasm for learning ethics from a TV show was motivating. Finally, thanks to all the friends who were early sounding boards for these ideas.

Andrew would like to thank his former student Anthony Gonzales, who told our Philosophy of Religion class that we should check out *The Good Place*, which had just finished its first season. Anthony did a great job of selling the show, including letting us know that it had a surprise twist ending to Season One, without giving away the details (though giving away that there was a twist ending at all was a sort of spoiler). Without Anthony's nudge, half of this book might never have happened.

Finally, the editors would like to thank each other. When you're paired with a stranger and told that you're going to work on a book about *The Good Place* . . . well . . . you get suspicious. So while this project could have been our own Bad Place masquerading as the Good Place, we are happy to report that it was filled with laughter, good feelings, and enthusiasm. This book was a real pleasure to put together.

I

The Demons in the Details

1
The Good, the Bad, and the Bureaucratic

JOSEPH WESTFALL

The basic conceit of *The Good Place*—from the very first scene of the very first episode—is that a sophisticated point-based system determines the merits and demerits of our actions while alive.

The point total, thought to be infallible, determines where each person spends eternity. Essential to this conceit is that the point system is not administered by any personal consciousness—in other words, the points accrue of their own accord, and the functionaries we see who administer the Good and Bad Places (most notably, demon-architect Michael) merely consult the tallies. Despite their various efforts at freedom, this structure remains a serious problem for the protagonists of the show, who must suffer without question the bureaucratization of morality and the afterlife.

The question of bureaucracy, and the related questions of power and freedom, are at the heart of the show's development over its first three seasons. Following on some of the insights of the philosopher Hannah Arendt, we can see that freedom is impossible in a bureaucracy. In a bureaucratic system of the sort that administers both the Good and the Bad Places, no one is genuinely free to do anything, since all action within the bureaucracy is pointless: when you play by bureaucracy's rules, the bureaucracy always wins. In the face of such immoral disempowerment Arendt notes that the only recourse good people have is violence against the system. By the end of Season Two, this is something that at least one of the characters understands, and it shapes the plot of the series throughout Season Three.

Did You Ever Reheat Fish in an Office Microwave?

In the first episode of Season One, *The Good Place* establishes the existence of a strictly mathematical and unfailing meritocratic system for evaluating a human being's actions over the course of his or her life, thereby determining that individual's destination in the afterlife upon the event of their physical death. As Michael notes in the orientation he provides to Eleanor and the other recently deceased in "Everything Is Fine":

> You were all, simply put, good people. But, how do we know that you were good? How are we sure? During your time on Earth, every one of your actions had a positive or a negative value, depending on how much good or bad that action put into the universe. Every sandwich you ate, every time you bought a magazine, every single thing you did had an effect that rippled out over time and, ultimately, created some amount of good or bad. You know how some people pull into the breakdown lane when there's traffic and they think to themselves, "Ah, who cares? No one's watching"? We were watching. Surprise! Ha! Anyway, when your time on Earth is ended, we calculate the total value of your life, using our perfectly accurate measuring system. Only the people with the very highest scores, the true cream of the crop, get to come here, to the Good Place. What happens to everyone else, you ask? Don't worry about it.

The screen on which Michael's orientation video is played offers tantalizing glimpses of the sorts of actions that constitute "merits" and "demerits" within the system, some serious: End Slavery: +814292.09; Commit Genocide: −433115.25. And some significantly less serious: Maintain Composure in Line at Water Park in Houston: +61.14; Use "Facebook" as a Verb: −5.55; Began to Compose Social Media Post about David Bowie Dying and Then Thought "The World Doesn't Need to Hear My Thoughts on David Bowie": +220.95.

As show creator Michael Schur has noted, the point system-model of the afterlife has its origins in a comparison to video games: it's "an omniscient system, like we're all playing a video game that we don't know that we're playing. And someone's keeping score, and the ten highest scores out of every ten thousand people get rewarded with their initials in the thing. That was the idea" (Adams interview). That the system is "omniscient" means, in this context, that it is impossible to appeal the ultimate determination of your eternal fate: as everything you've ever done is included in the calculation, without exception, and the same calculation is performed with regard to every human being in precisely the same way, "there's no questioning the system." This leaves the recently departed with no options for improving their final scores, despite the fact that, until they have died, they really have no idea what game they're playing. Thus, we have an omniscient point system which evaluates the relative moral worth of each action performed by every human being without ever telling the human beings under evaluation what it is they should be trying to do (or not to do).

We learn more about the nature of the system later in Season One, when Eleanor reveals to Michael (and everyone else in "the Good Place") that her admittance has been a mistake. As Janet cannot retrieve Eleanor's file, Michael opts to conduct a "pen and paper" evaluation of the moral worth of Eleanor's human life:

MICHAEL: Since Janet can't retrieve your file, I need to find another way to determine what kind of a person you were. This is a quick litmus test. Handful of questions designed to tell whether you were fundamentally good or bad. Question number one: Did you ever commit a serious crime, such as murder, sexual harassment, arson, or otherwise?

ELEANOR: No.

MICHAEL: Did you ever have a vanity license plate, like "Mama's BMW," "Lexus for Liz," or "Boob Guy"?

ELEANOR: No.

MICHAEL: Did you ever reheat fish in an office microwave?

ELEANOR: Ew, no.

MICHAEL: Have you ever paid money to hear music performed by California funk rock band The Red Hot Chili Peppers?

ELEANOR: No.

MICHAEL: Did you ever take off your shoes and socks on a commercial airline?

ELEANOR: And socks? Ew, who would do that?

MICHAEL: People who go to the Bad Place, Eleanor, that's the point. And unless I can figure out a compelling reason to keep you here, you will spend eternity with murderers, and arsonists, and people who take off their shoes and socks on commercial airlines. ("Most Improved Player")

Whether we look over Michael's high-tech orientation, or the series of questions Michael asks Eleanor directly, the system is fundamentally the same: each person's fate in the afterlife is determined automatically by a point system established once and for all, which cannot be escaped, evaded, or even questioned. There is a single, universal rubric for determining a person's moral worth, a rubric which makes no exceptions and admits no mitigating factors, and as such, does not actually require a conscious evaluator to make the determination: the system runs itself.

Viewers of *The Good Place* know that the "big reveal" at the end of Season One is that Eleanor, Chidi, Tahani, and Jason have not been in the Good Place after all, but in a subsection of the Bad Place constructed (by Michael) to seem to them to be the Good Place—a new mode of torture Michael has envisioned that prefers psychological torment and anxiety to more traditional methods like twisting, penis-flattening, or IHOP. But this fact does not seem to throw into question at all the evaluation system Michael describes in the orientation; throughout Seasons Two and Three, it seems that Michael Schur's omniscient "video game" system for evaluating the moral worth of human lives persists as the fundamental reality of the afterlife as depicted in the show.

Although we do learn of marginal cases (like Mindy St. Claire) and a very limited right of appeal (as indicated by the very existence of Gen, the Judge), these apparent exceptions to the universality and automaticity of the point system really serve only to emphasize even more strongly the significance of that system and the presumption of its omniscience. Despite the fact that she's a judge, Gen's power to adjudicate matters of the afterlife seems ultimately to be extremely narrowly focused: she can review the actions an individual has performed to see if their total score should be adjusted, but this is just the reimplementation of the same automatic decision-making process that was used in the first place.

He's Not God, He's a Bureaucrat

From the very first moments of *The Good Place*, we know that even if the afterlife is governed by an unquestionable automatic mathematical point system, it is not without its functionaries. Early on we meet Michael, who presents himself initially as an Architect overseeing the operations of a neighborhood in the Good Place, but whose real identity as a torturer in the employ of the Bad Place is revealed at the end of Season One.

Also near the end of Season One, we meet Shawn, Michael's supervisor (in both the fake "Good Place" and in the real Bad Place); numerous other immortal torturers who work in the Bad Place; and we meet Gen, who serves as an impartial arbiter of the afterlife point system itself. None of these characters is responsible for the creation of the point system, and none of them can undermine it altogether (even if there appear to be occasional opportunities to submit individual cases for reconsideration or review). Thus, although Vicky, Trevor, Chet, and Michael all report to Shawn, Shawn does not have the power to alter the system itself: he is as beholden to it as those he supervises are (and, in a certain sense, as powerless and subjected to the system as Eleanor, Chidi, Tahani, and Jason are).

As Michael Schur notes, "That's a thing Ted [Danson] locked into really early on. He's not God. He's a bureaucrat" (Egner interview). Being nothing more than a bureaucrat, Michael may appear as the face of the system to which Eleanor is subject; he may have designed "the Good Place" as a novel and innovative means of torturing condemned souls, and he may attempt to intercede at times on behalf of his victims/friends, but he is not in charge. Quite the contrary, as we learn from his interactions with both Shawn and Gen, he may have opinions of his own but he has very little real power. For her part, Gen can make rulings that reassign individuals from the Good Place to the Bad Place and vice versa, or in the extremely rare case, she can send one to an individualized Medium Place, but that's the extent of her power. The system is in charge, and yet no one operates the system.

This is, in its essence, the sort of power structure that the philosopher Hannah Arendt called "bureaucracy." What every bureaucracy has in common, for Arendt, is the fact that decisions are not made by those in positions of power nor by those directly affected by the decisions. Rather, bureaucracies are all characterized by the absence of centralized decision-making authority in favor of a series of interconnected (or networked) "bureaus"—offices or departments charged with efficiently and impersonally making one or more sorts of minor (often factual) determinations which, when aggregated, result in some semblance of social order. Think of the IRS, the postal service, or the customer service department of just about any American health insurance company. No one is empowered to make decisions on their own authority; no one in a bureaucracy possesses real authority at all.

As such, the individual who finds himself or herself subject to a bureaucratic process is confronted with a simple choice:

accept the determination the bureaucratic system initially spits out, or engage in a lengthy and typically meaningless series of interactions with parties who lack the authority—and often the will—to see you as anything but one more processed unit of data in a system designed to perceive everything and everyone as processed or processable units of data. The automated computer customer service system for my cable company doesn't care if I've been overbilled, and even if it did care, there's nothing it could do about it. As Arendt writes:

> . . . bureaucracy, or the rule by an intricate system of bureaux in which no men, neither one nor the best, neither the few nor the many, can be held responsible . . . could be properly called the rule by Nobody. Indeed, if we identify tyranny as the government that is not held to give account of itself, rule by Nobody is clearly the most tyrannical of all, since there is no one left who could even be asked to answer for what is being done. ("Reflections on Violence")

"Rule by Nobody," then, is in a way even more terrifying than traditional tyranny, wherein only one person legitimates, authorizes, and orders the enforcement of the laws which everyone else is required to follow—because at least *one* person is involved in the determinations of legitimacy, authority, and enforcement.

When we're confronted with the unthinking absoluteness of an impersonal bureaucratic system, however, we have no recourse to negotiation. At the end of Season Two, when she's given a second chance at her old life and Eleanor begins to see what's wrong with the exploitative telemarketing bureaucracy where she's employed, it is never the case that she could choose to change her workplace for the better: she can go along with the exploitation, or she can quit. (She quits.) And this is true always of bureaucracies, for Arendt: you can only ever choose to obey—or to resist.

According to Arendt, this is the opposition of power and violence: "Power and violence are opposites; where the one rules absolutely, the other is absent" ("Reflections on Violence"). Bureaucracies, in their intractable efficiency and singleness of purpose, deprive everyone subject to them (and everyone in service of them, including all the various functionaries and officials bureaucracy inevitably requires) of the power to act freely, to make choices that shape their own destinies, or to engage meaningfully in deliberate reform. No matter how many times you press zero to speak with an operator, no matter how convincingly you argue with the airport gate attendant, no matter how many forms you file to initiate another round of review—there's nothing you can do to change the way the system operates, and almost nothing you can do to alter outcomes. It's enough to give a person *ideas*.

> . . . the greater the bureaucratization of public life, the greater will be the attraction of violence. In a fully developed bureaucracy there is nobody left with whom one could argue, to whom one could present grievances, on whom the pressures of power could be exerted. Bureaucracy is the form of government in which everybody is deprived of political freedom, of the power to act; for the rule by Nobody is not no-rule, and where all are equally powerless we have a tyranny without a tyrant.

Bureaucracies systematically deprive everyone of power—even those initially "in charge" of the system lose what power they might have had over it, and can fall victim to it—and, as a direct result of that deprivation, bureaucracies inevitably inspire violence.

That's Not Supposed to Be Possible

No one denies that, according to the calculations made to determine her final score—and thus her quantitative moral worth—upon her death, Eleanor deserves to be sent to the Bad Place. First among his peers, however, Chidi comes to realize that there is, perhaps, something morally wrong not just with Eleanor, but with the point system itself. At great risk to himself, since he still believes he is in the Good Place, Chidi defends Eleanor's moral worth *after* death.

> CHIDI: Michael, I murdered Janet. I knew about Eleanor from the beginning. I've been trying to help her become a better person, and when she found out that your retirement meant that you would be tortured, she immediately tried to find a way to prevent it. Eleanor is learning. She's just doing it after she died.
>
> MICHAEL: I did enjoy her company. But, this is not Little League. There is no award for "Most Improved Player," Chidi.
>
> CHIDI: Well, maybe there should be. ("Most Improved Player")

This is the first time in the series when anyone suggests that there may be a problem with the whole system for evaluating moral worth and thus in the determinations made about who is sent to the Good Place and who to the Bad. So long as an individual remains free to make choices, to act, and to learn from her choices and actions—whether she learns this in life or in death—that individual remains capable of moral development and self-reform: she can become a better person even in Hell. And, becoming better, she may reach a point where she does not really deserve to be in Hell anymore.

The point is ultimately an important one, and it plants a seed in the viewer's mind (and in Michael's) that there is a potential problem here that might need at some point to be addressed. It will take *The Good Place* the entire second season to reach the point where the question is raised again, when Michael defends his human friends before Judge Gen:

> MICHAEL: The premise of our system is that a person's score during her time on Earth is final and inarguable. But, because of my accidental experiment, these four humans got better after they died. That's not supposed to be possible. Over and over again, I watched as they became thoughtful and generous and caring. And think about where they started . . .
>
> GEN: So, they got better in your little pretend world. That doesn't prove anything about what they were like on Earth.
>
> MICHAEL: No, see, I think it does prove something. If I'm right, the system by which we judge humans, the very method we use to deem them good or bad, is so fundamentally flawed and unreasonable that hundreds of millions of people have been wrongly condemned to an eternity of torture. ("The Burrito")

In this moment, Michael is not simply arguing in defense of Eleanor, Chidi, Tahani, and Jason. The strange case of these four humans proves, to Michael, that human souls are capable of growth after death—and, thus, that instead of eternal punishment what at least some of the condemned deserve is something like Chidi offers Eleanor and the Gang: lessons in ethics, by way of which they could become better. Such growth has even been shown to be possible for immortal beings like Michael, who also becomes better than he was before, learning to value human lives, and sacrificing himself for others. Michael makes a revolutionary plea: the whole system is corrupt. And the chief implication of his plea seems to be that the system thereby needs to be overthrown.

This is precisely the sort of violence Arendt argues is the only option left to those confronting absolute bureaucracy, but it also quite dramatically demonstrates Arendt's assertion of the powerlessness of individuals in the face of such bureaucracies. Eleanor, Chidi, Tahani, and Jason cannot change the system in ways that alter the outcome for themselves or others. Nor can Michael or Janet, despite their near-omnipotence. No one can fight the system. Even Gen, the most powerful character depicted in the show to this point, seems incapable even of challenging or questioning the system: her response to Michael's plea is to suggest creating four individualized and isolated Medium Places for the four humans, a way of pressing the pause button on their eternal damnation until she can conduct and finish her "recount" of the actions that constituted their lives. But a recount does not undermine or even challenge the system by which the counting is conducted in the first place; her response is to suggest that there may have been idiosyncratic or anomalous mathematical errors in these four cases, but not, as Michael suggests, that the way in which they have determined the ultimate fates of every human being who has ever lived may be fundamentally flawed.

And, as rewarding as it is for us to see new possibilities emerge for these characters, Gen's acquiescence to Michael's unprecedented suggestion that the four humans in question be returned to life so as to have the opportunity to make different choices and change their final scores is the opposite of revolutionary violence. Gen has simply plugged Eleanor and the gang back into the very same system that resulted in the injustice— or the perceived injustice—they (*and all human beings!*) suffered at the hands of the bureaucracy itself. Michael and Janet follow the newly extended lives of their human friends on a set of stock tickers, tape machines that at least in their earthly variants only report plusses and minuses, rises and falls, increases and decreases in the quantitative assessments of value. The way we talk about how a given stock has done well or poorly is precisely in these terms: it's "up three points," or "down a point-and-a-half." And if this is the way in which the ongoing fates of Eleanor, Chidi, Tahani, and Jason are being tracked, then the system has not been successfully challenged, or even questioned. Gen has merely agreed to accumulate more numbers, not to fight the number-based system for determining moral worth.

Even Gen, with all her power, is just another functionary in service to the system. She's not God; she's a bureaucrat. Which leaves the possibility of genuine revolutionary violence against the tyrannical bureaucracy governing morality and the afterlife in Michael's and Janet's hands. Despite Gen's injunctions that the humans must accumulate points fairly and without help from their immortal friends, in Season Three Michael persists in his prodding and cajoling interference. This interference constitutes an explicit undermining of the system (and disobedience of Gen) that *does* seem to have the potential at least to *challenge* the bureaucracy, if not revolt against it altogether.

While *The Good Place* is a show about ethics and human connection, it is also a show about the unquestionable authority of bureaucracy in the governance of human actions. So long as the system goes unchallenged, there can be no change: as Arendt so clearly explains, the first and essential consequence of any bureaucratic system is the disempowerment of all those subject to and in service of that bureaucratic system.

Powerless in the face of bureaucracy, we're left only to suffer absolute determination by the system—or to fight it, however one can. Hopelessly, futilely—impossibly, perhaps—but like Eleanor, Michael, and the rest, freely, too.

2
How Can Torture Be This Funny?

ANDREW PAVELICH

The Good Place is a very strange show. It's about a group of four dead humans who believe that they're in Heaven, but are actually in Hell, and are being tormented by the entity they think is their patron.

Eventually, they discover the deception, and the demon-tormentor has a change of heart and decides to try to help the dead humans escape from Hell. That's just the basic description, and it's already weird. We all love the show, but just imagine that you heard this description without knowing it was a Mike Schur show. You would probably think that it's some kind of experimental, dark, prestige drama. But *The Good Place* is a situation comedy.

Think about that for a moment. *The Good Place* is a comedy where the situation is that some humans think they're in Heaven. We're meant to laugh at their foibles and flaws, and even when we find out that they are in Hell (because they were, in fact, deeply flawed people) we're still supposed to like them and laugh with and at them. All of the positive feelings we had for them and their patron are supposed to remain in place even as their moral character shifts and reverses before us. This show is forkin' weird. How exactly does it pull off being this funny?

First, let's consider the possibility that the first season is funny just because we didn't actually know that the humans are in Hell and being intentionally tortured by Michael. It's true that the first season is played as a kind of comedy of errors, with poor put-upon Michael having to deal the insanity caused by the humans. There's a long history of television comedies working this way, from *Green Acres* to *The Office*—

one straight character trying to deal with the wackiness of some screwball characters.

This seems to be the formula of Season One, but it really isn't. And Season One is still funny on second, third, and fourth viewing, when we know what's really happening. The humor comes from something a little more fundamental.

Philosophy and Comedy

Most philosophers I know are very funny people, but for some reason, when philosophers talk about humor, they seem to get really boring. According to Ludwig Wittgenstein, you could write an entire book of philosophy using only jokes, but he never actually wrote such a book, and as far as I know he never put a single joke into one of the books that he did write.

Nevertheless, there are a lot of philosophers who talk about why something is funny. The general consensus is that comedy comes from a clash between what we expect and what we get—technically described as an incongruity of expectations. We hear a horse riding up in the distance, and then see some weirdo clapping coconuts together. Or, to take one of my favorite moments from *The Good Place*: at the end of Season One, when Michael has been doomed to retirement (or so we think, at least), and he retreats from his party to Eleanor's bedroom, he dejectedly says "This is the worst day of my life" as the clown doors close and circus music plays. Clown music is incongruous with the dour tone of Michael's dejection, and voilà!, it's funny.

On a large scale, this kind of incongruity is a big part of what makes *The Good Place* funny, especially after the reveal at the end of Season One. We can think of it as the *Hogan's Heroes* effect: if we can laugh at a comedy set in a prisoner of war camp, with Nazis no less, then it's entirely possible to set a comedy in Hell. The very fact that it's a comedy set in Hell is incongruous, and funny. It's also the case that the supposed tortures don't really land, and if they do, they're not as serious as the demons think they'll be (more on this later).

You can see this same fundamental incongruity from another angle. One of the great things about Season Two is that we get a pretty good look at the working of the Bad Place. I like to think that in the background of *The Good Place* there's another sitcom going on: a workplace comedy about demons going about their business of torturing terrible humans. Most of the time these tortures don't really work out, but that's fine. The comedy comes from the juxtaposition of people being tortured with the mundanity of an everyday workplace. In general, the juxtaposition of the tone of the show with the setting of the show is a masterful meta-example of this kind of comedy.

There's another ingredient that some philosophers (like Henri Bergson) think is essential to comedy: that the person we're laughing at (or whose predicament we're laughing at) somehow deserves to be embarrassed. According to this view, comedy is a form of social control—it helps us put people in their place, and ridicule them when they step out of bounds. This is why we like to make jokes about elites, or the pretentious: socially speaking, we use comedy to reinforce the idea that you shouldn't make a big deal about yourself. The recurring joke "This is why everyone hates moral philosophy professors" sort of fits this mold—it's funny because it takes moral philosophy professors down a peg, and importantly (the idea goes) they actually deserve it because they don't know any more about morality than the rest of us.

It has also been my experience that not everyone hates moral philosophy professors, and that not every moral philosophy professor goes around telling people what they should do, at least not without being asked. These two facts are probably related.

At least in the early episodes, this "moral justice" aspect of comedy applies the most to Tahani. Even though we don't know (at least the first time through) that it was intentional torture, it was still funny that this high-society woman who liked nothing more than to name-drop was coupled with the one person who could not acknowledge or participate in her pretensions. We also can see this in "Everything Is Great (Part 1)," the first episode of Season Two—there the joke is on Michael, whose plans are thwarted 802 times in succession. His repeated failure is funny in part because we (the audience) come to think that he deserves to fail.

The Trolley Problem

We can see where at least some of the humor of *The Good Place* comes from, but we still have to deal with the fact that this is humor at the expense of people suffering. Let's focus this discussion on just one episode (a real highlight of the series): "The Trolley Problem." We'll look at this episode for two obvious reasons: first, there is real suffering going on, and second, it's really funny.

As a reminder, this episode finds Michael taking "good person lessons" along with the humans. It's important to remember that at this point Michael has basically agreed to a mutually beneficial alliance with the humans. To stop Vicky from telling Shawn that his experiment has failed over 800 times, he has agreed to take ethics lessons with the humans, and they have agreed to not reveal that they know they are in the Bad Place. At this point in the show Michael has not genuinely come over to the humans' side, and he also has not acknowledged that he really cares for them. He's just in it to save his own skin. It's while Chidi is introducing the gang to Philippa Foot's famous runaway trolley thought-experiment that Michael transports them all to an apparently real runaway trolley, to put Chidi's theories to the test. Naturally, chaos ensues.

Before getting to the suffering that Chidi is put through (and that we as the audience laugh at), there's another element of suffering to look at: that of the people that the trolley runs over. There's a really quick exchange where Michael says that the people being run over by the trolley are "not real, but the pain is." This is quick, and funny, and a little dark. And it might even be darker than it seems at first.

I don't want to make a huge deal about this, but I'm not even sure that what Michael said is possible. How can there be suffering with no one to feel the suffering? It might be that there's nothing to the beings who are suffering over and above their suffering, but suffering is *just* felt, and it therefore has to be felt by someone (or something). So I think that Michael really was creating people, just so they could suffer and die. At the very least, Chidi (and the audience) are meant to think the people under the trolley, people who include Chidi's friend Henry and at least five William Shakespeares, really feel the pain (of course, Michael could have been lying about the fact that their suffering was real, but I don't think he was).

That part sounds pretty horrifying, and their deaths are equally grotesque. Parts of the trolley-killed people went down Chidi's throat. And yet it was really funny. Every single version of the Trolley Problem that Michael creates is hilarious. The same joke, each of them about a random act of decision or indecision that results in a painful death of one or more people, with splatter, keeps getting funnier every time they tell it. Eleanor and Michael both find it hilarious, and so does the audience. Either there's something wrong with the audience and comedy does encourage bad virtues (by desensitizing us to the suffering of others) or something else is going on. But let's back up from the fact that it's funny (which is predicated on our not really taking seriously that people are being run over), and think about what's actually happening in the show. It is, I think, a really good example of just how cruel Michael can be.

The fact that Chidi has to make a choice—and he really does have to make a choice—about whether one person or more will die, is what makes the Trolley Problem a problem in the first place. Either way he chooses, someone dies. If he chooses to take an assertive action, then fewer people die, but he's more directly responsible. If he chooses to do nothing he's less personally responsible, but then more people die.

(One more side note—later, when Michael says that he has solved the Trolley Problem, he is clearly wrong. The Trolley Problem isn't something that you solve—it's a dilemma because there are two choices, and both of them seem pretty bad. If the driver of the trolley could sacrifice themselves to save everyone, as Michael does when escaping the Bad Place, then it wouldn't really be a moral dilemma. The Trolley Problem is a famous problem precisely because it's not clear what a good person would do).

So, who's being tortured here, and how? In a sort-of famous article, philosopher Bernard Williams argued that the person who sets up that kind of situation is the one that is really doing wrong. Whatever choice the person in the trolley makes, they are not committing a moral wrong, since they are not responsible for being in the situation in the first place. Now, in Philippa Foot's original article, you just find yourself in the trolley— nobody put you there. But that's not Chidi's situation—Michael put Chidi in the trolley, and then just sat back and watched.

At the end of the episode, Chidi accuses Michael of torturing him by using teaching—the worst thing you could do to Chidi. This is sort of true, but it's not so much the teaching that Michael uses; it's much more fundamental. Chidi is defined by the fact that he agonizes over decisions—and in particular over moral decisions. To put him in the middle of the Trolley Problem is to make him the instrument of his own suffering, within his own milieu. Chidi wants to be free of his constant agonizing over moral issues, but not via time running out and people exploding into bloody hamburger.

In "The Trolley Problem" we get the comedy of juxtaposed expectations with the sudden shift from a classroom to the trolley. We also get the shock of blood and gore splashed in our protagonist's face—something that this show had never done before. And we get the social justification of the pedantic professor suddenly caught off-guard when his classroom teaching is taken into the real world. Funny, in other words. But also torture. Unfortunately, to take the next step in answering the question how torture can be so funny, we now have to turn our attention to actual, terrible, real-world torture.

Torture, for Real

We get the idea from more serious television and movies that real-world torture is about information gathering—ticking time bombs and all that. But we know that this is not how it works, since information gained under torture is notoriously unreliable. In the actual world torture is usually about punishment—it's about someone with power making their enemies suffer. Torture is not done to gain information, but just to make a person suffer. But it's more than that. Torture in the real world is about dehumanization. We talk about someone "breaking" under torture, and I think that it is too easy to take this word lightly. Torture really is often about breaking people. Making them broken.

Now imagine that someone was tortured like this for years. Imagine the worst person you can think of. Of course, we're all thinking about Hitler, but we really want to think about someone who's been tortured for centuries. So let's think about someone like Vlad the Impaler, or Attila the Hun, or Torquemada. People who have been dead for centuries, during which they've been tortured in the Bad Place. We can even confine our imaginations to the kinds of tortures that we're told about on the show: acid pits, pulling out fingernails, penis flattening, twisting spines, burning and biting people, etc. (the "etc." obviously includes butthole spiders). It's funny when we hear about these things (again, when they're presented as a sort of mundane work-place comedy everyday idea), but they really are tortures. The kinds of suffering described would likely kill a mortal person, but of course in the Bad Place you would just continuously suffer, and not die.

The show is very intentional about not showing actual, physical torture—it's a part of how they maintain the comic tone. This is why it was so jarring (for me, at least) when Chidi briefly showed up in Season Two with needles stuck into his face ("Janet and Michael").

I imagine that fairly quickly into an eternity of torture, the person who suffered would entirely cease to be the person that they were before they got to the Bad Place. They would sort of cease to be a person at all. They would just become a ball of suffering. They might look like Attila the Hun or Vlad the Impaler, but looking like someone and being that person are not the same—especially in the afterlife of *The Good Place*. Imagine that you travel to the Bad Place, and meet two people who have been suffering the worst possible tortures for decades. You don't know who they were, or what they did in their human lives. All you know is that they have spent lifetimes being crushed, beaten, twisted, and bitten by bees with teeth. I would venture to guess that you wouldn't be able to see any difference between the two; they would be indistinguishable. And here's the problem (at least for the torturer): if you wanted to actually torture someone for a long time, the torture couldn't be the kind that would quickly eliminate the personhood of the person you're torturing. There is just no way to torture someone in Hell in the usual ways for an indefinite amount of time. The suffering would last, but the person would not be the same.

If you want to actually torture Torquemada or Attila the Hun, or Grog (the first person to murder someone for trying to be altruistic) for centuries, you could only do it by allowing them to maintain their sense of self. This would mean not breaking them, but just making their life kind of crappy. Just enough crappiness so that they wouldn't really enjoy anything, but not so much that they break, since after that you wouldn't really be able to torture them any more.

Imagine that someone had punched Chidi in the super-market while he was having his psychotic break in "Jerimy Bearimy". It wouldn't have bothered him, since you can't actually hurt someone once they're already broken. He would still feel the pain, but it wasn't really Chidi at that point—he was literally not himself. No—the only way to torture someone for eternity is to do something very much like what Michael was trying to do to the humans in Season One. Michael's plan really was diabolical.

Michael and Eleanor as Moral Heroes

The Good Place gives us a picture of people undergoing genuine torture, but does so in a way that makes it funny. These two things actually go well together. Torture—if the goal is to make people suffer for as long as possible—must be something in the line of everyday crappiness. And everyday crappiness is funny—especially if our main characters either kind of deserve it, or quickly get over it. But if you keep up the everyday crappiness long enough—years, centuries, or millenia—it becomes genuine torture.

So here's the answer to our question: Torture on *The Good Place* is funny when we only see it in small doses (say, about twenty-two minutes at a time). It's still torture, but only torture on a kind of time scale that we can't really see. We live human lives, and we watch the show in human terms. But the characters are not living twenty-two-minute lives—they're living for centuries. If we really saw centuries of everyday crappiness, we would not be able to see it as a comedy.

The fact that we have a hard time taking a centuries-long perspective is not surprising. Lots of philosophers have thought about the afterlife, and about the possibility of living for eternity. Some think that it would be boring to live so long, and others think that we could continue to enjoy our afterlives. Personally, I agree with those philosophers (like Mikel Burley) who say that we just can't know what it would be like to live for eternity—it's just too far beyond what our minds are capable of grasping.

This is probably enough to understand how a show about torture can be funny, but it also points to something that I find really interesting about the moral center of the character of Eleanor. If we accept that the plan for the "The Good Place," as we see it in Season One (and the first episode of Season Two) is as I have described, then I would argue that Michael was among the worst of all the torturers of the Bad Place. He had devised a technique that would allow his subjects to actually suffer indefinitely, while remaining who they were. In addition, he really took the initiative to get his project going—he didn't just do what the other demons do as an everyday part of their jobs. He was committed to hurting people for centuries. And he seemed to really enjoy himself. But then he changed. He got to know the humans so well over the course of the reboots that he started to actually care about them.

Michael's change was a big deal, but Eleanor's was even more dramatic. Eleanor—and eventually the rest of the humans—forgave Michael for his previous torture and accepted him as part of the team. She actually did this twice—once in Season Two, and the second time in Season Three. Since these were basically independent timelines, it suggests that her forgiveness is rooted deep in her character. Not only that, but she forgave Michael after actually seeing the centuries of torture he subjected them to during the reboots.

Eleanor was the only human who used Janet's VR device to see the tortures, and in so doing she actually got a glimpse of the centuries-long perspective that is so hard for the rest of us. That someone with such a long history of selfishness could forgive someone whom she knew had wronged her in the most egregious way is remarkable.

So yes, this is a weird comedy about torture, and that's a hard thing to pull off, but it's also a show about people who are trying to be good, and pulling that off is even more impressive.

3
Sympathy for the Devils

Kyle Bromhall

With my apologies to Michael, the human members of The Soul Squad all deserve to go to The Bad Place.

Yes, they have shown some moral growth. Eleanor is less selfish, Chidi is less indecisive, Tahani is less self-absorbed, and Jason has shown some progress in being less impulsive. These are all improvements, and they are all better people because of it.

The problem is that moral growth isn't enough. Being a slightly better person isn't enough. Only one thing matters in *The Good Place* when it comes to being sent to The Good Place for eternal reward or The Bad Place for eternal torture: the number of points you've earned in the infallible, precise calculation of your moral nature. When you think about the consequences of that idea and what it means for the moral value of actions, you see that The Soul Squad's moral growth is not enough to earn passage to The Good Place.

Context and The Good Place's Moral Calculus

The points-based afterlife is one of the most novel and interesting aspects of *The Good Place*. Of course, we only know so much about it, but we do have enough to go on. That the points system is real is undeniable after Season Three, as members of The Bad Place and The Good Place have both talked about it, as have neutral parties such as Neil from Accounting and Judge Gen. We know from Judge Gen in the episode "The Brainy Bunch" that there is a threshold to reach The Good Place, but not what it is—only that Doug Forcett, despite devoting his entire life to maximizing his point total (as seen in "Don't Let The Good Life Pass You By"), is nowhere near it. In fact, we know that no one has reached The Good Place in 521 years.

Given what we know about the points system, we need to treat it as the definitive moral system to which we must defer all our previous judgments of good or bad. Points are awarded or deducted based on whether an action added more happiness or unhappiness to the universe over time. There is no other source of what constitutes a 'right' or a 'wrong' action.

In fact, we need to let go of the whole idea of an action itself being inherently good or bad. If points were awarded because an action was inherently good, then things like intentions and motivations wouldn't matter. Holding the door for someone would always be three points, regardless of who was holding the door, or for whom. But we know that motivations *do* matter. Eleanor's public relations blitz in the episode "What's My Motivation?" was a colossal failure because her motivations were corrupt. The same is true for Tahani. Despite all her humanitarian efforts on Earth, she is in The Bad Place because it was all done to try to upstage her sister. Unsuccessfully, at that.

This makes the points system what philosophers might call 'contextualist'. In a contextualist system, whether an action is good depends on who does it, in what way, for which reasons, and under which conditions. In other words, whether an action is good or bad depends on the context. In the show, this means that the number of points earned by the same action would depend not just on your intention, but also how well-received that action was—the amount of happiness it added to the universe.

A keen eye on the orientation video ("Everything Is Fine") provides a good example. In the list of positive and negative actions, the video states that the action "fix broken tricycle for child who loves tricycles" is worth +4.79 points, but that the action "fix broken tricycle for child who is indifferent to tricycles" is worth only +0.04 points. In both cases, your intention would likely be to make the child happy, but if she didn't really care, then you've added less good to the universe.

Or, imagine that the child hates tricycles. In that case, the action "fix broken tricycle for child who hates tricycles" might even *cost* you points, because "fix broken tricycle" is only worth good person points if it causes happiness, and fixing a tricycle for a child who hates tricycles might add unhappiness!

Regardless, it could be the same person fixing the same tricycle, but whether fixing the tricycle will count for or against you will depend on whether the child for whom you're fixing the tricycle likes tricycles, and how much.

For another example, consider when Eleanor promises to dog-sit for her friend Paula (in "What We Owe to Each Other"), but then breaks that promise to go see Rihanna in concert. If Eleanor had been a random person off the street, then Paula likely wouldn't have been as unhappy by her betrayal. If Paula didn't care about her dog's health, she wouldn't have been as unhappy about his newfound bulbous shape. If Eleanor had instead skipped out to, say, save a child from a burning building, then Paula would have probably been less scathing in her rebuke of Eleanor's choice. Or, finally, if Eleanor had *intended to go to the concert all along*, or had intended to make Paula's dog fat all along, then Paula would (rightfully) have been even more upset with Eleanor. Each of these contexts are different. Being different, they would have each had different points losses, proportionate to the amount of unhappiness that Eleanor caused. But the action itself—in this case, "breaking a promise"—is only bad *because* of the unhappiness that it generates in this context, and not due to being inherently bad.

This line of thinking is confirmed in the episode "The Book of Dougs," when Michael describes the same action performed by two Dougs at different points in history. Both Douglas Wynegar and Doug Ewing performed the action "gave twelve roses to grandmother for her birthday." But because of the different contexts in which the Dougs performed the action, they received a different number of points. Douglas Wynegar, who lived in 1534, received +145 points for this deed. A close look reveals what helped determine this value: that the gift was thoughtful (+41 points), picked by his own hand (+31 points), and also *that the gift was received well* (+31 points). Doug Ewing, living in 2009, ended up losing 4 points because although the gift was thoughtful and received well, he ordered the roses on his cell phone (−61 points) and the roses themselves were artificially grown (−46 points). The same action, performed in a different context, is worth a different number of points.

The point is that we can't just look at The Soul Squad's moral growth as an action by itself. We must look at the context in which that growth happened, and the amount of good that it created in the universe. Here's where things start to get a bit dicey for the humans.

What Is the World Like?

In *The Good Place*, moral growth has no inherent goodness. Becoming a better person can only get you to The Good Place if it affects your point total, and points are only awarded if your actions make the world a better place. This system is close to the moral system described by the late-nineteenth-century American philosopher William James. His thoughts on the context of moral action put *The Good Place*'s moral system on surer footing. James believed that human action only has a special place of significance in the universe because we can, through careful and effortful choice, change the world for the better or the worse,.

James noted that human choice would only be meaningful if the universe existed in such a way that those choices had consequences. This has some striking implications for the old debate between determinism and free will (*The Will to Believe*, pp. 117–18). If you're a determinist, you think that all your actions were determined, be it by God, the Big Bang, the laws of physics—whatever. Whatever you do is what you were always going to do, and there is no way to change anything or escape the hand of fate. In that setting, there is no real choice, and (of course) there are no consequences for our choices.

On the other side, if absolutely all our actions were entirely free, then we couldn't predict how the world would change because of our choices (*Essays in Psychology*, p. 272). If your choices were not limited in any way by how the world is, then how the world responds to you would not be limited either. There needs to be some predictability about the consequences of our actions for those actions to have moral value. Otherwise, it's all just a crapshoot and we can't be held responsible for the consequences of our actions.

But it's not just the world's responsiveness to our choices that gives our actions moral value. Our choices also have to be permanent. James thought that while the future was open-ended, and the present was malleable (or, in his words, 'plastic'), the past is set in stone. Once something happens, it happens, and can't be undone. James thinks that we all understand this at a gut level: We often know that we must act, but also that once we act, we don't get a do-over (*The Principles of Psychology*, p. 1137). A consequence of this, along with the idea that the world is responsive to our choices is that the world is shaped, at least in part, by human choice (*Pragmatism*, p. 137).

James called this view "meliorism." It states that if we really try, then we can, both individually and collectively, improve the state of the universe (*The Will to Believe*, p. 84). Yet this is not because of anything special we do—it's a by-product of the way the world is and how we engage with it.

We need to look at the kind of context in which people act, to determine whether or not actions are even capable of having moral worth. Taking a cue from Darwin, James believed that the world is constantly changing, adapting, and growing. It's not finished yet. But because it's unfinished, we can direct it to grow in some small ways (*Pragmatism*, p. 138). In fact, the universe grows so much and has so much potential that it ends up like Chidi trying to choose between two hats. Without something steering it, it tries to grow in opposite directions. In these cases, James thought that we could give the universe a nudge to grow the way we want it (*Pragmatism*, p. 138).

So, there are two conditions we must think about for actions to have moral worth: the world needs to be responsive to our actions so that the consequences of our actions are foreseeable; and our actions need to be permanent, with no do-overs. Only in that kind of system will actions have moral worth.

The Place of "The Good Place"

The problem for The Soul Squad is that the afterlife—The Bad Place, "The Good Place," and The Good Place—is not the kind of environment where actions can have moral worth.

It's true that the Powers That Be in the afterlife can interfere, in some way, with Earthly life. We know from the early episodes of Season Three that eternal beings may travel to Earth, and that their mere presence has a measurable effect on the world. It may not be divine intervention, but I don't think Jags fans care *why* they're suddenly better, just that they were.

Yet even with the presence of Michael, Janet, and Trevor, the Earth is still the same purposeless, directionless place brimming with possibilities for growth that James describes, that we experience on a day-to-day basis, and that Judge Gen got to experience in "Chidi Sees the Time-Knife." Whatever the humans did during their time on Earth could legitimately be rewarded with points, and it is appropriate to sort them into The Good Place or The Bad Place based on their end-of-life point totals. It is the right kind of context where moral growth has moral value.

The Afterlife in *The Good Place* is not like that. It's not an environment that changes in response to human choice but is indifferent towards which choice is made. Humans in "The Good Place" try their best to adapt to the world around them, but the world doesn't repay the favor, because everything is a construct meant to either deceive them or undermine them.

Michael, Judge Gen, or any of the higher beings can shape reality around the humans any way they see fit, including subjecting them to experiences that would be impossible on Earth. If things go wrong, they can wipe the humans' memories whenever they want without consequence. The humans are merely passive recipients of whatever the higher beings want them to see.

Actions only have moral value in the right context, and the right context has two features: there must be foreseeable consequences to your actions; and your actions must be permanent. Even if the humans aren't aware of it, nothing they do in "The Good Place" is consequential. They don't really know what the consequences for their behavior will be, because Michael can change the rules of the simulation at any time.

The last time I checked, having giant shrimp flying around was not a foreseeable consequence of stealing shrimp, and having garbage fall from the sky was not a foreseeable consequence of hiding garbage. This is something completely new to the humans, because the rules of "The Good Place" are not the rules of Earth. Nothing they do is permanent, either: at any point, Michael could simply snap his fingers and undo it all, making all of their hard choices meaningless.

Will No One Think of the Demons?

For the sake of argument, let's say that Michael's intuition is correct, and the post-death behavior of the humans has moral value; that is, that it's appropriate to award points for good behavior in The Bad Place. Would their moral growth be enough to send them off to The Good Place?

Again, we can only consider human action in light of the amount of good or bad the action adds to the universe. For their moral growth to be worth any points, it must therefore add good to the universe. But how much good has been added to the universe because of their moral growth? Is anyone really happier because of it?

It doesn't seem to make the humans any happier. Eleanor is glad to be rid of the little voice that warns her when she is about to do something wrong, but on Earth she quickly lapses into her old patterns of behavior because of the lack of tangible reward for doing good deeds. Chidi is less indecisive—at least in some of the reboots—and is more willing to sit with moral ambiguity. Yet he was assigned to The Bad Place because he made everyone else's lives miserable, and he still has a grating effect on the others when he starts to get his stomachaches. Tahani thinks of others and doesn't use everyone for her own ends, but her condescension, name-dropping, and cluelessness still frustrates the fork out of everyone, especially Eleanor. Jason has shown signs that he is developing some impulse control—especially in Season Three, when he cheerfully sleeps in a dumpster rather than taking advantage of a drunk Tahani, in "The Brainy Bunch"—but he still suffers from a lack of seriously considering the consequences of his actions. They're no happier, and they haven't improved the lives of those around them, so they haven't added much good to the universe, if any.

But what about the other side of the equation? Does their moral growth add any badness into the universe? Well, yes! And a considerable amount, too. The more the humans grow, the harder time that *Michael* has trying to keep the experiment on the rails. While most of his panicking in the front half of Season One is purely to keep up the deception, in Season Two he is honestly suffering. This suffering only intensifies when he is trapped on Earth in Season Three, unable to return to the afterlife for fear of immediate retirement. The more that the humans grow, the more they come together to overcome their circumstances, the more they show true warmth and friendship even though they seemed constitutionally incapable of friendship at the beginning of the series, the unhappier Michael gets.

Michael is not the only one who suffers. All the demons playing characters in "The Good Place" are indirectly affected by The Soul Squad's actions. As Michael continually reboots the neighborhood, their misery increases. We may be tempted to write off their happiness and their feelings—I mean, *they're forking demons*—but the algorithm doesn't care about the benefit of the good or the target of the bad. It only cares whether the net good or bad increases because of their behavior.

The Bad Place is special because what is considered good or bad according to its inhabitants is so different from what we would consider good or bad. For the demons, torture, the racist portions of The Nixon Tapes, epic farts, and mirrors in toilets are all good things. When the demons visit the Neighborhood in the Season One episode ". . . Someone Like Me as a Member," they disable the hangover filter because they like them.

Hangovers contribute to demon happiness, and so causing a hangover would have positive moral value.

Trevor is unrepentantly—maybe even gleefully—sexist. Even that godawful Puddle of Mudd song has positive value in The Bad Place, because things that we think are crimes against music are considered good. Making demons miserable by denying them the opportunity to torture you or by forcing them to grow morally would have the effect of adding more badness (for the demons) into The Bad Place. The Soul Squad's moral growth generates bad points for the humans because of the unhappiness that they cause for the demons.

In Season Three, we see that it's not just the demons who are affected, either. Michael's plan is the occasion for The Soul Squad's moral growth and this causes Judge Gen considerable distress. If we accept Michael's claim that actions are evaluated "over time," then the humans are responsible for Judge Gen's unhappiness, too.

This means that even if we grant that human action has moral value in "The Good Place," it would not help them much, as their moral growth has caused more unhappiness—badness—in the universe than it has goodness. Ironically, by becoming better people in "The Good Place," The Soul Squad shows that they belong in The Bad Place!

But Then Again . . .

That said, not every member of The Soul Squad belongs in The Bad Place. The context of The Bad Place does not give *human* action moral value, but they're also not the only ones who have shown moral growth. For his growth, *Michael* deserves to go to The Good Place, even if the humans don't!

Remember the three criteria for moral value to be possible in a context: there needs to be some consequences for actions; actions need to be permanent, with no do-overs; and, according to the criteria by which good actions are determined, actions need to add good into the universe.

All these conditions are met *for Michael*. There is a significant consequence for failed Architects: 'retirement', otherwise known as "the eternal shriek." As Michael describes it, it sounds very much like Hell for demons. It's also tailored specifically towards the punishments fit for an otherwise eternal being. There are real stakes for Michael's behavior. This is a point he realizes in the Season Two episode "Existential Crisis," when Michael has, well, an existential crisis. He comes to grasp what non-existence means, and that it is a very real possibility for him. As Chidi points out, it's the first step to understanding human ethics. The humans don't need to contemplate the empty indifference of the universe, because they're already dead and will not have to face the uncertainty of the afterlife. Even if they're tortured forever, they don't have to worry about oblivion! Hey, it's something.

Michael's actions are also permanent in the way that they aren't for the humans in "The Good Place" but are for the humans on Earth. Michael can't simply snap his fingers and undo any of the actions in The Bad Place outside of the Neighborhood. His decision to give Eleanor the final pin ensuring safe passage to the Judge represented a real and enduring sacrifice ("Rhonda, Diana, Jake, and Trent"). He can't just snap his fingers and undo his decision, just like how Shawn can't snap his fingers and undo Michael's treachery. Michael has shown tremendous moral growth throughout the series. He has gone from dedicating his life to maximizing human suffering to honestly trying to act fairly, justly, and to bring about the most good.

That really is the key: Michael's actions after he starts learning about ethics *do* add good to the universe. If his plan to revolutionize the algorithm, as hinted at during his arguments with The Judge, actually pan out, then he will be adding significant good to the universe through his actions and self-sacrifice. Even if it doesn't work out, he has still added good to *his* universe by helping the human members of The Soul Squad. Michael, having been trained to understand the point of ethics and the weight of acting ethically, chooses to make the leap and act selflessly in the face of possible retirement. For that, he deserves a spot in The Good Place.

But he'd be there without his human friends. Because, despite their moral growth, they belong in The Bad Place.

4
Can We Do Enough Good?

JUSTIN FETTERMAN

If I'm right, the system by which we judge humans, the very method we use to deem them good or bad, is so fundamentally flawed and unreasonable that hundreds of millions of people have been wrongly condemned to an eternity of torture.

— MICHAEL, "Somewhere Else"

When Michael learns that Doug Forcett would not reach The Good Place despite living a life full of explicitly doing good actions, he immediately assumes that demons from The Bad Place have been tampering with the points system. It's a natural conclusion. Michael is himself a demon and well aware of the lengths they'll go to in torturing humans. But it's a conclusion achieved from a long series of asking the wrong questions.

In the Beginning

The first question of *The Good Place* is whether Eleanor belongs in The Good Place. It's fairly short-lived, with the obvious conclusion that she was an Arizona dirtbag so no, she does not. It's also clear that Jason doesn't belong there and it's eventually made clear that neither do Chidi and Tahini. The Judge believes quite firmly that all four of our human protagonists belong in The Bad Place, but Michael is persuasive enough in questioning the system that he earns them a second chance at life on Earth.

This move introduces Chidi's four-part lecture, viewed online by Eleanor at the end of Season Two, which begins with the question, "Why do we choose to be good?" But he's assuming that we have any choice at all. Perhaps we each have a nature that is either good or bad, angel or demon, and that is all we'll ever be. When upset over Michael's trolley problem antics, Chidi cites the adage that a "tiger can't change his stripes."

Thinking that a bad person is born bad and will always be bad absolves us of any responsibility for improving them. Eleanor attempts to console Chidi: "This isn't your fault. You've been teaching him ethics for half an hour and he's been evil since the beginning of time" ("Existential Crisis"). Since Michael is literally a demon (or at least accepts that slightly-racist designation), it's his nature to act like a demon: to lie and to torture humans. Per Eleanor, again, in Season Three: "I can't be mad at a demon for being evil" ("Worst Possible Use of Free Will"). He simply cannot change.

If his nature is immutable, then it's pointless to try teaching Michael ethics. But it would also be pointless to try teaching Eleanor ethics, as her long history of selfish behavior would be evidence of *her* bad nature. Judge Gen puts it bluntly: "You're supposed to do good things, *because you're good*" ("Somewhere Else"). Therefore, the opposite must also be true: "If you do bad things, it's because you're bad." Chidi's question would be moot. No one *chooses* to do bad or good; they simply behave in accordance with their nature.

Philosophers, however, have argued that human nature cannot be judged as either good or bad, ethically speaking. Thomas Hobbes famously described the theoretical life of people "in the condition of mere nature" to be "solitary, poor, nasty, brutish, and short." Such a life would be governed by the need to simply survive. There would be no place for an ethical code as selfish desires would be the motivation behind each and every action.

There was, however, a way to begin stepping past those moment-to-moment concerns. Simone, Chidi's research partner and girlfriend, describes this, in Season Three, as the problem of "me versus us." Humans would have to learn "to sacrifice a little individual freedom for the benefit of a group" ("The Snowplow").

People = Good

Simone is expressing theories like that of Jean-Jacques Rousseau, who thought that humans seek the preservation of our whole species, especially our kin and offspring. Rousseau believed in the principle of universal compassion, which he described as "a disposition suitable to creatures so weak and subject to so many evils as we certainly are" (in his *Discourse on Inequality*). Since we find ourselves living in a world that constantly threatens our well-being, it is beneficial to band together, even when it means making sacrifices.

Consider the little voice in Eleanor's head that speaks up whenever she does something bad. Michael suggests it might be her conscience, and showrunner Michael Schur confirmed on *The Good Place: The Podcast* (episode 26) that he believes all humans have such a voice. We may be able to ignore or silence it (and may often do so), but the moral guidance it provides is an essential part of our nature. Rousseau believed that our compassion, hardwired into our being, causes us to feel repugnance, which is his version of the voice in our head which points us away from doing bad.

If this is correct, our natural condition is pointed towards ethical goodness. Actions that help the community are good, and actions that hurt the community or help only ourselves are bad. Chidi's initial question has become relevant again: "Why do we choose to be good?" Though perhaps the better question is better framed as: "Why do we choose to be bad?"

A Train to The Bad Place

Simone knows that we have more work to do, that we still struggle with the problem of "us versus them." The voice in our head, our compassion, is telling us to do things that benefit others, even sometimes to our own detriment, but it can be very selective about who those others are. Simone cites racism and nationalism as notable examples, but the world is not short on these issues.

Though Eleanor strives to avoid all group membership, it's a fruitless endeavor. Humans are social creatures. We need family and friends and other associates. This need began in the fight for survival (described by Hobbes), when these connections helped us find food, build shelters, and raise children. It grew as societies formed, offering emotional connections and a structure for enhanced security and comfort. Today, humans continue to seek communal physical and emotional support in the form of co-workers, research partners, and dance crews.

But we still haven't overcome our original selfish tendencies; we've simply reframed them from the original "me versus us" into the ongoing "us versus them." When Jason framed Donkey Doug's girlfriend for boogie board theft, he was doing it to save an entire sixty-person dance crew, not just himself. It was still done to serve his own ends, those ends were just designed to also benefit other people. It's unclear whether

Jason has a specific little voice in his head, but Rousseau and Schur would argue that something in him would feel regret and repugnance at having hurt Donkey Doug's feelings and relationship.

So why does he do it? Why do any of us do bad things when our compassion and conscience are telling us not to? Are those original selfish instincts just too strong to overcome?

Why Were You Like That?

Human nature began with an instinct towards selfishness, but then we evolved a positive compassion as part of communities. The mix of the two creates the "us versus them" mindset. On the one hand, we want to bond with other people, which is easiest to do with those who are similar to us. This is why Tahini thinks she and Chidi may belong together: she sees them as two intellectuals in a sea of Eleanors and Jasons. But then that smaller homogenous community comes into contact with other, dissimilar people and the clash triggers our selfish instinct. So yes, Jason is compassionate towards the members of his own dance crew, but he still lashes out at other dance crews and individuals that threaten his community.

The Good Place emphasizes the importance of these communities, especially during our formative years. All four humans on *The Good Place* have pasts that reinforced their selfishness and dulled their compassion, pushing them towards adulthoods that offered certain securities but not goodness:

- **Jason's childhood is spent at a school made of tugboats lashed together in a junkyard, where the main skill taught is how to sell magazine subscriptions. It should be no surprise that he can't think of solutions to problems beyond robbery and Molotov cocktails, even if he loves his dance crew.**

- **Little is known about Chidi's youth, except the negative reactions of schoolmates to his anxious personality. In response, Chidi seeks out a life in academic philosophy, where his overthinking and constant desire to find the "right" answer finds some reward, though he never has a satisfying romantic relationship and even his friendships are torn about by lies about boots and being best man.**

- **Tahani's parents fail to provide support for any of her natural talents, setting impossible standards and inducing numerous psychological complexes. As an adult, she surrounds herself with celebrities from whom she gains secondhand** notoriety and feelings of accomplishment, but seems to have no close friends and certainly has no close family.

● Eleanor also receives no support at home, being exposed only to the models of her irresponsible and inattentive parents, a situation which results in Eleanor's legal emancipation and ability to rely only on herself. The friends she finds as an adult are equally self-interested and hold Eleanor to very low moral and social standards.

Bundle Theory of the Self, Baby!

Can these difficult communities, which reinforced selfishness over compassion, excuse bad behavior? Michael's argument to the Judge hinges on this understanding: the bad behavior that sent the humans to the Bad Place only happened because they had such poor communities. He believes that with exposure to a better community (specifically with each other), they would have been and can still become good people.

This attitude largely resembles David Hume's bundle theory, a highlight of Chidi's syllabus. In the bundle theory, no objects (including people) have an existence outside of their properties. For example, there is no such thing as an orange beyond the combination of color, texture, flavor, and scent of an orange. Indeed, Hume says it would be impossible to even conceive of such a substance divorced from its properties.

The bundle theory can be extended to the concept of the self, as some Buddhist philosophers have done. It begins with the doctrine of non-self: the belief that there is no static and permanent self or soul. A person exists only as a collection of parts, attitudes, behaviors, and beliefs, which are changeable and influenced by their surroundings. It follows that being surrounded by people behaving badly would make you bad, but finding a new community of good people could make you good. Chidi follows this concept when suggesting Eleanor spend time with Jianyu (who Chidi still believes is a Buddhist monk).

A positive, nurturing community is not one made up of strictly good people (since this theory doesn't believe that anyone is naturally and completely good or bad). Rather, a positive community is one where individuals are trying to do the right thing and exercising their compassion, where they're seeking to better both themselves and each other, and where their constituent parts and properties support and enhance one another towards positive attitudes, motivations, and behavior.

Michael tells the Judge that the humans only need the little push towards a positive community and they can become truly good people. Indeed, the show continually returns to the concept of togetherness, creating first Team Cockroach and then the Brainy Bunch which eventually becomes the Soul Squad. For anyone who questions why Jason might belong in The Good Place, perhaps it's as simple as his understanding that everyone needs a team to succeed, from Dance Dance Resolution to the Jaguars.

Try to Do Good

So that's that, right? The group is together and even though they may have been damned for eternity by learning about the afterlife and Jeremy Bearimy, they're all together and they can still be good. Eleanor finally decides to start listening to the little voice in her head, her compassion, and she encourages the others do the same, to help others by going out and being good people. But they still haven't answered, or even really asked: What does it mean to be a good person?

Much of their help is focused on specific people from their lives, especially family like Donkey Doug and Diana Tremaine (née Donna Shellstrop). But they're still somewhat stuck in the "us versus them" mindset, helping only those who are part of their in-group. When they turn their attention outward, to seek a model of goodness for all humanity, Michael and Janet are significantly let down by the promise of Doug Forcett. In his all-consuming quest to earn points, Doug has created a miserable existence largely divorced from any community whatsoever. He leads a terrible life on Earth, and Shawn later reveals that Doug is *still* going to The Bad Place. Michael blames this on The Bad Place Crew, but he's still missing the point.

The problem lies in Doug's ultimate humanity. Rousseau spoke of community as a kind of goodness in itself, a way to protect and nurture each other. But the "us versus them" problem shows how communities can struggle to exemplify compassion towards all, because they are made of imperfect individuals. Doug is occasionally going to forget someone's name, and he may step on a snail now and then. He is, after all, only human. Can humans ever be truly good?

All Too Human

This is where Friedrich Nietzsche has our back. He acknowledges the "hereditary habits" that make us "human, all too human" (the phrase that titles his book quoted here). But like Hobbes before him, Nietzsche says that we cannot be held morally responsible for those kinds of actions. In it only once humans become truly social and form communities that we have to worry about ethics. Yes, he believes that being raised or welcomed by good people has the effect of making you good as well, but not in the way Michael has formulated it.

The contrast exists in how 'good' is defined, and by whom. In Michael's attitude, people who are good form a community that can instruct new members on how to be good. The Nietzschean attitude, however, says that community arises first, without a designation of "good" or "bad," and then defines *itself* and its customs as good. It begins to teach and enforce those customs upon others, including future generations, so that "to be moral" comes to be synonymous with "to act in accordance with custom." And, of course, they mean their own custom, not the customs of other communities.

This is the epitome of the "us versus them" conflict. Humans are taught to have compassion for those within their own community, with those who they describe as "good," but they are also taught to reject others who lie outside the community, whom they now call "bad." When the Judge's test forces Jason to play Madden football *against* the Jacksonville Jaguars, his initial struggle is that he has to switch around which team he sees as "good" and which he sees as "bad."

In this light, the various communities of *The Good Place* protagonists are less obviously destructive. They were each surrounded by a community that valued certain kinds of behaviors and defined them as "good." The humans were specifically taught ways of being that held value in their limited communities. But these attitudes and behaviors were not valued in the larger world community, from which the characters had become isolated.

- **For Eleanor, it was self-sufficiency largely secluded from all but the most basic interaction with the rest of society. This allowed her to survive the difficulties of her parents and to navigate towards gainful employment and relationships that provided the bare necessities of connection without asking her to self-sacrifice.**

- **For Jason, it was segregation from the wider public, relying only on his best friend and his dance crew as guidelines for desires and actions. Though many of their behaviors were illegal, they were valuable in maintaining their connections and necessities, like rent money.**

- For Chidi, it was restricting himself to a professional sphere that valued at least some of his personality and interests. He was able to contribute to the university's mission and had relationships that accepted his issues and limitations in small doses.

- For Tahani, it was denial of her own interests, desires, and skillsets to serve a performance of community good and celebrity. She built connections and raised funds that certainly achieved some good in the world, but at the cost of forgoing her personal dreams and having only superficial relationships.

The Soul Squad community might be able to counteract those formative issues and bring our protagonists into the wider community of humanity, but even that won't get them into The Good Place. The problem is not the number of points, but where those points come from.

Oh, *This* Is the Good Place!

The derivation of Good Place Points is presented as infallible, with billions of accountants always agreeing on the values. But how are those accountants deciding what is "good" and what is "bad?"

For demons, The Bad Place is actually great! Demons love biting and twisting people. Everything that is torture for humans is fun for demons. In fact, Trevor thinks that being in The Bad Place could be positive for Eleanor because, even though she'll be tortured, the behaviors and values she picked up from her community on Earth are similar to the customs in The Bad Place. If it were up to the demons, it might not even be called The Bad Place.

Therein lies the entire problem. It's the community of accountants who get to call their customs "good" and are able to apply that logic to all of humanity. Any human who follows those customs earns points and goes to The Good Place; any who go against those customs loses points and goes to The Bad Place. But that community is clearly biased. For some reason, "rev a motorcycle" costs a person ten times more points than "fix a broken tricycle for a child who loves tricycles" earns.

What demons call "good" is not what humans call "good." What the accountants call "good" has some basis in human ethics, but clearly has its own divergences. But they're in charge of the points, so everything they like gets to be "good":

holding doors, being vegan, never discussing your veganism unprompted. And everything they don't like gets to be "bad": sexual harassment, poisoning a river, the Red Hot Chili Peppers. They've been applying their own in-group customs, preferences, and morality on all of humanity.

It should be enough that Doug is saving every stray dog and minimizing his carbon footprint, but it isn't. It could be enough that Mindy St. Claire created an organization to help kids all over the world, advance human rights, revolutionize agriculture, and just improve every nation and every society in every possible way. But it isn't. It's quite possible that no human could ever be good enough to earn their way into The Good Place. However, Michael shouldn't be blaming The Bad Place and asking how they're getting away with tampering. He should be asking a more fundamental questions: who gets to decide what's good?

Call it The Frozen Yogurt Problem. The universally knowledgeable Janet knows it's "kind of a bummer" but if everyone in the neighborhood thinks it's good, then why isn't it good? Why doesn't humanity get to assign its own points based on its own values?

There's a New Angle I Should Consider?

Chidi's question of "why do we choose to be good?" may completely miss the mark. Instead, we must ask if we even *can* do good. Or, at least, can we do *enough* good? When put up against the customs set by the accountants and The Good Place, the answer is almost universally "no." The problem isn't about knowing why we do good, or even how to do it. Knowing all about the points can't get Doug Forcett into The Good Place because he was still too fallible. No amount of compassion and community, no Soul Squad, could ever achieve enough points to meet the customs of The Good Place.

The Good Place committee has a lot to answer for. Nietzsche argued that customs and traditions "have nothing to do with good or evil" and are only "directed at the preservation of a community." Michael's challenge of The Good Place's judgment threatens that preservation, but doesn't go far enough. Michael shouldn't be content with asserting that humans (and demons) can learn to follow the customs and be deemed "good." He needs to start questioning those foundational customs themselves.

5
One of Us Is a Manipulative Demon

Daniel P. Malloy

Michael and Eleanor's discussion of free will versus determinism ends abruptly when Michael pours iced tea on Eleanor's head. It's pretty satisfying, but doesn't really answer the question.

And it's a real question that the show has to deal with, since it seems that there was a contradiction at the core of Michael's "Good Place" from the beginning. On the one hand, Eleanor, Chidi, Tahani, and Jason must have free will in order to have earned their spots in the Bad Place. If they didn't have free will, then they had no control over their actions, and therefore can't be held responsible for them. So, they must be free beings to deserve their torture in Michael's "Good Place."

On the other hand, Michael's plan for the "Good Place" wouldn't work if he couldn't predict their actions. If the humans have free will, Michael would have no way of knowing with certainty that they will torture each other. And if our actions are predictable, then they are the result of factors Michael can control, which means they aren't free choices.

That said, Michael admits that he can't predict everything that will happen in his neighborhood. The effectiveness of Chidi's "good person" lessons, and Eleanor's resulting confession, came as surprises to Michael, which shouldn't be possible if the humans don't have free will. This seems to leave us with two possibilities. Either the humans in Michael's "Good Place" have free will, and hence can act in ways that it would be impossible for even an all-knowing being to predict, or humans don't have free will and are completely determined, but Michael doesn't know all of the factors that lead the humans to act in the ways that they do.

So which is it? Do the humans have free will or not?

Jason's Snorkel

The first possibility to consider is that maybe they have free will, but their actions are also totally predictable. This is called compatibilism. So what is compatibilism? I'll explain by looking at one incident in *The Good Place*: Jason's death ("What's My Motivation?"). Jason died when he suffocated in a safe he'd locked himself inside as part of a robbery attempt, but we wouldn't call his death a suicide. Why, even though he chose his actions? For compatibilism, the key is the difference between internal and external reasons for acting.

We act on internal reasons, or motives, when we do what we would have done, regardless of external pressures. We are acting freely as long as our motives are what push us to act. And if we act freely, then we're responsible for what we do. So, when Jason climbed into the safe with his snorkel and his whippets, he did so freely. His own ambition and ignorance were the only forces that led to that action. No one pushed Jason into the safe; Pillboi wasn't pointing a gun at him. So, Jason was responsible for getting into the safe.

What happened once he was inside is a different story. Jason didn't run out of oxygen because of any internal reason. Once he realized the problem, his desire to survive pushed him to get out of the safe. But by then it was too late. Jason's fate was as sealed as the safe he was in. His motives led him to get into the safe, but there was an external reason, or cause, that kept him in it and killed him—namely, the safe's locking mechanism and air-tight seal. He acted freely, and then died because of his choices, but he didn't choose to die—his death came from the outside. This is compatibilism: you can make free choices, but still be subject to predictability due to outside factors.

Eleanor's Confession and Chidi's Moral Quandary Grimace

If compatibilism is right, then there is no contradiction between Michael's design and the goal of the "Good Place." Humans are responsible for their actions, as long as they act on their own motives, so they can be punished for those actions. But, at the same time, Michael's torture works because the humans in *The Good Place* each have their own strong motive that makes their actions predictable. Tahani wants the recognition and appreciation her parents never gave her. Chidi wants to do the right thing so badly it paralyzes him. Jason wants whatever shiny thing happens to be in his field of vision at the time. And Eleanor wants what she thinks is best for herself, regardless of the consequences to anyone else.

But then Eleanor confesses that she's not supposed to be in the Good Place, and Michael's whole scheme goes out the window ("Eternal Shriek"). She behaved unpredictably. How do we account for that? Well, for the compatibilist it isn't terribly hard—we simply look for what motivated the unexpected action. In this case, Eleanor tells us explicitly: she confessed because she felt bad. By this point, Eleanor had changed enough to be uneasy continuing her lie. So, her internal change gave rise to this new internal reason for acting. Eleanor freely and predictably confessed. Michael could have seen it coming if he'd just paid more attention to Eleanor's progress toward becoming a good person.

But Eleanor didn't become a better person on her own, and she didn't confess without external pressure. As she says, she confessed because of the look on Chidi's face. Had Chidi not been there, or had he managed to conceal his discomfort, Eleanor would've kept right on lying. In order for Eleanor to confess, things had to be just right. She had to be on the way to becoming a good person; she had to have forged a bond with Chidi; Chidi had to be uncomfortable with their lies; and he had to have his "moral quandary" grimace on. Given all those factors are in place, there's no way Eleanor doesn't confess—but which element was decisive? For the compatibilist case, it had to be her feeling of guilt; that is, it had to be the factor internal to Eleanor that pushed her to act in order for her act to be free. But it's unclear whether that feeling can be separated from other internal factors, like her feelings about Chidi, or external factors like her role in creating the quandary and Chidi's grimace. Which means that it's unclear whether what led to Eleanor's confession was internal or external, and hence unclear whether Eleanor chose to confess or was forced to.

For compatibilism to work, we have to be able to draw a clear line between internal motives and external causes. But that often isn't possible. Eleanor makes different—usually bad—choices when Chidi's not around. And Chidi is more decisive when he's with Eleanor than when he's on his own.

What Makes Humans So Much Fun

If compatibilism is wrong, then it must be that either the humans don't have free will, and therefore don't deserve to be punished for what they did on Earth, or they do, and Michael can't predict what they are going to do at all.

The Good Place seems to favor free will. It's not just that the whole Good Place/Bad Place system only makes sense if humans have free will and can therefore deserve to be rewarded or punished for their actions. It's that no choice would matter if they weren't free. If we had no free will, then Chidi's constant deliberations about whether to help Eleanor, what kind of soup to order, whether to use almond milk on his cereal, whether to use markers and a whiteboard or pen and paper in preparing Eleanor's defense, whether to tell "real" Eleanor he loves her, whether to tell Eleanor that he loves her, wouldn't just make no sense, they'd be pointless. If he wasn't in control of his actions at all, there'd be no reason for him to worry about them. Nothing would be his responsibility if he didn't have free will to choose it.

In addition, the humans constantly surprise Michael. Given that Michael possesses cognitive capabilities that allow him to see in multiple dimensions, can process massive amounts of information in seconds, and has total recall of every aspect of the humans' lives, nothing they do should surprise him. Michael claims that he knows enough about humans, specifically these four humans, to predict how they will behave when they are forced to be around each other. And yet the fact that Michael's design failed time after time could shore up the evidence for free will even more. In 802 tries, Michael couldn't pull it off. He could get the humans to torture each other, but only for a little while. It kept falling apart, because humans are just unpredictable, because they kept making free choices.

What Does Michael Know?

But the free will explanation of Michael's failures raises a few problems of its own. The big puzzle for Michael isn't why he keeps failing. It's why he keeps failing in exactly the same way. No matter how he arranges things, no matter who he pairs the humans up with or what sorts of restaurants he populates "The Good Place" with, the humans always band together, start helping each other, and figure out that they're in the Bad Place. Two things explain why this happens in every version of "The Good Place," and both of them count against the free will theory.

The first one is that Michael's knowledge is exaggerated. He knows a lot more than the "dummies" he's torturing, but he plainly doesn't know everything. If he did, he wouldn't have had to rely on Janet to propose frozen yogurt as the perfect food for his "Good Place." He would have known that Vicky was plotting behind his back. He would have known that Jason and Janet, and later Jason and Tahani, had started romantic relationships. A being with all the information that Michael claims to have should have been able to predict all of the humans' actions and keep the "Good Place" version 1 going forever. But Michael just isn't that smart. If Season Two of the show reveals anything, it's that Michael has a lot to learn about humans. Rather than explaining Michael's inability by saying that humans have free will and therefore their actions are unpredictable, we could say that human actions are predictable but only if you know enough about the humans in question and the circumstances they're in. Michael knows plenty about the circumstances—he designed the neighborhood, after all. But he just doesn't understand humans well enough to know how they'll respond.

The other problem for the free will theory is just how predictable humans actually are. In all 802 versions of Michael's "Good Place" some things remained constant. Eleanor always sought out Chidi and asked for his help. Chidi always helped Eleanor. Eleanor always hated her house. Tahani always hated Eleanor. Jason always hated playing Jianyu. And, with one notable exception, Eleanor always figured out that they were in the Bad Place. If the humans really had free will, unpredictable behavior would be the rule, not the exception. If at any moment, any of the humans could do anything they chose to, Michael's experiments would all last about as long as the accidental butt reboot.

Bad Faith in "The Good Place"

The philosopher Jean-Paul Sartre (1905–1980) has an answer to this puzzle. The thing about being free is that it means we're also responsible. If everything is a matter of choice, then every choice is of the utmost importance. Chidi is right to be paralyzed by indecision, but if we all do that, then nothing ever gets done.

To solve this problem, according to Sartre, humans live in bad faith. Bad faith is a sort of self-deception where we trick ourselves into believing that our choices are more limited than they actually are. Often, we do this by overly identifying with the roles we play. Consider Chidi's idea of paradise: as he describes it, "doing paradise things" means sitting in a boat with a good bottle of wine and a book of French poetry. But when Eleanor sets Chidi afloat in his idea of paradise, he panics. Chidi didn't want what he said he wanted, because his paradise fantasy was a bad faith fantasy. He had, without any real desire, simply adopted other people's ideas of what paradise would be like and fooled himself into believing that that would be paradise for him as well.

Tahani is an even clearer example. Tahani lives her whole life in bad faith, doing everything not because she wants to, but because she thinks it will win her the approval and acceptance of others. What makes her life one of bad faith is the fact that Tahani won't admit to herself that that's her motive. Her true motives become clear in her final moments, a fact that Michael reveals to her with devastating effect. It's why Michael was upset that she got drunk at the opening night party instead of Eleanor—Tahani genuinely believed she was a good person, who did good things because she cared about people. She was well aware of her jealousy of her sister and need for her parents' approval, but managed to convince herself that they didn't matter. They were there, but they weren't motivating her. She was doing good, she thought, because she was good.

Eleanor, on the other hand, seems to live in good faith. She knows she's an Arizona trash bag. Although, in Eleanor's encounter with Trevor, he convinces her that she is living in bad faith by trying to be good. Eleanor is, in her words, a selfish ass. But in the "Good Place" she's been trying to become a good person, and she's been making progress. Trevor convinces her that she's just lying to herself—she really is just a selfish ass. In fact, Trevor's argument is actually encouraging bad faith. It's easy for Eleanor to be an Arizona trash bag; it excuses all of her bad choices. She's just doing what a trash bag does. But Eleanor isn't an Arizona trash bag by nature. Eleanor is only a trash bag because she chooses to be.

In order for bad faith to serve the purpose we've put it to— explaining why humans are so predictable—most people would have to be living in bad faith most of the time. Sartre doesn't have a problem with that; he thinks that's the case. But I'm not sure that makes sense. Bad faith involves a fairly complex mental state of holding two contradictory ideas at once. If Sartre's right, most of us are doing this most of the time—even Jason, who is only just barely capable of holding one idea at a time.

She Even Namedrops in Hell

This leaves us with one viable theory, and unfortunately it's the worst one for *The Good Place*: determinism. Determinism is the theory that our actions are like every other event in the universe: ruled by cause and effect. The causes of our actions are complex, but they don't include anything like "choice" or "will." Given a particular cause or set of causes, a particular effect always follows. Put Eleanor in the "Good Place," and she will always, always do what it takes to stay there. Show her an unlimited shrimp buffet and she will, inevitably, eat until she gets sick.

The evidence for this theory is largely the same as the evidence against free will: it starts with the fact that human beings are largely predictable. To give just one further example of this, consider what happens when the Judge tests Eleanor. After deliberating every possible angle, Eleanor figures out that "Chidi" isn't Chidi because he behaves incorrectly. Under no circumstances would the real Chidi Anagonye "forget about ethics for a second" ("The Burrito").

Michael's "Good Place" designs never worked because he could never predict how the humans would react in every situation. But they did work to some extent because he could predict how they'd react in most situations. Determinism tells us that the reason Michael couldn't predict their actions in all cases isn't because of free will, but because of Michael's ignorance. He simply didn't know enough to predict the humans' actions.

And it's easy to see why Michael wouldn't be able to predict everything. Human beings are complicated, and what makes us do the things we do isn't simple. For any action we take, a number of conditions have to be met to cause it.

Humans are unpredictable to the extent that they are complicated, which means that our actions rarely have simple causes. Under normal circumstances, if you put Eleanor near an open bar, she will get drunk. The opening night party in version 2 of the "Good Place," however, was not normal for Eleanor ("Everything Is Great! [Part 1]"). She felt extra pressure. She was trying to conceal the fact that she didn't belong there, giving her a reason to refrain from drinking—alcohol loosens tongues. Plus, she had her big speech to give. And she had to find Chidi. And her soul mate kept ditching her when she tried to talk to him. All of those extraordinary things led Eleanor to refrain from drinking—for a while. When she broke down and poured herself some shots, the only thing that prevented her from following her natural instincts was hearing Chidi's name.

Chidi's Choices

If all of our actions are determined by causes, why does Chidi spend so much time worrying about making the right choice?

Why do any of us, if we don't, in fact, have any choices at all? The answer is the same as the explanation of our supposed unpredictability: we're complicated creatures. There's never a simple one-to-one correspondence between a cause and an action, any more than there's a one-to-one correspondence between any cause and effect. For a cause to give rise to a particular effect, many conditions have to be exactly right. What that means is that, for any given decision, there are a number of conditions present that could push events in one direction or the other. Chidi's indecisiveness is caused by his awarensss of these complications.

Consider a single choice, one where Chidi seems somewhat decisive: his choice of a soul mate in version 2 of the "Good Place." Forced to decide whether Angelique or Pevita is his soul mate, Chidi deliberates ("Everything Is Great! [Part 1]"). He knows whom he feels most connected to. He knows how rejection will make one of them feel. He knows how he will feel about the rejected person's feelings. He can predict how he'll feel if he winds up with the wrong person—and how that person will feel. And yet, even with all of this weighing on his mind, when asked what he thinks, Chidi clearly makes a choice. How do we explain this uncharacteristic bout of decisiveness? Simple. In this case, unlike many cases for Chidi, the conditions for his opting for Angelique over Pevita simply piled up.

Chidi's indecisiveness isn't evidence against determinism. It's just evidence that human actions are determined by complex interactions of a wide variety of causes. As further evidence of this, consider Jason. Jason is never indecisive; just the opposite, Jason is impulsive. Why is he so impulsive? Because, unlike Chidi, Jason isn't aware of all the different factors pushing and pulling him all the time. Jason's awareness is pretty much limited to what's in front of him at the moment. When you're only conscious of one thing at a time, that thing tends to dictate your action.

It's Not Fair!

The most important takeaway of all this for *The Good Place* is that Michael's right about how badly flawed the whole Good Place/Bad Place system is. But he's wrong about why it's flawed. Michael thinks the system is flawed because it unfairly condemns people to the Bad Place. In fact, the system is wrong for punishing and rewarding in the way it does at all.

It may seem that if determinism is correct, then reward and punishment go out the window. But that isn't quite correct.

What is true is that if determinism is correct, then reward and punishment need to be rethought a bit. Usually, we talk of doling out rewards and punishments based on what people deserve. Good people deserve to be rewarded, and bad people deserve to be punished. That is the logic underlying the whole Good Place/Bad Place system.

But, if determinism is correct, then no one deserves anything. Deserving requires choosing, which requires free will. If there's no free will, then there's no desert. This doesn't mean that we don't reward some people and punish others, but only that rewards and punishments need to be understood as ways of encouraging or discouraging behaviors. Under determinism, we reward good actions to encourage their repetition and punish bad actions to discourage them. Rewarding and punishing isn't about what a person has done, but about what they will do.

Which brings us to the flaw in the Good Place/Bad Place system. People in the Good Place are being rewarded, eternally, for actions they didn't choose to take and have no chance to repeat. And since no living person actually knows about the Good Place, it can't even serve as an incentive to be good. Similarly, people in the Bad Place are being punished for actions they couldn't help and are not being given the chance to learn from their punishment.

II

Somewhere Else

6
A Better Bad Place

DANIEL GROSZ

Near the end of Season Two, Eleanor, Chidi, Tahani, and Jason (hereafter, "Team Cockroach") meet Gen, an impartial judge who rules on matters involving the Good Place and the Bad Place. Gen seriously considers consigning Team Cockroach to suffer in the Bad Place for all eternity. But is it ever right to consign someone to eternal suffering?

Christianity and Islam, among other religions, claim that there is a divine person whose job it is to judge human beings for the earthly lives they've led and decide whether or not to permit them to enter eternal bliss or to send them to eternal torment.

The Bad Place and Proportional Punishment

The traditional view among most adherents (both lay and scholar) of Christianity and Islam is that it is just (for God) to relegate some people to Hell, a place of eternal suffering. However, this view faces an obvious objection. When doling out punishments, doesn't a just judge make sure that your punishment fits your crimes? Justice requires only punishing people in proportion to the wrongs they have committed. But eternal suffering seems like a disproportionate punishment for the number and types of wrongs most people have committed on Earth.

The members of Team Cockroach have been selfish, indecisive, careless, and jealous (and more) on Earth. But it seems obvious that none of their faults, taken individually or collectively, are infinitely bad. And if not, justice doesn't call for an infinite amount of punishment in their afterlives. Thus, it would be unjust for Judge Gen to send Team Cockroach to suffer eternally in the Bad Place.

Infinite Beings and Infinite Punishment

That conclusion has its critics, however. There are at least a couple of ways monotheistic philosophers and theologians have sought to defend a doctrine of eternal Hell. One of the most historically significant ways rests on the idea that *sinning against (wronging) an infinite being deserves infinite punishment*. And since God is an infinite being and all sins are sins against God, any act of wrongdoing, however minor it may seem, deserves infinite punishment. We can understand this defense of Hell better by noting that it involves at least the following three claims:

1. **(INFINITE) God is an infinitely great being.**
2. **(SIN) Every sin is a sin against God.**
3. **(GREATER) The greater the type of being sinned against, the greater the punishment deserved.**

Within the monotheistic traditions, (INFINITE) and (SIN) are the least controversial. Concerning (INFINITE), the medieval philosopher-theologian Anselm (1033–1109) claims that God is a being "than which none greater can be conceived." So understood, God is a perfect being who has every great-making characteristic (such as goodness, knowledge, and power) to the maximal extent possible. So, among other things, God is infinite in power, goodness, and knowledge. Regarding (SIN), if there is a God, one way to understand sin is as a departure from the way God intended us to live. Every instance of wrongdoing, on this picture, is a kind of subversion of God's purposes for human beings. And God, as creator, rightfully has a say about how humans should live.

So (INFINITE) and (SIN) make some sense, at least within a theistic worldview. But what about (GREATER)? While not as obviously true as either of the first two claims, it has some plausibility. After all, we tend to think that while destroying a large tree may be bad in some cases, destroying, say, a dog is morally worse and deserves more punishment. Further, destroying a human being is worse than destroying a dog and deserves yet harsher punishment. The differing degree of punishment deserved for these acts is reflected in the severity of the legal punishments associated with vandalism, animal cruelty, and murder, respectively. It might be objected that we really don't think that the greatness of a being factors into the moral blameworthiness of wronging that being. For example, assaulting a president or a king should garner the same punishment as assaulting an ordinary citizen. However, this is perfectly compatible with (GREATER), which says that the greatness of the *type* of being sinned against is what affects the severity of the appropriate punishment. Kings, presidents, and ordinary citizens are all the same type of being, namely, human beings. So this objection is unsuccessful.

Let's suppose that, *if* God exists, (INFINITE), (SIN), and (GREATER) are all true. What would this imply about the justice of sending Team Cockroach to the Bad Place? One thing that's immediately noticeable is that it is not clear that God exists on the show. God, understood as a being than which none greater can be conceived, simply gets no airtime or even a mention on *The Good Place*. Now, of course, for all we know, God could well exist on the show. After all, we haven't yet caught much of a glimpse of the actual Good Place yet. Perhaps that is the only place in the afterlife of *The Good Place* where God can be experienced. But, since we can't know either way at this point, God's existence cannot be assumed in a defense of the Bad Place.

A defender of permanently sending people to the Bad Place might reply that, while there are no beings such as God against whom the members of Team Cockroach committed wrongs, there are other great beings on the show against whom they might be said to have sinned. Gen, while an impartial judge, seems fairly morally good. Michael, while obviously morally flawed, is an immortal being, along with Gen. However, neither Gen nor Michael act as if Team Cockroach has committed wrongs *against them*, even while the former shows concern that rules be followed. In addition, while it's true that Gen and Michael arguably have some "great-making" characteristics that God has (moral goodness, everlasting existence, respectively), neither is an infinitely great being. Thus, even if Team Cockroach is morally blameworthy for a variety of moral failures, the punishment deserved for such failures would be finite. Consequently, we have so far failed to see how eternal consignment to the Bad Place could be a just punishment for Team Cockroach.

Once a Sinner, Always a Sinner?

One way to defend the justice of everlasting afterlife suffering involves conceding the point that the earthly sins people commit during their lives don't merit infinite punishment.

However, so this argument goes, the people who are sent to Hell are already naturally inclined to sin, and so they continue sinning after death, meriting ever more punishment. As a result, those sent to Hell never leave and so suffer eternally. To illustrate this view, consider someone who commits a robbery and is sentenced to a few years in prison. While serving his prison sentence, the thief continues to steal and commit other crimes. As a result, his sentence is lengthened to punish him for offenses he committed in prison. We can imagine that this continues.

This view has some initial plausibility when applied to *The Good Place*, since it appears that most of Team Cockroach hasn't significantly improved their moral character during their time in the afterlife. At the end of Season Two, Gen gives each member of Team Cockroach a test to see how much progress they've made improving their moral character. Jason is sent to a room to play *Madden NFL Football 2018* against the Jacksonville Jaguars (his favorite team) using their rivals, the Tennessee Titans. But he ultimately proves to be too engrossed in the game and, thus, still seriously lacking in impulse-control.

In order to test her ability to not care what people think of her, Tahani is forced to walk down a hallway and bypass every room, in which people from her life are discussing her and voicing their honest opinions of her. While she refrains from walking in on at least some enticing conversations, she is unable to resist opening the door with her parents' names on it.

Chidi is placed in a room and asked to choose between wearing a grey or a brown hat. Like Jason and Tahani, Chidi is bested by one of his bad habits (indecisiveness), taking over an hour to choose a hat to wear. Thus, most of Team Cockroach couldn't help but continue on in their destructive habits in the hereafter. Assuming such habits are moral failures, it would make sense to punish the members of Team Cockroach indefinitely, assuming they persist in such habits.

The Traditional Bad Place

But the plausibility of the idea that those sent to Hell would continue sinning indefinitely arguably depends on what Hell is actually like. For example, if Hell is such that people can't continue sinning while there (or can, but not in a way that deserves extra punishment), then the continuing-sin model of Hell fails. The Bad Place that Team Cockroach hears of at various times is depicted as a place of brutal physical torture and intense suffering. It has such instruments of torture as lava monsters, eyeball corkscrews, bears with two mouths, volcanoes full of scorpions, butthole spiders, and bees with teeth. Further evidence from the show indicates that the denizens of the Bad Place could have their arms peeled like bananas, have their eyeballs pulled out through their nostrils, be stuffed with or made into hot-dogs, or be partially decapitated. Thus, people in the Bad Place experience intense physical suffering.

According to this picture of Hell, is it plausible that people would continue sinning? Arguably not. It is unlikely that I would continue sinning during moments of intense physical torment. If I were to get my eyeballs pulled out of my nostrils or have my arms peeled like bananas, the pain would be so intense that I wouldn't have the time or inclination to be, say, greedy, lustful, gluttonous, slothful, envious, or prideful (to mention some of the seven deadly sins). My focus would be entirely consumed with the pain I was experiencing. Therefore, it's implausible to think that the people who would enter the Bad Place, including Team Cockroach, would just keep on sinning and earning ever more punishment.

Another problem with this model of Hell is that it doesn't allow for a meaningful chance at moral reform. In states of intense suffering, it's hard to reflect on your wrongs and how you could improve morally. Thus, those in the traditional Bad Place are not given a reasonable chance to improve. Someone might object that neither Gen nor anybody else has a duty to provide an opportunity for those entering the Bad Place to improve themselves morally. After all, sometimes we on Earth perhaps rightly conclude that some criminals are beyond the possibility of reform and, consequently, we sentence some of these to death. However, even if it is true that some persons are so bad that they don't deserve a chance to improve and would likely not improve anyway, that doesn't imply that nobody deserves a shot at developing a virtuous character. In fact, we seem to tacitly accept the idea that in general people should be given a chance to reform, since most prison sentences (in principle, if not in practice) allow for the possibility of reflection and correction of the behavior that landed the individual in prison. So, it doesn't seem like it would be just for anyone, including Gen, to implement the traditional version of the Bad Place.

The "Good Place"

Perhaps the "Good Place," Michael's version of the Bad Place, is a version of Hell that can make sense of the idea that people continue sinning indefinitely upon entering Hell. Michael sets up the "Good Place" in a way designed to fool Team Cockroach into thinking they are in the real Good Place. In so doing, he intends to bring intense psychological pain to the members of Team Cockroach, whom he thinks will end up torturing each other. He does this by structuring their living situations in a way that would bring maximum discomfort. Eleanor feels the pain of being around people whom she sees as morally superior. Tahani, who loves to converse, is paired with Jason, who initially feels compelled to pretend to be a silent monk. Rigid and indecisive Chidi is paired with free-wheeling Eleanor.

Thus, Michael intends for the members of Team Cockroach to function as instruments of their own suffering. As mentioned above, by the time they are tested by Gen, most of the members of Team Cockroach still have certain vicious character traits. So, perhaps it's not a stretch to think they would continue sinning in the "Good Place," resulting in more deserved punishment.

But there's a significant problem with pointing to Michael's Bad Place as an example of morally justified eternal suffering. The problem is that the "Good Place" appears incapable of actually doling out eternal punishment, at least as far as Team Cockroach is concerned. Michael designs the "Good Place" as a version of the Bad Place that depends on the members of Team Cockroach not knowing they are in the Bad Place. But Michael is forced to reboot different versions of his "Good Place" hundreds of times because someone (usually Eleanor) always figures out that they are in the Bad Place (and not always because of any moral improvement).

You might think that Michael could simply allow his "Good Place" experiment to continue to produce suffering even after Team Cockroach figures out what's going on. However, since he is a demon (and has not yet joined forces with Team Cockroach), he would presumably continue the experiment if he thought enough suffering would ensue. Thus, based on his decisions to reboot the experiment, we can conclude that he doesn't think the hundreds of versions of the "Good Place" he has tried were capable of rendering substantial eternal suffering for Team Cockroach. Therefore, it's doubtful that Team Cockroach could experience significant eternal suffering in the "Good Place," even if their sins warranted it.

The Bad Place 3.0

In considering whether it would be just for Gen to consign Team Cockroach to eternal suffering, we've so far assumed that the main purpose of Hell is retribution. That is, we've assumed that punishing someone in Hell is simply aimed at giving them what they deserve, rather than reforming their character, or deterring future bad behavior. But this way of thinking about punishment seems wrongheaded in some instances.

Suppose Jason were punished for throwing spray paint cans at flamingoes on Earth by being forced (in the afterlife) to endure being hit by speeding spray paint cans. Suppose further that the flamingoes hurt on Earth will not benefit by Jason's being punished and that Jason will not morally improve by being punished. The net result of the punishment will simply be an overall increase of pain, Jason's pain. In this case, it just seems that Jason's punishment would involve needless suffering and, thus, should not be carried out. At least one major ethical theory, utilitarianism, implies that Jason should not be punished in this case. Utilitarianism says that an act is right just in case it maximizes happiness, and wrong just in case it fails to maximize happiness. Since forcing Jason to be hit by spray paint cans will not increase anybody's happiness and will only make Jason less happy, it would be wrong to punish him for his transgression in this way. Thus, any plausible conception of Hell will not assume that retributive justice is always appropriate.

To take a more extreme approach, we might consider whether there could be an entirely non-retributive version of the Bad Place to which Gen would be morally justified in sending Team Cockroach. I submit that there could be such a version of the Bad Place, whether or not afterlife administrators on *The Good Place* would be willing to implement it. This new Bad Place (we can call it "Bad Place 3.0") would be reserved for people not morally equipped to spend their time in the Good Place. The purpose of sending someone there would not be to give them deserved punishment, but to do what's best for them.

How might sending someone to the Bad Place 3.0 rather than the Good Place be best for them? We can illustrate by considering Eleanor, who is inclined to compare herself to others, in part due to her perceived and actual moral deficiencies. We're told on the show that only the most ethically superior people enter the Good Place. So, it seems that, due to her tendency to compare, Eleanor would experience intense suffering if sent to the Good Place upon death. She would likely find it maddening to see so many truly good people and know that she is not one herself. Thus, given her current moral character, it may be better for her to be elsewhere. Something similar could be said for the other members of Team Cockroach. To take one more example, Jason might also be better off somewhere other than the Good Place, since he may find the likely disregard for Joe Francis, dearth of ball taps, and absence of Taco Bell references disheartening. Thus, the Bad Place 3.0, understood simply as a place where those not allowed into the Good Place go, might be the best place for people whose characters are not currently up to par.

What would people in the Bad Place 3.0 experience? They would be allowed to persist in their vice and suffer whatever natural consequences result. The suffering resulting from bad behavior may motivate some to improve, but the Bad Place 3.0 would not include torture, physical or psychological, since this may hinder moral reformation.

For those who end up improving their character, the Bad Place 3.0 would act as a kind of purgatory, readying them for the Good Place. For those content with their vicious behavior, the Bad Place 3.0 would be Hell, since they would experience any pain or dissatisfaction resulting from such behavior, potentially for eternity.

A similar view of Hell is portrayed in C.S. Lewis's *The Great Divorce*. It looks like Gen could be justified in sending some people, potentially members of Team Cockroach, to the Bad Place 3.0 for eternity. Of course, it would be up to those who enter to determine whether or not they'd suffer there forever.

7
Eleanor and the Meaning of Afterlife

Eric Yang

We're all going to die. And unless you are Seventies Canadian stoner Doug Forcett, it's unclear exactly what to expect afterwards. Thinking about our inevitable death often forces us to reconsider what really matters and whether our lives are meaningful or not. That's what happens to Michael in Season Two.

Damned if You Die

When Eleanor Shellstrop and the gang team up with Michael, he agrees to learn ethics from Chidi. But Michael doesn't take the lessons very seriously, and the gang believes it's because he's an immortal being. They do find out, however, that it's possible for Michael to die and go out of existence through retirement—where his essence would be scooped up with a flaming ladle and the molecules of his body placed on different stars ("Existential Crisis"). As Chidi invites him to imagine retiring and entering into a state of "nothingness—empty, black void," Michael falls into an existential crisis. His conclusion is that "searching for meaning is philosophical suicide," and he wonders how anyone can do anything "when you understand the fleeting nature of existence."

In that episode, Chidi introduces Michael to some of the ideas in Todd May's book, *Death*. As May elaborates in that book,

> if I had died—that is to say, if I had not been immortal . . . Those joys which meant so much, which gave me the life I realized I did not regret, would be over. (*Death*, pp. 3–4)

Death reminds us that our existence is finite, and not just for human beings. Many physicists believe that the universe will end in "heat death," where all the energy will eventually be used up. What remains will be particles floating further and further away from each other. If this is the end of everything, then what does it matter whether we achieve great things or fail in all our endeavors? The book of Ecclesiastes in the Hebrew scriptures reminds us that kings, peasants, and dogs all end up with the same fate—so why does it matter which path in life we take? Living for a finite duration, then, appears to threaten the value or meaningfulness of our lives. So we might be led to believe that we can have meaningful lives only if we live forever.

Damned if You Live

Unfortunately, this side of the coin also appears to be problematic. As it turns out, Eleanor and the gang will live forever, and as long as Michael doesn't retire, he will too. It's obvious that if the gang lived in The Bad Place for eternity, then their lives would be miserable and meaningless. But what if they lived forever in "The Good Place" (the place they mistakenly believed in Season One was The Good Place)? Or what about Mindy St. Claire's situation, living forever in The Medium Place? Whether in The Good Place, "The Good Place," or The Medium Place, Eleanor and her friends might be doomed to meaningless lives. So, we face the following dilemma: whether we die as finite creatures or live forever, our lives turn out meaningless.

Now why should we think that immortality yields a meaningless life? May explains the worry quite clearly:

> . . . if I were immortal I would neither have had a chance to reflect on my life nor known what it meant to me to have lived this particular life. None of that would have mattered . . . and whatever joys I had had, they would have lost a bit of their luster with my knowing that I might experience those same joys an infinity of times again . . . When there is time for everything it is hard to make anything matter. (p. 62)

So an immortal life appears to be meaningless because it will lead to utter boredom.

Suppose Eleanor remained in "The Good Place" for all eternity, never figuring out Michael's deception and where they really are. Her life would be filled with an eternity of eating frozen yogurt (or clam chowder, depending on which rebooted version), engaging in continual deception by pretending to be the "real" Eleanor, or learning ethics from Chidi—plus never being able to curse! It's easy to imagine how boredom can creep in for Eleanor and her friends. When you do the same things over and over again, you eventually get bored. Activities that used to be exciting, such as driving when you're a kid, become tedious when you are constantly doing it. Even if Eleanor got to do some of the more fun or amazing activities, such as flying ("Flying"), that too would become boring if she did it every day for a billion years.

We can extrapolate the same lesson for the other places. Even if the real Good Place includes many of the common elements of Paradise that the gang is hoping for, doing the same things over and over again will eventually get boring. You might think that there is a plethora of activities available to prevent them from becoming bored—they can simply ask for whatever they want from Janet. But imagine having done everything (that's the story of Dr. Faust and the ancient Greek gods). Once you've done it all, what's left but to do everything all over again. And after you've done that a million times, you still have the rest of eternity to do it again. The same goes for the Medium Place. There's only so many times one can read the same issue of *People* magazine or watch *Cannonball Run II* (as well as engage in carnal pleasures) without becoming bored.

Some might be tempted to think that boredom is avoidable if we change our personalities or character over time. As we change, we form new interests and desires, and that may help prevent boredom. Perhaps. But with an eternity, even small changes will eventually lead to big changes, and so the person Eleanor is in year one will be drastically different than Eleanor in year five trillion. Those two stages of Eleanor will be so disconnected—and the later Eleanor might not even remember being the earlier Eleanor—that they seem like two different people.

In fact, Eleanor and the gang do experience something similar to that: Eleanor, Chidi, Jason, and Tahani have their memories wiped every time Eleanor (and that one time Jason) figures out that they are really in The Bad Place. With each reboot, they don't remember any of the experiences from previous versions and so start from scratch by being welcomed to "The Good Place." Their lives in each reboot are disconnected from earlier and later versions of themselves in other reboots. The reboots are a quicker version of the personality changes that can occur over a lengthy period of time. But both cases appear bad in a way similar to an individual with severe amnesia.

So that's the predicament for Eleanor. Either she goes out of existence, thereby making her life meaningless and devoid of lasting value and purpose, or she lives forever and ends up utterly bored for all eternity or disconnected with her future and past selves.

Does The Good Place Need God?

Some philosophers, such as Albert Camus, concede that life lacks meaning and is indeed absurd and pointless. Camus raised the famous example of the Greek myth of Sisyphus. As punishment from the gods, Sisyphus is doomed to roll a rock up a hill only to watch it roll back down, and he is assigned to this fate eternally. The problem isn't that the task is a difficult one—we could change the example of taking a penny and flipping it over every five seconds. The problem is that it is a pointless task. Nevertheless, Camus believed we can still press on with courage even if life exhibits this kind of pointlessness.

However, many people strongly believe that life is meaningful and has a purpose. Immortality by itself may not guarantee it. Some claim that what more is needed is God, an all-powerful, all-knowing, and wholly good being who can provide the relevant meaning and purpose to our lives.

The Good Place includes only a point system, quite similar to karma. But is having a point system enough? What guarantees that justice will be correctly administered without a personal God? Perhaps having Gen, an all-knowing, burrito-eating Judge of the universe is enough for sustaining or conferring meaning in human lives, or maybe a more traditional conception of God is required for meaning.

It's difficult to see how having an all-knowing scorekeeper such as Gen can confer meaning, at least not without knowing more about the role Gen plays or how the afterlife system originated. Who (or what) established the point system? Who (or what) put Shawn and the other demons in charge of The Bad Place? Without answers to these questions, it's unclear how Gen can infuse Eleanor's life with meaning. And since God doesn't appear in *The Good Place*, does that mean Eleanor and her friends are doomed to lead meaningless lives?

Doing What You Want

Not necessarily. Even without God—and even without immortality—there might still be hope for Eleanor and the gang. Some of the goods in life that they can acquire may be satisfying after experiencing them only a single time. It might be enough for

Jason to watch Blake Bortles win the Superbowl only once. But the gang can also engage in repeatable goods, ones that can be enjoyed while retaining the desire to have more of it.

Even after befriending Chidi, Eleanor may want to make more friends, which she does. Eleanor can also engage in intellectual pursuits, studying moral philosophy; and she can move on to other areas in philosophy as well as studying other disciplines. She can also partake in sensual delights, which she does in some of the romantic encounters she has with Chidi in some of the reboots. Part of the problem with boredom stated earlier was thinking about doing the same thing over and over again. But Eleanor and the gang don't have to do that. They can rotate different repeatable pleasures. Some days Eleanor can eat frozen yogurt. She can then spend several years doing something else, such as sitting on a boat reading Aristotle or Kant or falling in love with her alleged soul mate. She can then try different fine meals at the restaurant, The Good Plates. Then after many years, she can go back and try frozen yogurt again. By rotating different repeatable pleasure, boredom may not be inevitable. John Martin Fischer makes this point in "Why Immortality Is Not So Bad".

But even avoiding boredom, will Eleanor's life be meaningful? That depends on what it takes for life to be meaningful. Some philosophers claim that the meaning of life is entirely subjective, that it depends only on the attitude of a person. One well-known version (advanced by Richard Taylor) suggests that a life is meaningful just in case an individual is able to fulfill her desires or goals—whatever her desires or goals may be. If Sisyphus were injected with a serum that made his life ambition to roll a rock up a hill over and over, then we might stop feeling bad for him but think that he's doing what he loves doing.

If Chidi's ultimate goal is to write a book on ethics, then as long as he is engaged in that project, his life is meaningful. So Eleanor's life in "The Good Place" may count as meaningful since she is fulfilling her desires, which is keeping up with the ruse of pretending to belong in order to deserve belonging (Season One) or trying to figure out how to escape from The Bad Place and make it to The Good Place (Season Two).

One worry that might be raised arises from the belief that some lives are intuitively meaningless even if they involve someone who is fulfilling her goals or desires, because some goals or desires are simply inane and pointless. Many are not inclined to regard as meaningful a life filled with hanging out in the "budhole" and playing video games for all eternity—even if that is Jason's ultimate goal. We can also imagine someone who wants only to eat frozen yogurt and does it every waking moment of every day. Maybe those should be regarded as meaningful lives. But for philosophers who disagree, it is because they believe more is needed than merely doing what you want to do.

Loving What Deserves to Be Loved

We get a clue of what more might be needed when Eleanor returns to Earth ("Somewhere Else"). Her near-death experience leads her to re-evaluate her life, and she decides to pursue more worthwhile activities such as undertaking projects related to environment awareness. This transformed outlook is not uncommon. When coming to the end of their lives, people don't typically wish they had played more video games or spent more time at work. Usually they wish that they had spent more time with family or traveled more to see marvelous sights around the world. Those who have a terminal illness often try to spend their remaining time with loved ones or having valuable experiences.

So what makes life meaningful might require combining both the subjective element of desire and the objective element of being worthwhile. If you're doing what you love, and what you love deserves to be loved—it's worthwhile—then you are living a meaningful life. According to this view, advocated by Susan Wolf, a life of eating only frozen yogurt is not a worthwhile one. But even in "The Good Place," Eleanor is able to pursue worthwhile endeavors. She is able to seek intellectual engagement by learning more about moral philosophy. Her goal of becoming a better person, strengthening her friendship with Tahani, or cultivating romance with Chidi are the kinds of goals that we usually regard as worthwhile.

So Eleanor and her friends can live out meaningful lives, and this may be so even without bringing immortality or God into the picture. If this is right, then Eleanor and her friends can live meaningful lives even if death is the end and they won't live forever.

Writing Our Own Stories

We've looked at the problem of boredom, but we haven't yet dealt with the problem of Eleanor and her friends being rebooted eight-hundred-and-two times, which is similar to the problem of disconnection mentioned earlier. A clue to resolving this worry arises when examining the order of events in Eleanor's life. She went from manipulating older people to purchasing ineffective pills to striving to become a better person through studying moral philosophy and performing acts of kindness. However, if we reversed the events, where she started out as a student of moral philosophy and trying to be kind to becoming a manipulator whose favorite book is Kendall Jenner's Instagram feed, then we probably wouldn't regard her life as meaningful. So the order of events in someone's life can affect whether we regard it as meaningful or not. It's also important that the characters are not manipulated or coerced into becoming better—they need to be freely choosing to do so in a way that makes them authors of their own lives, engaging in creative self-expression. These issues are discussed by John Martin Fischer in "Free Will, Death, and Immortality."

By bringing in the importance of free choice and the order of events, certain reboots can still make room for meaning. Some reboots may not since they are too short, such as the eight-second version where Michael accidentally does a "butt reboot" ("Team Cockroach"). But in most of the attempts, Eleanor and her friends freely choose to work at becoming better people. We can even think of each reboot as analogous to individual episodes of a television series—a self-contained story that has plot twists and turns but is usually resolved after twenty-two minutes. Each television episode has its own self-contained meaning, and the same appears to be true for many of the reboots that the gang endures.

Eleanor and her friends may even be better off than they realize. Even if they don't directly remember previous reboots, they have ways of finding out. For example, Eleanor discovers Mindy's recording of Eleanor and Chidi professing their love for one another. That event influences Eleanor's feelings and actions towards Chidi in the final reboot (at least through Season Two). Another example is Eleanor's secret message to herself written on the title page of T.M. Scanlon's *What We Owe to Each Other* right before they are rebooted, which causes her to look for Chidi in the second reboot and to once again work towards becoming a better person. Those with retrograde or anterograde amnesia are able to send themselves messages so that even without directly remembering, their past selves and future selves can still make a difference. So memory wipes do not necessarily yield disconnectedness.

Hope for Eleanor

If these views on meaningfulness are correct, then we can conclude that Eleanor and her friends are able to lead meaningful lives. If they are pursuing worthwhile goods that they love, such as forming bonds of friendship or becoming better people, then their lives are meaningful. Or if what matters is the order of events and acting freely, then Eleanor and her friends can lead meaningful lives by creatively expressing themselves through authoring their own stories—and this is so even if they have to endure rebooting.

However, Eleanor and her friends may end up choosing imprudently or immorally and thereby engage in later events (in later seasons) that alter and ruin the meaning of earlier events. We're going to have to wait and see whether they continue to make good choices and end up with a good story. Perhaps that's the most we can hope for any of us.

8

The Death of God and the Death of Meaning

MATTHEW MONTOYA

What happens to us after we die? Why am I here? What's the point of it all?

These are some of the most common questions in human experience. We all, at some point, wonder about the possibility of there being an afterlife, a God or higher power, or even just a purpose to our seemingly short lives. Going all the way back to Socrates and Plato in ancient Greece, we have wondered what the purpose of existence was for ourselves and whether there was something that would come after death. Well, compadres, time to hold onto your mother-forking shirt-balls because in *The Good Place* we have been given some of these answers.

Moments into the first episode, we learn with Eleanor that after the moment of death people are sent to either the Good Place or the Bad Place. These two places aren't your traditional ideas of Heaven or Hell as depicted in Western Philosophy or Christianity, but they have some similarity. As Michael describes in the very first episode, "Every religion gets about five percent right" ("Everything Is Fine").

As the show progresses, we end up going through a very entertaining ride of moral learning as we discover that the Good Place is really the Bad Place, that Eleanor and her friends are all being tortured, and that Michael is really a demon. This leads to even further zany adventures, but at the end of the day the show is about morality.

The Good Place is all about these ethical questions as our group of neighbors (Eleanor, Chidi, Jason, and Tahani) all attempt to make their way through the rigorous obstacle course that makes up morality. However, towards the end of Season Two a very good question arises about their moral journey so far. That question is, why do they desire to act morally?

The Judge puts the idea out there that they aren't actually becoming better people and that they don't want to become better people for the sake of morality. Instead, the Judge argues that our group of friends simply want to be good out of a fear of the Bad Place. They are looking for, as she puts it, moral deserts ("Somewhere Else").

What makes an action real or authentic? Well, strap in as we prepare to go Maximum Derek and explore these questions by looking at the ideas of nihilism, existentialism, and their relationship to the Good Place.

Chidi, the Death of God, and the Madman

We can begin our journey into nihilism with the philosophy of a man named Friedrich Nietzsche (1844–1900). You may even recall Nietzsche's philosophy from Season Three in the episode "Jeremy Bearimy." In this episode, Chidi and the rest of the Brainy Bunch learn that they are just a metaphysical experiment for demons and an all-powerful Judge, and that they have been tortured by demons for approximately three hundred years.

Chidi, not knowing how to process the fact that every metaphysical possibility he has studied is likely wrong, begins to have an existential crisis. He is wandering around aimlessly when he is approached by a man who asks Chidi if he wants to talk to him about God. Chidi looks this man in the face and simply replies, "God is dead. God remains dead. And we have killed him . . . Who will wipe this blood off us? What festivals of atonement, what sacred games shall we have to invent?" ("Jeremy Bearimy").

Chidi is quoting from a story by Friedrich Nietzsche known as "The Parable of the Madman," from his book *The Gay Science*. This story is about a Madman who would go from town to town screaming about the death of God. This Madman would go up to people on the street screaming, "God is dead. God remains dead. And we have killed him" (*The Gay Science*, p. 181).

Many people often use this quote out of context, and try to claim that Nietzsche was either being literal or making an atheistic statement about God. What Nietzsche originally meant was more of a metaphor. He meant that the concept of God has lost its place of central importance in society. For large portions of human history, religion has served as a central figure in the western world. God has served as the answer for all of the central questions that we had about the world, reality, and humanity. However, after the Enlightenment, religion began to fall by the wayside. It no longer served the central position of importance that it once had. For Nietzsche, to claim that "God is dead" is to say that God has been replaced by logic and science.

Nietzsche was claiming that after the death of God all we have left is an absence of meaning. Previously, God had given us a purpose. When bad things happened it was because of God's plan. Our faith in God was enough to move the world forward and to give us meaning in life. However, after the death of God all we are left with are the cold and calculated answers of logic and science. These remove any real meaning from existence that we may have felt under God. Our entire existence can be broken down to nothing more important than chemicals and formulas. It is this cold calculated reality born from the death of God that we call nihilism

Nihilism is the idea that existence has no genuine ultimate meaning. There is no metaphysical plan but, instead there is simply the cold indifference of a universe that really just doesn't care about us. We as human beings constantly attempt to seek meaning for our existence. Yet, with nihilism, human beings are no more special than other animals, dirt, or rocks. To the nihilistic universe, we are all the same, meaningless.

Chidi and company have just learned that there is a Heaven and Hell type afterlife. However, beyond learning the truth of existence, they have learned that, regardless of what they tried to do or how they lived their lives, they were condemned to be tortured forever. There was no hope for them. Their desire to find meaning and purpose for their lives has been reduced to pure absurdity. No matter what they chose to do they were met with the reality that they would still fail. Chidi's entire existence has been made meaningless as everything he has spent his life studying and pursuing has been shown to him as worthless because he will still end up dead and tortured. He feels as though he has no real control or purpose to his existence because it will always end the same for him now that he knows about the Bad Place.

This realization of meaninglessness that Chidi feels is what Nietzsche argues would happen because of the death of God. Nihilism would begin to take hold of many of us. However, Nietzsche didn't claim that this was the end of meaning for humanity. Nietzsche himself was not a nihilist—he was not resigned to accepting a meaningless existence—but he did believe that, given time, humanity would find itself at this point.

For Chidi, a man who has spent his entire life attempting to understand philosophical concepts of reality, morals, and choice, to be told that his life has but one end is jarring. He has had all choice and freedom stripped from him. The meaning and purpose he once felt in life has been replaced with nihilism. He has been filled with a feeling of insignificance as he is now being met with the cold and calculating indifference of the universe.

Existentialism and the Absurdity of Living

You might be thinking to yourself that just because God doesn't give us meaning then that doesn't mean we can't find meaning for ourselves. You would be absolutely correct. This is a common reaction to the feeling of nihilism, leading to what we call existentialism. Existentialism is a reaction to nihilism, and existentialist philosophy could not have come into being if nihilism had not come around first. Our need to search for a meaning to our own existence is what fuels existentialism, and our sometimes inability to do so leads us to having what is known as an existential crisis.

In *The Good Place,* we have seen an example of an existential crisis before, with Michael in Season Two. In the episode "Existential Crisis," Michael is faced with something that all of us learn when we're children. He is forced to think about his own mortality and the possibility of his own non-existence. As human beings, we all learn about this possibility very early on in life. Whether it's by the death of a family member, a story on the news, or the loss of a pet, we all at some point ask what happens to us after death. It's this line of thinking that causes us to begin wondering if there is a life after death or maybe that there is nothing.

With the emergence of nihilism, we more and more lean toward the idea of there being nothing after death. Our lives become the only certainty that we have. We don't know whether or not we have meaning or purpose, and we don't know whether there is a life after death. All we know is that we exist, and that death could be the end of that existence. We're faced with the possibility that all our efforts simply lead to our non-existence.

In this episode, Chidi realizes that Michael, as an immortal being, has never had to deal with his own potential non-existence. As far as Michael has known, he would always be. The possibility of retirement, his version of death, is so unlikely that most demons do not even worry about it. Due to this, Michael has never had to face the nihilistic fear that we human beings begin to fear at a very young age. We even see the moment when Michael comes to realize that he might no longer exist. We see him as this look of realization and horror comes over his face and his body language almost become childlike as he utters the words, "Huh . . . So, you're saying I would be . . . no . . . me?" ("Existential Crisis"). Michael has now entered a full-on existential crisis as he becomes so overwhelmed with the realization and fear of non-existence that he can almost no longer function.

So, how do we deal with the concept of the nothingness found within nihilism so that we do not turn into a miserable ball of existential despair? Well, there are two main existentialist thinkers in the early twentieth century who wanted to give us an answer to the question of nihilism. The first of these two thinkers is Albert Camus (1913–1960).

Camus's philosophy is best known for telling you to ignore the meaninglessness of existence and to just live your life in a way that keeps you living. Essentially, you need to live in a way that makes you happy and prevents you from killing yourself while ignoring the meaninglessness of existence. We can either continue to search for metaphysical meaning and purpose in a universe that clearly doesn't allow for such meaning, or we can embrace this fact and find meaning for ourselves. Camus argues that to do anything else is absurd. It is this concept of absurdity that fueled a large part of his existentialist philosophy.

Camus describes the concept of the absurd through the story of a Greek king, Sisyphus, who was condemned to an eternity of repetitive absurdity. The Gods tasked Sisyphus to painstakingly push a boulder to the top of a hill. Sisyphus would push the boulder to the top of the hill but then it would always roll back down to the bottom and he would have to begin again. He would do this over and over again for all of eternity, and the boulder would always roll back to the bottom. Sisyphus would never succeed. Camus sees this type of repettive behavior as an example of the absurd.

We as human beings still continually search for metaphysical purpose in a universe that is just indifferent to us. We, like Sisyphus, are constantly stuck in a pattern of behavior that is absurd. Camus believed that by embracing the absurd nature of the universe we could accept that there is no grand purpose. Instead, we could find our own meaning in the things that make us happy.

We see this type of mentality in Michael's initial reaction to his nihilistic revelation. Michael shows up like a man going through a midlife crisis. He has gotten a new car, given himself and Janet makeovers, and he constantly wants to have a good time. He's attempting to make life a party that never stops. He's attempting to find meaning through these actions. These actions allow him to ignore the meaninglessness of his existence, and instead to live a somewhat happy life. Michael is, without knowing it, attempting to embrace the absurd.

Eleanor and the French Soldier

The other philosopher who gives us a possible solution to the question of nihilism is Jean-Paul Sartre (1905–1980). Jean-Paul Sartre claimed that the best way for us to react to nihilism was through existentialism, and, for Sartre, this would mean making what he called authentic choices to live a life that was beneficial not just for ourselves but for the people around us.

In Sartre's essay *Existentialism Is a Humanism*, he explains what it is to be an existentialist. To become an existentialist one needed to embrace the premise that our purpose, or essence, came after our birth. In other words, our "existence precedes our essence."

For a large part of history humanity has assumed that "essence precedes existence." They believed that God created them with a purpose. However, in the face of nihilism this premise falls apart. Sartre believed that this idea has another flaw. He believed that by saying our essence comes before our birth we can try to shift the blame for all of our moral failings and shortcomings onto God, rather than ourselves. Sounds like a classic Shellstrop move.

Instead, if we believed that "existence precedes essence," then we would have no one to blame but ourselves when we did something bad or when something didn't work out. The idea that we would bear the full responsibility for our actions due to the removal of God is called abandonment (*Essays in Existentialism*, p. 27). This is the fear that we will be the only ones to blame if something goes wrong. It is a terrifying thought. It becomes even more terrifying when we add what Sartre called anguish, or the idea that our actions will affect other people (p. 25).

When we must accept that our actions are our own and that they will cause happiness or pain for other people then we really begin to consider their consequences before we perform them. We must realize that we are the ones who bear responsibility, and as such we are the ones who determine what it is to live a good and meaningful life. It is the acceptance of this responsibility in making our choices that allows for us to be what Sartre called authentic.

Consider Eleanor for a moment. When she arrives in the Good Place she is rude, selfish, holds no respect or regard for anyone else, and constantly tries to blame others. However, as she begins to learn ethics and as she begins to care for these people around her she begins to take responsibility for her actions. She accepts that what she is choosing has an impact on other people's lives and that she no longer wants to be responsible for their pain. When she reveals to Michael in Season One that she does not belong in the Good Place, she does this out of a human sympathy for Chidi. She knows she will be punished for it but she accepts responsibility. She makes an authentic choice in that moment. Granted, there is constantly a back and forth for Eleanor in her willingness to accept responsibility, but she is growing and that is what Sartre wanted. To demonstrate this, let's look at one of Sartre's most well-known examples, the French Soldier.

The French Soldier example asks you to consider a man who was living in France during war time. He lived with and took care of his mother. He was her whole world. Unfortunately, the man's brother had recently been killed in the front line of the war. He felt like he had a moral and social duty to go and avenge his brother by fighting in the war, but if he did this then he would have to leave his mother behind. She would surely die without him. Sartre asks, what should the man do? Should he stay with his mother where he will make a huge impact on a single person's life, or should he go fight in the war where he will make a small impact for a much greater cause?

The answer to Sartre's example is that there honestly is no correct answer. No one can tell this man the right thing to do. Only by choosing for himself and accepting the full responsibility for his choice could the man claim to have made the right decision. This is because he would be making the choice authentically, or true to himself.

We've seen Eleanor make this type of decision multiple times in the show. She makes this type of decision when she reveals to Michael that she doesn't belong in the Good Place. However, she also makes this type of decision when she is undergoing her test with the Judge. She chooses not to abandon her friends and go to the Good Place without them because she doesn't believe it to be right. She lies to them and tells them that she failed her test too when really, she is the only one who passed. She is making the decision to be unified with her friends rather than blaming other people. Maybe she isn't condemned to the classic Shellstrop move all the time. Eleanor has grown and become a more authentic, true to herself, person.

Moral Behavior in the Face of Existentialism

Normally, existentialism is a reaction to the realization that there is no ultimate purpose to existence. But our four heroes have all been shown the opposite. They have seen the Bad Place, been told of a Good Place, and have been shown that their lives are merely the playthings of greater metaphysical creatures. However, they are all seemingly becoming better people. They are becoming better versions of themselves. The Judge argued that this evolution of their moral character didn't mean anything because they were simply looking for some kind of moral desert or reward.

We can probably agree with the judge, at least as far as our characters' motives existed when she met them in Season Two. However, in Season Three our heroes have been told that there is no hope for them. That they will never make it to the Good Place because they have had their motives corrupted. This is what leads to Chidi's breakdown. Yet, by telling them that there is no hope, have Michael and Janet actually given our heroes their only chance at true moral and existential redemption?

If they truly believe that their futures are damned, then every choice they make has no bearing on metaphysical existence. Instead, they are left making their own meaning for what time they have left to be alive, just like the rest of us. The revelation of an afterlife is no longer impactful when told that they will still fail. Their decisions to help Pillboi, Eleanor's mom, and more in Season Three are motivated by their own wants and desires. They are authentically choosing to help the people they love, as well as others, because they truly and authentically want to be good people. They are embracing their abandonment and anguish to become moral examples for those that they love. In doing so, they become better people themselves.

Sartre believed that a people are what they make of themselves, and our friends in the Brainy Bunch have chosen to make themselves, and each other, much better people.

III

Everything Is Fine

9
Send *The Good Place* to The Bad Place?

ZACHARY SHELDON

Isn't it interesting that *The Good Place*, a show about ethics and doing the right thing, tells a giant lie to its audiences for an entire season?

As we all know by now, the Season One finale, "Michael's Gambit," features the revelation that Eleanor, Chidi, Tahani, and Jason have *not*, in fact, been living in the Good Place, but have actually been residing in a new, experimental version of the Bad Place where they were torturing one another by design.

This now iconic twist, which some have called one of the greatest twists in television history, actually turns the entire show—again, a show all about ethics—into an ethical paradox in its own right. Is it alright that a show about morality lies to its audience? To explore this question, we first have to look at just how exactly *The Good Place* engages in deceiving its audience.

One easy response is that all fiction is, to some extent, a lie. Many of us actually learn to distinguish between non-fiction and fiction by remembering that "fiction" and "fake" both start with the letter "F" (or at least I did). But an answer to this accusation is that fiction is not necessarily a lie so much as it is *not real*. Fictional stories don't try to pretend that they're about real people or events. In fact, fictions celebrate that they aren't constrained by such limitations to tell stories about spies or forbidden romances or adventures on far away planets—or about people in a screwed-up version of the afterlife. So, recognizing *The Good Place* as fiction is to recognize that the story is not lying at its core by being the type of story that it is.

Another way to look at lying in fiction is to consider the idea of "truth in fiction." For instance, suppose that you're watching a movie about ten-foot-tall aliens invading the planet, and early in this film it's established that the conquering species is entirely impervious to gunfire or ballistic weapons of any kind. And then, in the action-packed finale, a group of rogue soldiers with machine guns somehow takes down the alien leader and turns the tide of the battle to save humanity. Isn't that cheating? Isn't it a kind of *lying*? The idea of truth in fiction is that fictional stories establish rules for themselves and their characters that they must then abide by in order to remain consistent and "realistic"—even if the story happens to be about ten-foot aliens invading the world.

Here again, *The Good Place* generally passes as being truthful. Though each episode reveals new rules and understandings of the way the Good Place or Bad Place work, going back and re-watching earlier episodes reveals that the show doesn't deviate from the logic that it puts in place even as it progresses. In fact, one major issue for Eleanor and her compatriots, especially in the second season, is how rigid the rules of the show's universe really are. So, once again, *The Good Place* does not explicitly lie in this particular sense.

The way that the show *does* lie is in its informal, unspoken contract with its audience. By watching the show, viewers effectively agree to believe in the story of the show as it is presented to them. But, as we know, by the end of Season One the show actually reveals itself to be the exact opposite of what it said it was at the season's start. In this way the show actively supports and even encourages one interpretation of its characters and events, only to pull the rug out from viewers and reveal that this interpretation is entirely false.

The show, in short, deceives. On the one hand, this is not necessarily a problem: we do know that *The Good Place* is fiction. And, of course, twist endings can be fun for audiences (just ask M. Night Shyamalan). But what makes the deception in *The Good Place* so very interesting is that it takes place in the context of a show that is all about teaching moral lessons, and which actually comments on the moral problem of lying.

Given that it seems like *The Good Place* puts itself in something of a paradoxical relationship to the idea of lying, it is worth looking at what both creator Mike Schur and the show itself say about lying as a way of seeing whether or not the show offers an embedded justification or rationale for its own deception.

In interviews before the show's airing, Schur compared the sitcom's world-building to the show *Lost*, which, famous for its twists and turns, probably should have clued some viewers in to the fact that they should suspect that not everything was as it seemed, even early on in *The Good Place*. And following the conclusion of Season One, Schur admits that he knew that the twist would happen even before he began writing the pilot episode: "The explicit idea was to have the [Season One] ending be something that completely changes everything you've seen so far," Schur said (Berkowitz interview).

There was no specific instructional or philosophical reason behind the twist, either; it was mainly just a way for Schur to know that his idea for the show could sustain more than a single season. But one consequence of the twist, according to Schur, is that some people ended up liking the show better because they weren't expecting what came at the end. The fact that it surprised them drew them into the world even more. One example of this is viewers who went back through Season One to investigate any clues from earlier episodes that may have hinted at the fact that Eleanor and her compatriots were actually in the Bad Place—of which there were several. ("We felt like we had to layer in these clues," Schur said. "We had to do things so that when you saw the twist, you would think back and realize, *Oh, of course, Michael's a demon*.")

When asked about the pressure to create an equally compelling twist for the end of Season Two, Schur demurred: "You don't want to suddenly make it a totally different show, but at the same time, part of the reason why they liked it is that they didn't know it was going to happen. If you play right into their hands and do another big twist, that might be the least shocking thing you could do" (Chaney interview).

What both Schur's foreknowledge of the plot and this statement reveal is that his major commitment is—perhaps rightly so—to the viewing and entertainment experience of the audience. Schur wants to make sure that the audience is engaged with his fiction, and so works to deliberately draw viewers into the intricate workings of his universe. Deception, it seems, is inherently a part of this. But this doesn't entirely eradicate the pesky reality that the show is ostensibly about teaching good, moral behavior. So, what does the show itself have to say about all this?

Liar, Liar, Boots on Fire

"The Eternal Shriek" is the main episode in Season One where the question of lying is addressed head on. The episode begins with Michael announcing that he recognizes himself as the source of all the neighborhood's problems, and so he will have to leave the neighborhood and go into retirement. Michael asks Janet to call him a train, which he explains is the only way that anyone can leave a neighborhood, with Janet being the only entity capable of summoning a train.

Eleanor is pleased with this turn of events, as she sees it as a kind of vindication—with Michael gone, she no longer has to worry about being found out as an imposter. Chidi, as is perhaps to be expected by this point, has problems with this "solution," namely that Michael isn't the problem, *Eleanor* is. Therefore, Chidi concludes, they have lied to Michael by making him think that he's the source of the neighborhood's trouble, a position that he finds untenable to say the least. This sets off a discussion about lying between Chidi and Eleanor that will be carried through the rest of the episode.

Chidi's history with guilt and shame about lying is illustrated in a flashback, where we see Chidi interacting with a colleague on campus, Henry, who has just purchased a pair of red cowboy boots that are *ostentatious* to say the least. When asked if he likes the boots, Chidi quickly answers, "Yes!" which has an extremely positive effect on his friend and yet sends Chidi into a nearly crippling ethical bind—the truth, of course, is that he *hates* the boots. That night, he agonizes over the lie that he told, prompting discussion with his girlfriend, Allesandra, about the ethics of lying. Kant, Chidi notes, believed that lying was never appropriate, no matter the circumstance. Allesandra counters with the argument that ethical philosophy in the abstract isn't the end of the matter; in order to get along in society, sometimes people say things just to be polite. But, she says, if Chidi really feels this way, then maybe he ought to confess to Henry about how he doesn't actually like his boots.

Naturally, the situation is further complicated when Chidi goes to confess to Henry, only to find out that Henry has purchased Chidi his own pair of red, bejeweled boots, proudly proclaiming that he and Chidi are now "boot brothers" united by their unique footwear. This particular situation comes to a head some time later, when Henry is in the hospital about to undergo surgery for an aneurysm with a fifty-fifty chance at survival. He jokes to Chidi that now would be the time to say anything that he'd been meaning to say to him, which nearly prompts Chidi into confessing his distaste for the boots, which Henry is wearing even in the hospital (they are the only things that give him any comfort). Chidi does not say anything, however, except that he is there for Henry at this difficult time. But—following the successful completion of Henry's surgery, Chidi confesses his hatred for the boots, admitting that he has been haunted by the lie he told and his desire to come clean. A deflated Henry flatly states: "This is why everyone hates moral philosophy professors" ("The Eternal Shriek").

Flashbacks to Chidi's life on Earth portray the Kantian position that Chidi takes here in the Good Place: that there is no appropriate, moral circumstance in which lying is acceptable. Eleanor, naturally, fights back against this logic, looking for something to fix her problem without revealing herself as the true source of the neighborhood's instability. Eleanor's search for a solution ends up placing the crosshairs of her plotting directly on the neighborhood's artificially programmed guide, Janet, specifically focusing on Janet's role as the sole conductor of trains in and out of the Good Place, with Eleanor intending to "kill" her, making the argument that the ends justify the means, which Chidi calls out as a Machiavellian position that can only result in more lying— something he has already explained is never justifiable according to Kant.

Eleanor proceeds anyways, and the events that transpire result in Chidi accidentally "killing" Janet, thus trapping him in a secret lie of his own. While the rebooted Janet has no memory of who "killed" her, so that Eleanor sees everything as continuing to work in her favor, Chidi is beside himself with guilt. That night, Michael gathers the neighborhood to tell them that the murder of Janet is most likely related to whatever is causing the neighborhood's problems, meaning that Michael himself is not the only problem.

Michael asks anyone with any information to speak up, a request which makes Chidi even more visibly upset, the lies he has told and become involved with clearly eating him up inside. Eleanor sees this and takes action. She stands and comes clean: "Michael," she says, "the problem in the neighborhood . . . is me. I was brought to the Good Place by mistake. I'm not supposed to be here" ("The Eternal Shriek").

The following episode, "Most Improved Player," is dominated primarily by Michael dealing with the fallout of both Eleanor's revelation and Janet's murder, but offers two additional moments of commentary on the problem of lying. First, while discussing the conundrum of how best to talk to Michael about the predicament she, Chidi, Tahani, and Jason all are in, Eleanor makes reference to Chidi's position that lying is always morally wrong—even citing Kant while doing so, which Chidi takes note of. And second, later in the episode Chidi ultimately confesses to his role in the murder of Janet.

Pepto for Chidi's Stomachache

Now, let's take a look at all of this and what it seems *The Good Place* is telling viewers about lying. One major implication we can draw out is that Eleanor's position of harmless lies doesn't seem to hold water. All that her actions and deceits seem to do is to get everyone around her into more and more trouble, just adding layers of complication to an already complex situation. Chidi's approach of complete and utter honesty *also* complicates things but is portrayed in a manner that seems to dissolve or simplify the overall situation when the truth finally comes out.

In fact, it seems that the primary implication of the show's take on lying is that confession is key to absolving the guilt that accompanies lying. The flashbacks to Chidi's colleague with the boots end with Chidi feeling relieved and refreshed at having confessed his earlier lie. Eleanor's confession prompts further questions and problems dealing with her ultimate fate in the afterlife, but also brings some of the neighborhood's issues to a close and demonstrates that Eleanor has at least developed *some* sense of selflessness. And Chidi's confession to Janet's murder once again relieves him of an intense burden of guilt.

None of this quite absolves these lies entirely. Henry, of the bedazzled boots, is visibly upset with Chidi's admission even as Chidi himself feels relieved. And Eleanor faces dire consequences and relocation to the Bad Place as a result of her confession. But the show positions the revelation of each particular truth as a kind of release of tension in the narrative—things and situations kept getting more and more convoluted and precarious, and these confessions simplify events such that many minor problems may be ignored in the name of addressing bigger, more important issues. There *is* still fallout from the lies that are told, but the dramatic tension of the situations is resolved in such a way that the lies *feel* absolved. This is modeled in both Eleanor and Chidi, and in the show itself: the revelation that what we thought was the Good Place is actually the Bad Place pulls the rug out from under viewers, but, as Mike Schur points out, many viewers *liked* that they had been fooled. Viewers felt *good* about the twist, swept up in it rather than upset at it for its deception, even though the show really *was* deceitful.

Ostensibly, the show's revelation of its own deceit functions to absolve its own sins—but does it? As audience members we may not feel angry at this twist, or even feel exactly like we have really been deceived. Of course, this does not negate the fact that we *were* deceived, nor does it absolve or remove the question of whether or not this deception was right in the first place. But this may actually be the point of such a twist. What this twist introduces is the idea that *The Good Place* is actually *performing* ethical education rather than just participating in it. Each episode features discussions or illustrations of ethical and moral philosophy, often in the context of Chidi teaching Eleanor, subtly (and sometimes not-so-subtly) educating the audience right alongside her. But if the point of learning about ethics is to get away from abstraction in order to live out ethical codes and stances, then the show must do more than illustrate these concepts as entertainment content. By deliberately invoking an ethical paradox like this in its plot and presentation, *The Good Place* all but demands that a conversation around the ethics of the show itself take place, showcasing how ethical discussions may be incorporated into everyday life and thinking.

But this raises another intriguing question. However admirable the development of the show as an ethical lesson may be, the question remains: do the ends justify the means? Does the show involving its audience in productive ethical conversations justify its use of deceit as a means to do so? Chidi argues in "The Eternal Shriek" that this Machiavellian principle is abhorrent and untenable as a moral position, and the show's subtle support of his position over Eleanor's suggests that at least initially the show agrees with Chidi. *Initially* is the key word, there.

As we know, things get more complicated in Season Two, to the point that Michael teams up with Eleanor, Chidi, Tahani, and Jason to engage in an extended campaign of deception in order to save Michael's life and reputation and to try and get the four humans to the real Good Place. Chidi's involvement with these schemes is mostly attributed to his recognition that his life's work on ethics was largely unsuccessful, though he does continue to teach ethics to the group and particularly to Michael as a way of helping him become more human and understanding.

If Chidi is arguably the moral center of the show—as the only character well-versed in ethical problems and theory—then his acceptance of this course of action may be read as the show entrenching itself in the philosophy of the ends justifying the means, or at the very least leaning heavily on the question of whether or not such a philosophy is morally right, or ever can be. Given that Chidi earlier recognized such a position as indefensible, this too involves the show in another paradox that viewers must work out for themselves.

Chidi Becomes a Moral Particularist

Chidi doesn't end up being the *only* person in the show to teach about ethics. In the Season Two episode "Rhonda, Diana, Jake, and Trent," the four heroes (with Michael and Janet) find themselves in the *actual* Bad Place, on their way to see the Judge. When Eleanor, Chidi, Tahani, and Jason accidentally stumble into the reception for the opening of an exhibit in the Hall of Low-Grade Crappiness, Chidi's Kantian stance on lying is challenged by his need to play a part in order to survive a literal party in Hell.

When Chidi is initially (and very apparently) reluctant to go along with such a ruse, Eleanor steps to the plate, reminding him of the idea of moral particularism. This perspective, which she attributes most prominently to philosopher Jonathan Dancy, holds that there are no stable, immovable moral principles, but rather moral judgment and ethical behavior must be decided based upon the particulars of the case at hand.

So, Eleanor argues, while Kant may say that lying is never appropriate, what about a lie being told in order to do some good? Jonathan Dancy, she holds, would ardently support such an idea. Chidi is blown away that Eleanor was studying moral philosophy on her own time (and who wouldn't be?), and, ultimately (if reluctantly), swayed by her reasoning. He plays his part in the charade to the best of his ability, and so dramatically contributes to the group's survival.

The introduction of moral particularism raises further questions for the continued behavior of characters throughout the series, and, of course, for the series itself. While it may traditionally be wrong to deceive an audience in the way that a twist ending requires, the moral and ethical lessons that *The Good Place* is trying to teach arguably required such a twist in order to engage viewers in an ethical quandary and series of questioning just like the show's characters. A question for audiences to answer is whether or not this is valid reasoning, or an acceptable explanation of the show's behavior.

One final question worth considering here is: where does all this leave viewers, exactly? How are we supposed to feel, or what are we supposed to do, when a TV show about teaching and practicing ethics seems to subvert or maybe even disregard its own moral teachings? This is another great question that the show forces us to consider and invites us to answer for ourselves—*which is ultimately the point*.

If *The Good Place* maintains a coherent stance on anything, it is the importance of individuals' cultivating a sense of morality to guide their lives and interactions with others. Further, the implication is that this morality is best founded in a *system* of ethics rather than independent assessments of justice or right and wrong, even in the discussion of moral particularism introduced later in the second season. The show often strives to present and perform several different perspectives on complex issues that can affect our everyday lives. And so, determining what to do about these issues, or what to believe about certain ethical conundrums like lying, is both the great and terrifying responsibility we are left with as viewers.

10

A Love Story between Theory and Praxis

JOHN ALTMANN

Welcome, dear reader, to the tale I am to tell you this evening. It is a love story, and the love it concerns is one that has transformed the world continuously for centuries. It has started revolutions, it has guided the evolution of societies, and it has even liberated entire groups of people.

On a much smaller scale, this relationship has shown human beings individually how to best live their lives. This is the love story between two entities known as Theory and Praxis. Theory is brilliant but shy; Theory has all the knowledge of the world but has have never actually used it. Praxis, on the other hand, is an entity that loves living in the world, despite having never understood it. Theirs is a love that takes shape in a variety of ways across the world, but our story is one that sees this love actually transcend the Earth and dwell in a corner of the universe known as "The Good Place."

Theory takes the form of a moral philosophy professor by the name of Chidi Anagonye, a man who is well read in the thought of the philosophers who came before him but struggles greatly with living in the world and putting his education into practice. Any sort of conflict that forces Chidi to have to make a decision leaves him with terrible anxiety and stomachaches. In fact it was revealed by Michael, the man who runs "The Good Place," that Chidi once suffered a panic attack at a make-your-own sundae bar. Chidi always becomes indecisive in the face of the richness and complexity of the world, which makes him the perfect personification of Theory, who always prefers to be separated from the world.

Praxis takes the form of a rude and selfish woman known as Eleanor Shellstrop. Eleanor is a woman who likes to party, get drunk, hang out with friends, and ultimately has no problem actually making decisions and actively participating in the world and its offerings. The problem with Eleanor (as opposed to Chidi), is that Eleanor consistently makes the wrong choices, and in doing so hurts the people around her.

One of the worst examples of this was when Eleanor willingly became a salesperson for a fraudulent business that posed as a pharmaceuticals company selling fake medicine to the elderly. Because Eleanor had no appreciation for the broader consequences that result from her actions, she soon became the top salesperson there. Without the nurturing affection of Theory, Praxis, especially as the form of Eleanor in our story, is indiscriminate in her actions as it relates to them being good or bad. As a result, she never lives up to her fullest potential in helping the world and humankind. As embodied in Chidi and Eleanor, Theory and Praxis have found each other again in death in this paradise known as "The Good Place", and it is here where our love story begins.

The Evolution of Eleanor

Eleanor Shellstrop lived her life prior to coming to "The Good Place" as someone who never allowed herself to grow close to anyone, who was a liar and who deceived those around her so that she could always get ahead, and who was mean-spirited and self-absorbed in the face of other people's needs. When Eleanor met Chidi in the hopes of becoming a better person in the afterlife, her journey would ultimately reveal to them both how theory can promote mindfulness and goodness, as well as how praxis can take theory and bring it into the world and make it better in the aftermath. When Praxis took the form of Eleanor, she got by mostly on her deceptiveness.

In "The Good Place", this was a dangerous way of life, for Eleanor's lies caused chaos in that place, ranging from flying garbage, all the way to giant sinkholes. For the purposes of this parable, we can set aside the fact that we now know that Michael was causing these things, not Eleanor, since this did not factor into her path). Theory, taking on the form of Chidi, was able to show her not only how lying can be harmful, but how to best understand that harm and act to prevent it.

One of the theories that Chidi taught to Eleanor was Utilitarianism. Utilitarianism is the idea that what is ultimately moral is what brings the most happiness to the most people possible. Chidi explains to Eleanor that her current conduct is putting every citizen of "The Good Place" in danger with her lies tearing it apart. Chidi explains that Eleanor should let Utilitarianism guide her actions and by doing so, confess her lies and let Michael know that she does not belong there. Eleanor is not thrilled with Chidi's suggestion, because she doesn't see how acting in such a way benefits her personally. We can see here one of the main difficulties of putting a theory of how to live into practice: namely the fact that human beings are prone to being selfish and exhibiting the most care towards things in our personal life most of all ourselves. Such was the way of Praxis in her life as Eleanor, until she saw selflessness in action.

Eleanor experienced great difficulty in taking Chidi's lesson on Utilitarianism and carrying it out by telling the truth that she didn't belong in The Good Place. Eleanor illustrates a problem many of us face: we all have a difficulty accepting a theory unless we see it proven in action, especially when the theory goes against what we previously believed. Eleanor's selfishness prevents her from seeing how anybody could reasonably act in line with the rules of Utilitarianism, at least until Michael summons a meeting with every one of "The Good Place's" citizens to announce that all of its problems are his fault.

At first Eleanor is elated to see Michael take the fall for her, but when she hears that retirement for creatures like him is eternal torture, she tries to save him. In the end, when all of Eleanor's lies and plans fail (including the plan to kill Janet), she confesses the truth about her not belonging in "The Good Place." Eleanor seeing Michael being willing to take on eternal suffering by himself to spare the lives of everyone in "The Good Place," convinces Eleanor that the theory of Utilitarianism has legs to stand on, and decides to use them to walk a more honest path. That this was ultimately a lie doesn't change the fact that from Eleanor's perspective, she thought she was seeing something she had never thought was possible: someone acting on a moral theory that did not benefit them personally.

Chidi Breaks His Moral Bonds . . . and Becomes Better for It

Chidi Anagonye is a man who is incapable of lying. He finds himself in "The Good Place" by always trying to act based on the theories of German philosopher Immanuel Kant (1724–1804). Kant thought that the act of lying violated the spirit of what he called the Categorical Imperative.

The Categorical Imperative says that when a person is thinking about following a rule in their own lives, they should ask whether they would want absolutely every person to always follow the same rule. Kant's talking about theory here—the Categorical Imperative is a test of logical consistency—the idea is that if you can't desire everyone to follow your rule, then it's not really a rational rule for anyone (including you) to follow. So, say for example that somebody decided for themselves that stealing was morally right. If we applied this moral law universally for everyone to follow, the world would soon be plunged into chaos.

Kant puts lying on the same level as stealing, which is something Chidi would agree with, for both men believe that if everyone lied, no stable relationships in the world could exist, and that chaos would prevail.

But the world is more complicated than that, which Chidi would soon learn the hard way. Because when Chidi and his friends are trying to get through The Bad Place, Chidi has to adapt to the hostile environment and break his moral bonds, with his life and the lives of his friends in the balance.

When we think of a theory about the world or how to live in it, we have to think about the world as it is outside of our theory. In a world where grave dangers such as murderers exist, we know that if we ourselves or our loved ones were ever in their crosshairs and lying was the only way to save them or ourselves, chances are we would do it without a moment's thought of any potential moral violation. This is because strict obedience to a theory and its straightforwardness more often than not makes it useless when tested in reality with all of its complexity and nuance.

This is what Eleanor as Praxis tries to make Chidi as Theory understand. When you apply your theory to the world and your theory does not fully conform to how the world is, you must change your theory accordingly so that it may know greater harmony with the world. When Chidi is having trouble lying to the demons of The Bad Place and maintaining his Kantian moral principles, Eleanor tells him that he needs a new moral philosophy to get outside of his anxiety and to affect the world around him. Because, at the end of the day, if theory cannot inform how people act in the world and change it, then it is worthless.

Eleanor argues against Chidi's Kantian position as it relates to lying by talking about an alternative known as Moral Particularism ("Rhonda, Diana, Jake, and Trent," S2E11). Moral Particularism is unique in that it abandons the concept of universal rules and instead, believes that moral rules are created from the specifics of a given situation. In the case of the predicament of Chidi and his friends, if they do not lie to these demons and the truth gets exposed, they will be tortured in The Bad Place for eternity.

By Eleanor convincing Chidi to embrace Moral Particularism in their situation, we can see a bridging of the divide between Theory and Praxis. Theory is pure and uninformed by the goings on of the world, whereas Praxis concerns itself with nothing but the world but isn't always mindful about how it acts within it. Because Chidi has shown Eleanor different ways of living, Eleanor in turn was able to show Chidi that his philosophical principles will only keep him frozen before the world unless he starts to pay enough attention to what goes on around it. The love that Eleanor and Chidi share is what makes Theory and Praxis so beautiful: Theory is born in the world, but it is Praxis that allows Theory to thrive in it.

From Demon to Hero: How Love Transformed Michael

When Theory and Praxis find harmony with each other, their love touches people in the deepest of ways and transforms them. Because when people see firsthand that there are ways to change not only the hearts of human beings but also the world in which those hearts beat, people want to be a part of it. They witness something greater than themselves, something that actually can make the world or even just a single human being better. Such was the case with Michael, the demon architect of The Bad Place. Michael, who had designs to torture Eleanor, Chidi, and their friends for all eternity, saw how Chidi helped Eleanor become a better person. In time, this would lead him to become a kinder and more moral version of himself.

Michael was a demon who thought very little of humans and did not think that they were at all capable of change. He took delight in torturing them. His way of living—the theory that he abided by—was that the best way to live his life as a demon was through causing as much suffering to human beings as he possibly could for as long as he could. The praxis through which he brought about that vision of living was designing "The Good Place," which was a deceptive version of the actual Good Place meant to cause suffering to Chidi and Eleanor (and Jason and Tahani) by having them annoy each other given their opposite personalities. When Chidi and Eleanor actually end up befriending each other and even developing romantic feelings for each other, the flaws of Michael's praxis was exposed. Begrudgingly, Michael would abandon his praxis, and it would not be long before his theories about human beings and the world would follow suit.

Michael demonstrated his moral growth many times throughout Season Two, but it reached a definite high point when he sacrificed himself (or so he thought, at least), so that the humans could all get through the portal to the Judge's chambers ("Rhonda, Diana, Jake, and Trent"). This is a genuine Utilitarian act of selflessness. When he initially teamed up with the humans, Michael's only concern was self-preservation. By the end of Season Two, he had come to embody the best of moral theory. This happened slowly. It began when Michael saw Chidi changing Eleanor as a person, and then took a big step when Eleanor wanted to give Michael a similar chance.

Along the way, Michael started to no longer look at Eleanor and her friends as objects for him to torture, or to use for his own personal interests, but as his own friends who are worth saving. That is the power of the love between Theory and Praxis at work. Because once a theory has been proven or disproven out in the world—the theory in Michael's case was the idea that Eleanor was incapable of changing when in fact she was and did—then we can never look at the world the same way again. Michael's world was forever altered by these humans, and the theory he now lives by because of them is that people can change and become good. And his praxis? Helping his friends get to The Good Place by any means necessary.

What Is to Be Learned from This Love?

In the end, Michael would convince the Judge to give Eleanor and her friends another test, in the form of returning them to Earth and letting them prove the goodness they have gained in their time together, but without having any knowledge of the existence of their friends.

Eleanor is returned to Earth and after Michael saves her life, she sets out to be the best person she can be by doing honest work, engaging in eco-friendly activism, and all around doing good deeds. Eleanor would come into hard times however, and these struggles would convince her there is no point whatsoever in being a good person. She would revert back to her angry, selfish, and outright rude behavior.

Because Eleanor abandoned her moral education, she went back to hurting everyone around her and isolating herself. At least until an old friend got her back on track. She would unknowingly encounter Michael masquerading as a barkeep and after Eleanor had quite a few drinks, Michael reminds her about what we owe to each other. Eleanor wakes up the next day and on her laptop comes across a series of lectures given by moral philosophy professor Chidi Anagonye on the same topic that Michael had discussed with her the night before. Feeling engaged and inspired watching Chidi, she sets out to Australia to find him again so that he can teach her ethics, thus renewing the cycle of theory and praxis once more.

What can we learn from the love shared by Chidi and Eleanor, and more broadly by theory and praxis? From Chidi, we can learn to love ideas, to love the consumption of knowledge and from this consumption, the pursuit of goodness and meaning. From Eleanor we can learn to live life to the fullest, to indulge in the pleasures around us and to do so authentically. In the case of Eleanor however, we can choose superior pleasures to those like getting drunk or stalking Kendall Jenner's Instagram.

Our pleasures can come from turning our readings of the theory of utilitarianism into the practice of helping the homeless. We can take everything we learn over a lifetime about what it means to be in a society, and use that to either run for public office or promote civic goods like libraries, parks, and schools. Ultimately, we can be better people both to ourselves and our fellow human beings for after all; it is what we owe each other.

11
Those Agonizing Choices

Max Romanowski

> **Chidi:** You know the sound that a fork makes in the garbage disposal? That's the sound that my brain makes all the time. It's just this constant grinding about things I'm afraid of or things that I want or want to want or want to want to . . .
>
> **Eleanor:** Is it grinding in there right now, bud?
>
> **Chidi:** . . . Yep!
>
> —"Best Self"

In *The Good Place*, a primary topic of discussion is the question of what it means to be a good person. This is most frequently explored as Eleanor tries to better herself to fit in to what she believes is "The Good Place," then again when she sets out on a quest to get into the actual Good Place.

Chidi also grapples with similar questions about personal morality, to an even greater extent. While Eleanor tries to be a moral person after she died, Chidi struggled to do this his entire life, so much so that it crippled him with anxiety and ultimately led to his death. He was aware of how difficult it was to be completely moral, and it destroyed him.

Despite taking place largely in the afterlife, Chidi's journey in *The Good Place* actually functions as an effective mirror to a painfully relatable component of everyday life on Earth. One of the most enduring realities people are faced with as they get older in the real world is how complicated modern adult life actually is. For proof of this, listen to someone who is pro-choice debate with someone who is pro-life, two people debate about gun control, or any two people debate any of the countless hot-button issues that are infinitely more complicated than they seem at first.

Chidi may be irrational and fickle at times, but at the core of his dilemma is an authentic battle all people face at some level, albeit slightly hyperbolized—Chidi still frets over his decision to drink almond milk instead of dairy milk even while he's in the afterlife ("Dance Dance Resolution"). More than anything else, Chidi wants to be a good person and lead a moral life. He slaved at this task on Earth but ended up with nothing to show for it, still failing to get into The Good Place as a result of what his indecision put others through. However, since this is *The Good Place,* Chidi gets the opportunity to continue laboring in the afterlife. *The Good Place* thus is able to use philosophy not just as a gimmick to quip clever jokes or tell an elaborate story, but to actively and authentically explore its characters and their struggle with the nuances of leading a moral life.

Chidi's Life on Earth

MICHAEL: Listen, I don't need the Chidi who once had a panic attack during rock-paper-scissors because there were, and I quote, "just too many variables." I need the Chidi who stormed in here and told me to stop Eleanor's train without thinking of consequences.

CHIDI: Oh, boy, now I'm nervous about that decision.

MICHAEL: Retroactively? I mean, how do you even . . . ?

CHIDI: I don't know.

—"Chidi's Choice"

In "The Eternal Shriek," we get our first glimpse of Chidi before he died. In a series of flashbacks, we see Chidi interact with a colleague who purchases a pair of tacky and extravagant cowboy boots. In order to spare his friend's feelings, he lies and says he loves the boots. In traditional sitcom fashion Chidi's lie gets bigger and more elaborate, until he breaks down in agony and confesses that he hates the boots. For members of the audience, this is invaluable to understanding Chidi's ideas of moral principles. He follows the Kantian idea that principles are universally true, no matter the situation. He believes this so intensely that a simple and theoretically harmless lie eats him up inside until he has no choice but to confess. Crucial to the story here is that his friend does not embrace him or even thank him for his honesty. His friend scoffs in annoyance and grumbles the soon to be recurring lament, "This is why everyone hates moral philosophy professors." Despite following through on his principles, Chidi is not given the freedom of forgiveness, but is instead left to ponder if he made the right decision by telling the truth.

Opening the back half of the first season, "Chidi's Choice" offers the audience another preview of what makes Chidi tick. After Eleanor outs herself as the imposter in "The Good Place," the whole town works together to build a legal case to convince the powers that be to let her stay. As a moral philosopher, Chidi is left to make a myriad crucial decisions in order to determine the best way to persuade the judge to let Eleanor stay. This in itself begins to paralyze Chidi, but his day gets even more complicated as both Eleanor and Tahani profess their love to him in the span of several minutes. Left to choose between the two women, Chidi retreats into hiding with Michael to explore his options, while the audience gets another tour through Chidi's life on Earth to learn just how deeply indecisive he has always been. These memories vary from being unable to pick teams for recess soccer—"filibustering" recess, as his friends complain— to failing to make any crucial decisions as best man for his friend's wedding. Back in the afterlife, Chidi's decision is eventually made for him as Eleanor and Tahani both rescind their professions of love.

Even though the choice hinted in the episode's title is eventually made null, this episode is still able to communicate to the audience a great deal about Chidi's anxieties and his struggles with making any decision whatsoever. Chidi has so intensely studied the ins and outs of moral philosophy that it has infected every level of his life. Not only does he struggle with the big ethical conundrums, but also personal decisions both big (whom he's in love with) and small (whether to use a pen-and-paper or marker-and-whiteboard).

Exaggerated as it may be, Chidi's anxiety speaks to the universal struggle of trying to be a good person. All people may not get an ulcer trying to decide between Pumpkin Soup and Risotto, but life is still full of tough decisions where the "right" answer is seemingly impossible to determine. Which college do I go to? What job should I apply for? Whom should I marry? The list is endless and while it's fairly easy to feel good about a decision in hindsight when it has worked out well, the fear of choosing incorrectly and ruining everything is still very real and palpable.

The Theoretical Made Literal

In Season Two, when Eleanor, Chidi, Tahani, and Jason have all discovered that they are in fact in The Bad Place, they strike a deal with Michael for Chidi to conduct "Good Person" lessons in order to try to improve enough to get into The Good Place. One such lesson focuses on The Trolley Problem (originally proposed by philosopher Philippa Foot).

The thought experiment is fairly simple: imagine that you're driving a runaway trolley that will run over and kill five people unless you switch tracks and kill one other person. Chidi emphasizes to the group that there is no single answer to The Trolley Problem, but instead a variety of different scenarios and approaches to the problem.

Michael, of course, take this as a chance to exploit Chidi's fear of making choices. He manufactures a reality where Chidi is on an actual trolley and has to make the decision to choose between the life of one man or the lives of five. As the episode continues and the scenarios get more elaborate (including a scenario where Chidi runs over his old colleague from "The Eternal Shriek;" his blood splattered red boots flying into Chidi's face), Chidi becomes more distressed about making the right decision (because while the people may be fake, Michael assures him that their pain is completely real). By the end of the experiment, Michael finally relents and Chidi kicks him out of his house.

While this thought experiment takes up the majority of the episode, the show is very strict about never giving the audience the "right" answer. We still don't know whether we're supposed to switch the track to kill one person instead of five, harvest the organs of one healthy person to save the life of five, or any of the other horrible scenarios Michael creates for his own amusement and Chidi's agony.

The ultimate reality that sinks in by the end of the episode is that Chidi was right, as much as Michael and Eleanor (and Chidi himself) may wish otherwise, and there are no clean and simple answers to the difficult and complex issues in the world. As usual, Chidi is aware of that, and in this episode that awareness is exploited and used against him for the amusement of others. This is a snapshot of Chidi further on in his character development. He may not be ready to make concrete decisions, but he is now being forced to address them head on, whether he wants to or not. By the end of the episode Michael repents of his bad behavior and some form of status quo is achieved again. But the episode is clear that this doesn't make all of those tough problems go away. The rest of the group finds out through the remainder of the season that while The Trolley Problem may be hypothetical, its comment on the tough decisions humans need to make in life is still real.

The Chronicles of Riddick

Principles aren't principles when you pick and choose when you're gonna follow them!

—CHIDI, "Rhonda, Diana, Jake, and Trent"

In the group's quest to get into The Good Place, they must travel through The Bad Place in order to make their case to the head Judge. This requires them to don costumes and personas to sneak unnoticed through The Bad Place's treacherous landmarks. During their quest to stay hidden, they accidentally stumble upon a cocktail party in the Museum of Human Misery, forcing them to interact and overtly lie to various demons in order to blend in. While everyone in the group adapts into their roles quite nicely, Chidi is left feeling unsure about this deception. According to his Kantian principles, lying is always wrong, whether it's about his distaste for gaudy cowboy boots or about his identity in The Bad Place.

While certainly irritating to the rest of the group, Chidi does raise some reasonable concerns. The entire point of getting to the Judge is make a plea that they deserve a chance at going to The Good Place. Lying has the potential to be counterproductive to their entire mission, with Chidi noting, "What if I lie down here and I lose twelve points, and then we get in front of the Judge, and I'm twelve points short? Or what if the Judge won't even take our case at all because we lied to get there? Kant says that lying is always wrong, and I follow that maxim." Based on our knowledge about Chidi, this is a legitimate objection, and one he sticks to even as they venture further into The Bad Place.

In the back half of the episode, though, Eleanor offers a compelling counter argument to Chidi's Kantian principles, by evoking the philosophy of Jonathan Dancy. Dancy argues for the concept of Moral Particularism in his essay of the same name, suggesting that there is no one set of principles that apply to every scenario; that human life is too complex for one moral judgment to be true every single time (Dancy). Eleanor pitches this concept to Chidi using an elaborate example about going to the movies:

ELEANOR: Let's say you promised your friend you'd go to the movies. But then your mom suddenly gets rushed to the ER. Your boy Kant would say never break a promise.

Go see *Chronicles of Riddick*. Doesn't matter if your mom gets lonely and steals a bucket of Vicodin from the nurse's closet . . . But a Moral Particularist . . . would say there's no absolute rule.

> You have to choose your actions based on the particular situation
> and right now, we are in a pretty bonkers situation. ("Rhonda,
> Diana, Jake, and Trent")

Her example is charming and comedic in a way only *The Good
Place* can pull off. But several crucial ideas are being commu-
nicated here.

Firstly, her argument is actually quite compelling. Chidi has
raised a legitimate concern and she has responded with a legitimate potential solution. This isn't just a way to move the plot
forward and squeeze out a few jokes about *The Chronicles of
Riddick*; it's a genuine discussion of the ethical ramifications of
their actions, filtered through the philosophical writings of
Immanuel Kant and Jonathan Dancy.

Secondly, it allows Chidi to further his characterization.
Chidi adopts the mindset of a Moral Particularist and is able to
get out of their predicament without blowing their cover. He had
a decision to make and followed through when it was required
of him. This contrasts with his life on Earth where any insignif-
icant decision would send him into deep anxiety. Once again,
The Good Place uses the philosophical underpinnings of its
roots to allow its characters a chance to grow and learn how to
navigate the complexities of the world they're in. A definitive
correct decision is rarely offered, but a thoughtful examination
of the dilemma and possible solutions are always provided.

What We Owe to Each Other

> Why choose to be good every day if there is no guaranteed reward
> we can count on, now or in the afterlife? I argue that we choose to be
> good because of our bonds with other people and our innate desire to
> treat them with dignity.

> —CHIDI, "Somewhere Else"

In the final episode of Season Two, the entire group is given
another chance to live out good lives on Earth to see if they can
become worthy of making it into The Good Place. This allows
for the culmination of Chidi's arc and his fear of making concrete decisions. Before they get sent off, Chidi observes Jason
and Janet confess their love for each other, throwing caution to
the wind as they may never see each other again after this.
Janet admits that she'd been avoiding the issue in the past by
saying that the situation was complicated.

This admission in particular strikes a chord with Chidi. As a
person who has avoided making decisions his entire life because

of how complicated and confusing the problems were, Chidi finally sees things clearly. Even though his "brain is grinding like a fork in a garbage disposal" ("Best Self"; "Somewhere Else"), the entirety of the series has been leading to this realization. Life may be exhausting and terrifying and confusing with no easy answers, but that's still not an excuse to not act toward making things right. Chidi acts out this belief by walking over and kissing Eleanor, finally dismissing all of his fears and anxieties and making a concrete decision.

Immediately after this they get sent back to Earth, with no memory of each other. Due to a brief intervention from Michael, Eleanor eventually seeks out Chidi back on Earth, stumbling across some of his video seminars online. In these videos, Chidi outlines some of the most basic principles of his own personal philosophy, citing the philosopher Thomas Scanlon and his book *What We Owe to Each Other* (1989). Scanlon suggests that we as humans owe each other decency and humanity in how we treat one another because of the inherent desire that exists in forming bonds with other human beings. Chidi follows suit in his beliefs about how to treat each other and why treating each other with dignity is worthwhile.

Both of these scenes from "Somewhere Else" function as a type of bookend for Chidi's character. In his lectures, we have Chidi before he died; before he went through the trials of the afterlife. At the beginning of the episode, we have him after his journeys with Eleanor. On Earth we see him recite a lecture that emphasizes how important he thinks it is to treat each other with dignity. Retroactively this feeds into our understanding of all the asinine decisions Chidi has made—belaboring over lying about cowboy boots, not knowing how to respond to Eleanor's profession of love, even writing a multi-thousand-page manifesto on ethics and how indeterminate it all seems. He did this from a perspective of trying to answer the question Scanlon posed in his book.

Fast forward to his decision to kiss Eleanor and we see a version of Chidi completely transformed. One who still has not given up to the desire to be good or interrogate the hard questions of ethics and moral philosophy, but who also understands that things don't have to be as frustrating and complicated as he had always made them. It is the blossoming of a new era of Chidi's character. Continually, *The Good Place* allows this character work to be authentic and realistic while tethering it to the various philosophers discussed during the series. Chidi talks about Kant, Dancy, Foot, and Scanlon, and the show uses their ideas to grow him as a character. He doesn't just grow alongside the various philosophical musings of the show, but precisely because of them.

How Do We Live Life?

The Good Place may understand and effectively articulate the difficulties and nuances that come with attempting to live a moral life, but what statement is it trying to make about that reality? Looking toward Chidi may serve us well. No one is more aware of these difficulties and nuances than Chidi, and no one is more petrified by the implications a single action can have on those around us. However, as his arc over the course of the show indicates, just because we're aware of how tough living a good life is, that's no excuse for not taking action on what matters and what is important in life, just as Chidi does when he finally sheds his fear and indecision and chooses to be with Eleanor.

The lesson here is clear—inaction is understandable but cannot be the final position in which we find ourselves. The reoccurrence of the Trolley Problem showcases that as well. Despite there never being a fixed and determined answer to The Trolley Problem, Michael is forced to solve it for himself when choosing between saving himself or Eleanor from being caught as they are sneaking through The Bad Place. He informs her that he has "solved" the Trolley Problem, saying that, "the actual solution is very simple: sacrifice yourself" ("Rhonda, Diana, Jake, and Trent"), right before turning himself in so Eleanor can escape. While there is technically no philosophical rigor to back up what he is saying in the moment, his selfless act shows the growth he's undergone in their time together, becoming a more caring person as a result.

This sentiment stems back to Chidi himself and his reading of *What We Owe to Each Other*. The right answer may not be easy to determine, and we may not get it right every time, but there is still grace in the pursuit, as Eleanor tells Michael when he asks how she is still able to try and be a good and ethical person: "This ethics stuff, it's hard, and it's confusing. It is such a buzzkill. But, it does get rid of the little voice [in the back of my head]. Because at least I'm trying to do the right thing instead of the crappy thing, and I've got to say, man, I don't miss the little voice" ("Derek"). *The Good Place* is determined to remind us that even though it's hard, working to become a better person is worth it, if for no other reason than to treat our fellow humans with respect and dignity.

IV

The Brainy
Bunch

12
How the Fork Did I Get Here?

JOSHUA TEPLEY

Imagine you accidentally drop a bottle of margarita mix in a grocery store parking lot. As you bend over to pick it up, a runaway stack of shopping carts knocks you out into the street, where you're hit by a large truck.

Suddenly, you find yourself sitting in a comfortable armchair in front of a large desk. Behind the desk sits an attractive white-haired man who looks a lot like Ted Danson—the guy who played Sam in *Cheers*. The man smiles and tells you to relax; everything is fine. You're dead, but you're in the Good Place.

Whether you feel shock or fear or relief, there's a question that needs answering: How did you get there? I don't mean, "What did you do to deserve a spot in the Good Place?" but rather, "How are you, the person sitting there in that chair, the very same person as the one who just seconds earlier dropped a bottle of margarita mix in a grocery store parking lot?"

This is an instance of what philosophers call the "problem of personal identity." The problem is this: What makes a person at one time identical to a person at another time? The word "identity" can mean different things, and this sense of the word has nothing to do with how a person identifies him- or herself, such as male or female, religious or secular, liberal or conservative. Nor is it what philosophers call "qualitative identity," which is when two things share almost all of the same qualities, such as two freshly-minted pennies.

Rather, "identity" means "being the very same thing as." In this sense of "identity," George Washington is identical to the first president of the United States, and the Eiffel Tower is identical to the tallest structure in Paris. Philosophers call this "numerical identity," since it's the kind of identity expressed by the equals sign in mathematics.

The numerical identity of persons over time poses a number of puzzles. To give just one, consider Eleanor Shellstrop and her five-year-old self. What makes them the same person? Their bodies are very different, and so are their minds. In fact, if Eleanor had an identical twin sister, the two of them would probably share more in common now, at thirty-something, than Eleanor does with her five-year-old self. But in that case, what makes Eleanor numerically identical to her five-year-old self but not to her hypothetical thirty-something-year-old identical twin?

The problem of personal identity is extremely important when it comes to thinking about the afterlife. If there's an afterlife, and you want to get there someday, then somebody in the afterlife after you die had better be numerically identical to *you*, the person now reading this book. But how can that happen?

We know very well that when you die your body will remain here on Earth, either put in a grave or turned into ashes. Given this undeniable fact, how can you possibly survive your death? The inhabitants of "The Good Place" have bodies, but how did their bodies get there? Or do they have new bodies? And in that case, what makes them numerically identical to people who died on Earth? This chapter will try to answer these questions by carefully considering three different theories of personal identity.

Bodies

Let's begin with the simplest theory of personal identity, which I'll call the "same-body theory." According to this theory, two persons are the same person in virtue of having the same body. At first glance, this seems pretty plausible: the inhabitants of "The Good Place" not only have bodies, but their bodies look exactly like the ones they had on Earth before they died. So, perhaps Eleanor, Chidi, Tahani, and Jason make it to "The Good Place" simply because their bodies make it there. End of story.

Unfortunately, there are problems with this account. To start, what makes two bodies the same body is typically thought to be *spatiotemporal continuity*. This means that two bodies are the same body in virtue of there being an unbroken path between them through space and time.

For example, Eleanor's thirty-something-year-old body is numerically identical to her five-year-old body, despite their obvious physical differences, because anyone who started following around her body when it was five years old, and kept it up for thirty-or-so years, would eventually be following around her thirty-something-year-old body. At no point would Eleanor's body disappear and reappear at a later time, or jump from one place to another without going through a continuous series of points in between them.

The issue is that *The Good Place* provides no indication whatsoever that people's bodies literally travel through space from Earth to "The Good Place." Their bodies seem to simply appear in the latter, out of thin air, in which case there's a huge spatial gap between them and the corresponding bodies back on Earth. The former and the latter might be qualitatively identical, but they can't be numerically identical.

And there's an even bigger problem. Even if someone thinks that two bodies can be the same body without being spatiotemporally continuous with each other, there's the undeniable fact that people's bodies don't just disappear when they die. We don't know exactly what happens to Eleanor's body after it's hit by a truck, but we do know what sorts of things are likely: it's embalmed and buried, or maybe it's cremated and scattered. Either way, how can it *also* be in "The Good Place"? Think of it this way: What happens to Eleanor's body after she dies? Does it remain on Earth, or does it end up in "The Good Place"? The answer can't be *both*, for the same thing can't be in two places at once; and since Eleanor's body clearly *does* remain on Earth, it can't also be in "The Good Place."

For these two reasons, the same-body theory seems unable to explain how people can make it to the afterlife when they die. It's time to consider another theory of personal identity.

Minds

Imagine that Eleanor and Tahani both die and find themselves sitting together in Michael's office, but something strange has happened: one of them has Eleanor's mind and Tahani's body; the other has Eleanor's body and Tahani's mind. (By "mind" I mean "sum total of mental properties," including thoughts, feelings, beliefs, desires, and memories.) Who's who? The same-body theory says that people go where their bodies go, so Eleanor now has Tahani's mind, and Tahani now has Eleanor's mind. But doesn't this get things backwards? Isn't this better understood as a situation in which Eleanor now has Tahani's body, and Tahani now has Eleanor's body? If so, this suggests that persons go, not where their *bodies* go, but where their *minds* go.

Let's call this the "same-mind theory" of personal identity. According to this theory, two persons are the same person in virtue of having the same mind. What makes two minds the same mind? Surely, they needn't contain *exactly* the same mental properties, for people are constantly changing their thoughts, feelings, beliefs, and desires. If having the same mind required having exactly the same mental properties, then nobody would survive for more than an instant. Sharing a *vast majority* of mental properties is also too strict, for small changes over short periods of time can add up to large changes over long periods of time. Five-year-old Eleanor and thirty-something-year-old Eleanor have very few mental properties in common, but they're still the same person.

A better answer to our question is *psychological continuity*. Two minds are psychologically continuous if they're connected by a series of minds, each temporally contiguous pair of which shares a vast majority of mental properties. (Two minds are "temporally contiguous" if they exist immediately before and after each other—such as your mind right now and your mind a split second ago.) This allows persons to survive everyday changes in thoughts, feelings, beliefs, and desires. It also explains how five-year-old Eleanor and thirty-something-year-old Eleanor can be numerically identical, despite having so few mental properties in common. They're numerically identical because they're connected by a series of minds, each temporally contiguous pair of which shares a vast majority of mental properties.

The same-mind theory, understood in terms of psychological continuity, has no trouble explaining how people can make it to the afterlife without their earthly bodies when they die. So long as one's mind at death shares a vast majority of mental properties with the mind of a person who, at the very next instant, appears in the afterlife, the two persons are numerically identical—regardless of what bodies they have. So far, so good.

Reboots and Duplicates

Despite its initial promise, however, the same-mind theory has problems. Serious problems. To start, this theory runs into trouble with the first major plot twist of Season Two: the 802 reboots. Every time Eleanor, Chidi, Tahani, and Jason discover that they're actually in the Bad Place, Michael reverts their minds to the way they were when they first arrived in "The Good Place."

This involves a sudden and massive change in their mental properties. If the numerical identity of persons over time requires psychological continuity, then such abrupt and major mental changes arguably result in numerical differences—the end of one group of persons and the beginning of another. Throughout Season Two, nobody—not even Michael or all-knowing Janet—wonders whether the four characters survive the reboots. The only time anybody ever questions this is in Season Three, when Chidi tells Eleanor that he isn't numerically identical to the "Chidi" who fell in love with her in a previous reboot because he doesn't remember being that person ("Janet(s)"). Needless to say, nobody takes Chidi's suggestion seriously—least of all Eleanor, who accuses him of simply trying to avoid talking about his feelings.

In any case, the same-mind theory faces a far bigger challenge than the 802 reboots and psychological discontinuity they involve. Imagine that Eleanor dies and suddenly two people looking like her find themselves sitting in Michael's office. The two act just like Eleanor, too, for each of them has virtually all of the mental properties that Eleanor had right before she died. Both of them remember being Eleanor, and each of them even thinks that she *is* Eleanor.

This imaginary scenario seems harmless enough, but it's devastating for the same-mind theory. According to this theory, two persons are the same person if they have the same mind, which we're understanding in terms of psychological continuity. Since each of the two individuals sitting in Michael's office is psychologically continuous with Eleanor at her death, the same-mind theory implies that *both of them* are numerically identical to Eleanor. It's a principle of logic that if A = B, and A = C, then B = C, so it logically follows that the two people sitting in Michael's office are also numerically identical *to each other*. And this is completely absurd, for nothing whatsoever, not even a person, can be wholly in two places at once. In short, this perfectly coherent and seemingly harmless imaginary scenario has driven the same-mind theory into a contradiction. Any theory that even possibly entails a contradiction is false, so the same-mind theory must be false. Another dead end.

Souls

It's time to consider a third solution to the problem of personal identity. Perhaps we're more than just our bodies, and what carries us from moment to moment, and from this life to the next (if there is one), is precisely this non-bodily part of us. Perhaps, in other words, we have *souls*.

Philosophers have offered many different theories of the soul over the past 2,500 years. What they all have in common is that souls are in some sense *immaterial*—that is, they aren't made of matter (atoms). According to some philosophers, we actually *are* souls and not our bodies at all. On this view, we have bodies, but we're no more identical to them than we are to the clothes we wear. According to other philosophers, souls are *parts* of us, either because we are our bodies, and our bodies are compounds of soul (sometimes called "form" or "essence") and something else (usually called "matter"); or because we are compounds of which our souls and our bodies are parts. Fortunately, we needn't decide which of these conceptions of the soul is best. We can sidestep this issue by simply defining a soul as *an immaterial person or part of a person*, which is neutral with respect to these different theories.

There are, as you can imagine, a host of philosophical arguments both for and against the existence of human souls. Let's set these aside in order to focus on the prospect of using souls to solve the problem of personal identity. Perhaps what makes two persons the same person is simply the fact that they have (or are) the same soul. Apart from its commitment to the existence of souls, how does the "same-soul theory" fare? Does it solve our problem?

At first glance, it certainly seems to. The same-soul theory easily explains how we can make it to the afterlife without our earthly bodies. As long as people in the afterlife have our souls, those people are *us*—regardless of what bodies they have. This theory also explains how Eleanor, Chidi, Tahani, and Jason can survive having their memories partially erased for each of the 802 reboots, for there's no reason to think that having the same soul requires psychological continuity. Finally, the same-soul theory apparently avoids the problem of duplication, for whereas we can easily imagine one person being psychologically continuous with two different people, we can't easily imagine one soul belonging to, let alone being identical to, two different people.

But not all is sweetness and light for the same-soul theory of personal identity. The main problem with this theory comes into focus when we try answering the following question: What makes two souls the same soul? We might be tempted to say that two souls are the same soul in virtue of being psychologically continuous with each other, but that turns this theory into the same-mind theory, which then inherits all of its problems—including the problem of duplication. Nor can we say that two souls are the same soul in virtue of belonging to the same body, for that turns this theory into the same-body theory, which then inherits all of *its* problems.

Perhaps it would be best if we simply said that there are no criteria by which we can judge that two souls are the same soul. But in that case, we have no way of knowing whether two persons are numerically identical.

How do the four humans who find themselves in "The Good Place" know that they have the same souls as people who just died on Earth a few minutes earlier? In fact, how do any of *us* know that we have the same souls now that we had ten years ago, ten days ago, or even ten seconds ago? Without any criteria for judging that two souls are the same soul, we have no way of answering these questions.

Essences

At this point, someone might object that we've lost sight of the main purpose of this chapter, namely to understand how personal identity works in *The Good Place*. Regardless of any philosophical objections to the existence of souls or problems with using them to explain personal identity, don't they just obviously exist in the show?

For the first two-and-a-half seasons, I think the answer is *no*. It's true that there's a great deal of talk about "soul mates" and saving this or that person's "soul," but such talk is best understood metaphorically. It's also true that Michael twice mentions his own soul in describing the nature of demonic retirement (the so-called "Eternal Shriek"), but Michael, don't forget, is a demon; and from the nature of demons, nothing follows about the nature of human persons. Up through the middle of Season Three, the writers of *The Good Place* seem to leave it open whether the humans in their fictional universe have souls. Perhaps they do; perhaps they don't.

This ambivalence changes in "Janet(s)." In this episode, the four humans end up in Janet's "void" with bodies that are qualitatively identical to Janet's. What happened to their earthly bodies—the ones that were duking it out with demons in the Puking Moose Saloon? As Janet explains to them: "Your real bodies dematerialized when you entered my void, and your essences reconstituted themselves in this form." The word "essence" can mean different things, but the meaning that makes the most sense in this context is *soul*—more specifically, a conception of the soul according to which it's a metaphysical component of the human body along with what is usually called "matter" (roughly, a collection of atoms).

This theory of human persons—namely, that they are bodies, and bodies are compounds of soul (essence) and matter—is called "hylomorphism." Hylomorphism can be traced back to the Ancient Greek philosopher Aristotle, but its most famous proponent is probably the medieval Catholic philosopher Thomas Aquinas. Whether the writers of *The Good Place* realize it or not, they seem to be endorsing the traditional Catholic view of the human person. And with this theory of the human person comes a theory of personal identity: the same-soul theory. According to *The Good Place*, two persons are the same person in virtue of having the same soul, or essence.

The same-soul theory of personal identity has its share of problems, not the least of which is that it requires the existence of souls—immaterial persons or (as in *The Good Place*) parts of persons. Another problem, as we saw earlier, is that it seems to make it impossible to know when two persons are numerically identical, for we have no way of telling when two persons have the same soul.

Apparently, Janet is able to tell, but how? By what criteria does she judge that two persons have the same "essence"? The episode "Janet(s)" raises such questions, but it doesn't really answer them. Hopefully, *The Good Place* will tackle these and other problems with souls and their use in explaining personal identity in the final season.

13
The Vessel of Knowledge Who Stole Our Hearts

ELIZABETH SCHILTZ

While there are many traits that endear Janet to her fans and friends in *The Good Place*, the one that is most essential to her character is her charmingly unabashed and often repeated claim to know "literally everything."

As everyone's favorite "anthropomorphized vessel of knowledge," Janet can break it to Eleanor that Kevin Paltonic just wasn't that into her. She can carefully explain to Jason that Derek is her "son/rebound/booty call." She can even use her knowledge of everything about "computer programming and virtual reality and artificial intelligence and the human brain and everything else" to build a virtual reality simulator that allows Chidi to determine which break-up scenario is least painful for Simone (as she notes, she is "kind of a nerd") ("The Ballad of Donkey Doug").

Philosophers typically call the possession of all knowledge "omniscience," such that an omniscient being is one who, like Janet, "knows everything." The tricky thing, then, is how to define this state of "omniscience"—what, really, is it to "contain all the knowledge in the universe"? Is Janet omniscient in this way? And most importantly: is it possible that philosophical reflection on the nature of omniscience can help us to understand and appreciate Janet even more?

Janet and Omniscience

Many contemporary philosophers think that the definition of omniscience has to do with what we call "propositions"—roughly, objects of belief that may be expressed in declarative sentences. When Jason asserts that the approaching police officer can't arrest him if they quickly get married, he is uttering a sentence which expresses something that he believes—namely, that the world is such that spouses can't arrest each other, even if one is a police officer and the other is a criminal who has initiated a quickie wedding by offering half the stuff that he has just stolen. The proposition here is this view (or representation) of the world, and Jason is expressing his belief in it by proposing marriage to his arresting officer.

Some propositions are true, and some are false. While Jason really believes that spouses can't arrest one another, this is not actually the case—a fact that Jason quickly learns as "Officer K" proceeds to detain him. Many philosophers also think that it follows from the definition of knowledge that we can only actually know true things. We may say we know something that turns out to be false, but if we do that we're making a mistake: we, like Jason, may believe the false thing, but are wrong in saying that we know it. So, philosophers will point out that, while people can believe either kind of propositions, we can only be said to actually *know* true ones. According to this analysis, then, being omniscient is about believing all of the true propositions. (Some thinkers would want me to add that it also means not believing any of the false ones.)

This description of omniscience seems to fit very well with Janet, our beloved "walking database." Janet is repeatedly described in ways that suggest that she stores propositions and recalls them when requested: she is both "a vessel containing all of the knowledge in the universe" and an "informational delivery system." Her memory can be erased and re-installed. She holds and processes data, and even developing an attitude toward that data results in "glitches"—which may cause a frog to come out of her mouth or an earthquake to shake the neighborhood. If being omniscient is about knowing true propositions, Janet does indeed seem to be a candidate for omniscience.

Careful watchers of the show, however, will notice that there actually are some limitations to Janet's knowledge. Thus, for example, she doesn't seem to know that Michael has lied to her from the outset—that he is, in reality, a Bad Place architect and that the neighborhood she has helped him construct is actually designed to torture humans. She doesn't seem to know that Eleanor and Jason don't belong in the Good Place. In addition, she doesn't seem to know the future. Finally, Janet's knowledge also stops updating when she's on Earth. She can only identify winning lottery tickets that were printed before she arrived. She doesn't even know if Raul Benitez of Caracas, Venezuela, finished the ham sandwich he started immediately before they went through the portal—and it "makes her crazy"!

To be clear: there are true propositions about Michael's identity, the future, and current events on Earth, and Janet just doesn't know them.

So, there actually are some true propositions that Janet doesn't know. While she surely knows more than Chidi, Eleanor, Tahani, and Jason, it appears that she is not really omniscient—at least, not in the way philosophers usually think about that attribute. Interestingly, though, the ways in which Janet is *not* omniscient may help us understand and appreciate her even more.

God and Omniscience

Perhaps unsurprisingly, it is often the case that philosophers who study omniscience are concerned about it because they are trying to understand the nature of the divine. While this is an analysis of a TV show about the afterlife that quite pointedly does not feature a traditional God, a consideration of what philosophers of religion have said about divine omniscience can help us understand Janet's unique relationship to knowledge.

The idea that God is omniscient is a common one among religions. Many thinkers from Jewish, Christian, and Islamic traditions point to particular stories and claims in scriptures which suggest that the divine being possesses ultimate knowledge. Thus, for example, see Job 12:13, "With God are wisdom and strength; he has counsel and understanding," and the Quran 6:59: "Not a leaf falls without His knowledge."

But even beyond the particulars of religions and holy texts, many philosophers think that we can also come to know God's omniscience through reflection on the nature of the divine itself—that, if we think carefully about what it means to be 'God,' that we will conclude that a divine being must be omniscient. Thus, for example, the twelfth-century Islamic philosopher Averroës argues that, because 'God the Glorious' is the ultimate cause of all other things, it follows that He must also be omniscient.

Averroës asserts: "He knows things, because their issuing from Him is solely due to His knowing; it is not due to His being merely Existent or Existent with a certain attribute, but to His knowing, as the Exalted has said: "Does He not know, He who created? He is the Penetrating, the Omniscient!" ("On the Harmony of Religion and Philosophy," p. 212). In a similar way, the thirteenth-century Christian philosopher Thomas Aquinas argues that because God is "universally perfect," He has every excellence. As among those excellences must be the possession of "the most perfect knowledge," Aquinas concludes that "God knows all things whatsoever that in any way are" (*Summa Theologica*, I.14.9).

Now, Janet is not the ultimate divine being. As Eleanor tells her, she is indeed really great: "You contain all the knowledge in the universe, you have a rippin' bod, and you can literally do anything" ("Janet and Michael"). Still, in the quasi-corporate structure of the afterlife of the *Good Place*, Janet is the "informational assistant." She is created and employed by other eternal beings who themselves seem to be more middle management than CEO. While Janet is not God and it seems that Janet is not entirely omniscient, the philosophical association of the divine with omniscience leads to many more questions, some of which help us to see the strengths of Janet's particular type of sagacity.

Puzzles about Divine Omniscience

Once philosophers started to take seriously the idea that God was omniscient, they found that all sorts of questions quickly followed. One that causes a great deal of worry is about what seems to be a conflict between the idea of a divine, omniscient being and that of human free will. If a divine omniscient being knows all true propositions, then that being must know propositions about the past, present, and future. It doesn't just know that Eleanor stole shrimp from the welcome party—it also knows that she will steal shrimp again, at some particular future party. (Note that this is different in kind from the knowledge Michael has of Eleanor. While Michael knows everything about her past life, he is constantly frustrated that he simply cannot predict her future actions in the way an omniscient God could.)

However, this divine omniscience seems to conflict with our belief that our future actions are freely chosen—if God knows now that Eleanor will steal the shrimp, then she can't *not* steal the shrimp at that forthcoming event. An omniscient God's foreknowledge seems to eliminate human free will.

But wait: it gets even worse! If a divine being's omniscience means that our actions are not free, then we may not actually be the moral beings we believe ourselves to be, either. We generally think that people are only morally responsible for actions that are freely chosen from alternative possibilities. We wouldn't, for example, hold Janet morally responsible for the way she begs for her life as Chidi and Eleanor approach the kill switch. She simply can't help but lie that a stock photo of the crowd at the Nickelodeon Kids' Choice Awards shows her soon-to-be orphaned children Tyler, Emma and Philip, because, while wrong, that behavior is the result of a (brilliantly) pre-programmed fail-safe measure ("The Eternal Shriek"). While this does not seem to be the case with all of Janet's actions, her reactions to mortal danger can be known in advance, and are not up to her.

However, the claims above about divine foreknowledge imply that all of our future actions are not free either—that, while it *seems* that we could do otherwise, we really can't. As a result, this argument suggests that we aren't actually morally responsible for our actions!

One way that some philosophers try to respond to this difficulty is by saying that God doesn't know things in the same linear way we do. For example, the fifth-century Roman philosopher Boethius argued that God simply doesn't understand the world in terms of past, present, and future. As such, we don't need to worry that God has foreknowledge which makes our actions unfree, because it isn't quite right to say that God has foreknowledge at all. Instead, according to Boethius, God "sees all things in his eternal present," and this does not, in itself, impose any necessity on us. (Boethius explains that, just as our watching events unfold doesn't force them to unfold in a particular fashion, God watching us engage in actions doesn't force us to engage in those specific actions, either). In this way, according to Boethius, the existence of divine omniscience can coexist perfectly well with the existence of free and morally responsible creatures (*Consolation of Philosophy* V, Prose 6).

The Good Place suggests yet another way: as we noted above, our all-knowing being does not know the future at all! While we learn from Janet and Michael that time is Jeremy Bearimy-shaped, Janet's knowledge still seems to be limited to what, from our linear, human perspective, is the past and present. Janet can make precise predictions about the future—she knows that John the gossip columnist is twenty-nine percent likely to respond to Tahani's "savage insult" by saying "Oh, honey" "in a tone so devastating you will think of it every day for the rest of time" ("Pandemonium"). However, that is simply a conjecture based on her careful analysis of the past. She does not actually know what will happen, and so has none of the foreknowledge that might seem to threaten free will.

A second kind of question philosophers ask about omniscience is about the extent to which a divine being could genuinely know about humanity. If we understand a divine being as wholly perfect, it's hard to see how such a being could understand much about the lives of decidedly imperfect humans. In particular, it's difficult to see how such a being could understand what it's like to live a human life—especially one conditioned by decidedly imperfect knowledge. Think about how an omniscient being could possibly ever understand states like jealousy, frustration, and fear. If such a being could not, then is there necessarily something missing from that being's knowledge?

There's a thought experiment at the heart of Frank Jackson's famous article "What Mary Didn't Know" that can be read as illuminating these worries. Jackson tells the story of Mary who, for reasons never quite explained, grows up and is confined in a totally black and white environment. Literally black and white. Mary learns from black and white books and lectures played on a black and white TV, and in this way comes to know about the world. Even if she learns everything that could be learned, however, Jackson argues that "Mary does not know all there is to know. For when she is let out of the black-and-white room or given a color television, she will learn what it is like to see something red, say. This is rightly described as *learning* . . ." (Jackson, "What Mary Didn't Know," p. 291).

While Jackson uses the story of Mary to make a point not really related to omniscience (he was arguing that physicalism—the idea that the world is entirely physical—is false) we can use it to think about omniscience. Mary, like the traditionally conceived divine being, knows the relevant true propositions. Still, she learns something new when she experiences color for herself for the first time. Once again, it is a much-debated question whether Mary's new knowledge consists in knowing new propositions, or is a different kind of thing altogether. On either interpretation, though, we are seeing that a kind of direct experience improves understanding.

We can see the importance of this kind of understanding by considering another important character in *The Good Place*: Maya Rudolph's luminous Judge Gen. Gen, like Janet, is described as "all-knowing." However, when we meet her, her relevant knowledge seems to consist in knowing a great deal about the afterlife's structure and system of evaluation, punishment, and reward of humans. She has almost no direct experience of humans or human life—although she does admit to binge-watching *NCIS* and enjoying the occasional burrito with "the concept of envy" on top!

Clearly, Gen's TV watching helps her creatively imagine some things about what it is like to be a human—she at least grasps what is obviously the case, that it is nearly impossible to see Kyle Chandler as anyone except Coach Taylor. Still, this "all-knowing" judge of humans very clearly does not know what it is like to be a human. As Jason—Jason!—asserts, this is problematic: "You can't judge humans 'cause you don't know what we go through." Her later visit to Earth highlights what she didn't know—she discovers that "Earth stinks," in such a way that it is incredibly difficult to make the good decisions she has been expecting humans to make. Like when Mary steps out of her black and white room, Gen learns something new ("Chidi Sees the Time Knife").

One way that some philosophers try to resolve this difficulty with respect to a traditional God is by revisiting the characteristics that such a divine being might have. Philosopher Linda Zagzebski, for example, has recently argued that in order to truly have the best and deepest kind of knowledge, a divine being must also have what she calls 'omnisubjectivity': the "property of consciously grasping with perfect accuracy and completeness the first-person perspective of every conscious being." As Zagzebski argues, this would be an advance over the traditional view: "I think omnisubjectivity makes more sense as a model of how an omniscient being knows his creatures than the model of the deity reading off all the propositions about the world in his mental encyclopedia" ("Omnisubjectivity," p. 248).

Alas, our hero Janet can't go quite that far. Still, as the seasons progress, we see her steadily developing more and more human features—as well as more and more understanding of what it is to be human. Janet is initially introduced as a "walking database," a "foundational mainframe," and an "informational delivery system." She is, of course, not a human. However, her many adventures—and over 800 reboots—allow her to develop social awareness and abilities. We see her directly experience happiness, sadness, jealousy, and friendship. She moves from drawing conclusions about love from the "231,600 songs, movies, poems, and novels" that she scans in three seconds to inform her wedding vows, to bonding with and feeling genuine love for Jason ("Chidi's Choice"). She develops empathy and understanding. She goes from using her powers to help the group merely because she is programmed in this way, to doing so to help the Soul Squad because she is a key part of it.

Ultimately, it appears that our beloved Janet isn't really omniscient after all—at least not in the philosophical sense that is traditionally considered as one of the divine attributes.

However, I think that we should consider this a feature rather than a glitch.

As we've already seen, Janet does not know the future. On the one hand, it's hard to know what this would look like on a show that asserts that time is Jeremy Bearimy–shaped, anyway! On the other hand, for those of us trapped in a linear view of time, Janet's ignorance of the future preserves free will and moral responsibility in such a way as to allow for the development of the characters and action of the show.

We can now see that Janet also does not come to have the divine omnisubjectivity that Zagzebski describes. However, her developments are far from the defects they were initially believed to be. In *The Good Place*, Eleanor, Chidi, and Tahani— and even Jason and Michael!—grow and improve morally at least in part due to the deeper understanding they develop of themselves, the appreciation they come to have of each other, and the genuinely close bonds that follow from that learning. Janet does so as well.

Janet reflects the development of a kind of understanding that is usefully different from—and an important addition to— the kind of omniscience that consists in belief in all true propositions. While she may not be "all-knowing" in the sense described by many philosophers, her unique type of knowing allows for the moral growth of the characters—and the plot of *The Good Place*. Far from illuminating shortcomings, it seems that philosophical reflection on the nature of omniscience really does enable us to do what initially seemed impossible: to understand and appreciate Janet even more.[1]

---

[1] The ideas in this chapter benefited greatly from enormously helpful feedback from Steven Benko and Andrew Pavelich, as well as rich discussions with many of my students at the College of Wooster. Special thanks go to Mylo Parker-Emerson, '19, Margy Adams, '19, Teagan Robinson, '19, Maxwell Gregg, '21, Dzifa Adjei, '20, Erin O'Connor, '19, Anna Nacci WHS, '20, and all of the wonderful students in my 2018 First Year Seminar on the Meaning of Life.

14
Is Kant the Reason Everyone Hates Moral Philosophy Professors?

Guus Duindam

Imagine: you're being held captive in the Bad Place, surrounded by malicious (and remarkably inventive) demons. One of them is altogether too keen on biting. Your best chance at escape is to prove to the Powers That Be that you *deserve* to be in the Good Place. To do this, you must learn to be moral.

You could try to find an ally in one of your fellow captives: an arrogant, self-important party-planner, a failed DJ pretending to be a Buddhist monk, and a Moral Philosophy professor. *Clearly* the Moral Philosophy professor is your best bet at becoming a good person. *Right*?

This is roughly the situation in which Eleanor finds herself in Season One, though she doesn't realize it. And it does seem as if Chidi is her best bet, at least initially. It must be admitted that he's not entirely unsuccessful in his tutoring. But how reliable a guide is an ethicist who has himself been sentenced to eternal torture?

Chidi may be loveable and well-meaning, but he's also rigid, *incredibly* indecisive, and prone to constant unnecessary overthinking. His professional expertise doesn't appear to be terribly useful in practice. Michael tries to create his Bad-Place-in-Disguise *eight-hundred and two* times and Chidi never once discovers the ruse. Even our failed DJ—the very same who managed to asphyxiate himself in a safe during a robbery attempt—has a better track record!

Nor are we given the impression that Chidi's extensive philosophizing has made him a better human being. To the contrary, his obsessions over moral minutiae lead him to commit serious wrongs, as when he misses his mother's back surgery to help his landlord's nephew program a phone ("Michael's Gambit"). No wonder everyone hates moral philosophy professors!

Is It Kant's Fault?

Why is Chidi the way he is? It's tempting to suggest that it's because of his big philosophical hero, the German philosopher Immanuel Kant. Chidi's most exasperating moments are invariably accompanied by references to Kant's philosophy. Why not just let your friend believe that he can pull off those hideous boots ("Eternal Shriek")? Because Kantian ethics prohibits deceit. Why hesitate to lie—to *demons*, mind you—to escape from Hell? You guessed it. "Principles aren't principles if you pick and choose when you're going to follow them," Chidi tells Eleanor – a concise summary of Kant's ethics ("Rhonda, Diana, Jake, and Trent").

And though I have yet to see Kant characterized as loveable, he bears a striking resemblance to Chidi. Does everyone hate moral philosophy professors because of their rigidity? Tendency to over-think even the most mundane situations? To speak in complex and dense philosophical prose that no one can understand? Both Kant's rigidity and the incomprehensibility of his writings are legendary. Could *Kant* and Kantians be the reason everyone hates moral philosophy professors?

We kant[1] answer that question without knowing a little about Kant's ethics. According to Kant, whenever we do anything, we are acting on a principle of action (philosophers call this a *'maxim'*). This sounds complicated, but all such a principle involves is a goal and a means: when we do something, we've got to know 1. what we want (the goal) and 2. how we plan on getting it (the means). For instance, suppose I want some frozen yogurt (Fully Charged Phone flavor) and I go to Michael's Fro-Yo shop to get it, then my maxim is "When I want some frozen yogurt, I'll go to Michael's Fro-Yo shop to get it."

Kant's big idea (well, *one* of his big ideas) is that we can determine the moral rightness or wrongness of your behavior by looking at your maxim and subjecting it to a test, which he called "The Categorical Imperative." (JANET: If the Categorical Imperative were a person, it would stare at us disapprovingly over its horn-rimmed glasses.) This test consists of two questions, and your maxim fails the test if the answer to either question is 'no'. If this happens, your maxim is immoral, and you ought not to act on it. If the answer to both questions is 'yes', you've earned Kant's blessing and it is not immoral to act in accordance with that maxim.

---

[1] JANET: Fun Fact! Use of this terrible pun earns philosophers −100 points. That makes it 18.1818 times as bad as using 'Facebook' as a verb. Just goes to show that philosophy is a dangerous profession.

The first question a Kantian would ask is: Can we imagine a world where your maxim has been made into a law, binding on everyone? If we can't imagine such a world, then the action described by your maxim is wrong. Not just a little wrong, but *always wrong, wrong everywhere, and wrong without exception*. Acting on this maxim is going to cost you a lot of afterlife points. Here's an example: suppose that my maxim is: 'When I need something, I'll just steal it.' Can you imagine a world where that maxim is a law everyone agrees ought to be followed? It turns out, you can't.

Here's why: stealing means taking someone's property without their permission. Property means an object *I* have the rights to and no one else. But in a world where it's a *law* that when you need something, you can just steal it, there's nothing at all that I have the rights to anymore! There will be no property. The law is logically inconsistent: if property is something that you have a moral and/or legal claim on, but anyone can steal property without punishment, then there is nothing that anyone can make a moral or legal claim to own, therefore there is no such thing as property. By the same token, in world where it is lawful to steal whatever you want, there won't *be* any such thing as 'stealing' anymore.

Now there's a lot of bad things we *can* imagine as a law. That is why we need a second question for all the cases where we answer 'yes' to the first. That question is: if you can imagine a world where your maxim is a law, would it be rational to want to *live* in that world? If the answer to that question is 'no', your maxim is still wrong. It's not wrong *always and everywhere without exception*, like maxims that fail the first test. But in general, you should try not to act on principles that fail this second test.

For instance, it looks like pre-death Eleanor had a maxim a little like this: "I won't help anyone unless it benefits me." That selfishness is what got her into the Bad Place. Kant's second question helps explain why it's bad. We may be able to imagine a world where this is a law ('Don't help anyone unless it benefits you'). But would it be rational to choose to live in this world? Kant would suggest not. After all, in that world, you'd risk never being helped yourself. And it's inevitable that some day you will need help. (As Michael is always eager to point out, humans are *pathetically* weak and fragile). This means that, in general, Eleanor's selfish maxim isn't one we should have. Of course, everybody is selfish sometimes, and doing just one selfish thing shouldn't get you straight into the Bad Place. That's why it makes sense that this principle fails only at the second question.

Devilish Demons and Deranged
Ax-Murderers

Chidi does some exasperating things and tells us it's because of Kant. The one behavior that frustrates Eleanor the most is Chidi's refusal to ever tell a lie. Just as Kantian ethics makes all instances of stealing morally wrong, Chidi thinks, so too does Kantian ethics make all instances of lying impermissible. But does Kant's test really dictate that we can't lie? *Ever?* Even when we're trying to escape from demons who take pleasure in torturing us?

Turns out, Kant is not as rigid as all that—and he certainly doesn't prohibit all lies. In fact, he specifically distinguishes between lies that are morally innocent ('falsifications') and lies that aren't ('mendacious falsehoods'). So why would Chidi (or anyone) think that Kant would disapprove of lying to a demon?

Here, we can fairly say that Kant has only himself to blame. Remember when I said the incomprehensibility of his work is legendary? Well, I wasn't kidding. It is whispered in the halls of philosophy departments that Kant's publisher went into a major depression after reading (or trying to read) his first major masterpiece, the *Critique of Pure Reason.* So it's no surprise that many of Kant's first critics didn't understand his position very well. One of them wrote an article criticizing Kant's ethics in which he provided roughly the following scenario:

> You're visiting a friend's house. Just as he goes down to the base-ment to grab something, someone knocks at the door. You open it and—holy mother*forking shirtballs*—there stands a deranged ax-murderer who has it in for your friend. He politely asks if your friend is home. What do you tell him?

According to his critic, Kant would instruct us to tell the mur-derer exactly where our friend was. Sensible people, in con-trast, would lie. Simple logic tells us that, therefore, Kant was not a sensible person.

This criticism clearly put our friend Kant in a bad mood. He wrote a *very* crotchety response called "On a Supposed Right to Lie from Philanthropy" in which he hacks into his critic. At first glance, he seems to be doubling down, suggesting that lying is morally wrong even to an axe-murderer at your door. So, it wasn't all that unreasonable of Chidi to think lying to a demon is wrong, too.

But Kant didn't intend to defend this conclusion and is actu-ally just making an obscure legal point in his essay. It's still (posthumously) haunting him: philosophy students everywhere now scoff at Kant as the guy who said you can't lie to a murderer.

But when we apply his actual test, it seems as if lying to murderers to help your friend (not to mention lying to demons to escape from Hell!) is just fine. Can we imagine a world in which it's a law that, when a murderer asks for his victim's location, you should lie? It seems that we can. Could rational people want to live in that world? I would! Wouldn't you? (JANET: If your answer is 'no', you may want to reconsider your career choices.)

So Chidi needn't have worried. Lying to demons while trying to escape their clutches is, even for good Kantians, just fine. Chidi ought to assign himself the task of re-reading these important essays so that Kantians everywhere can avoid this unnecessary slander.

Trolleys, Murderous Doctors, Utilitarianism

When they are not answering house-calls from polite killers, Kantians around the world—like Chidi and myself—are locked in an eternal battle with their mortal enemies, the utilitarians. Utilitarianism is the moral theory which says that you should always do whatever benefits the most people while harming the fewest people. Given the rigidity that Kantian ethics seemingly inspires, utilitarians come off looking flexible, realistic, and practical . . . which just makes people hate (Kantian) moral philosophy professors even more. On the other hand, utilitarianism distinguishes itself by being the only moral theory which Jason has no trouble understanding. This should raise suspicion.

The fight between Kantians and utilitarians is the topic of one of the most important *Good Place* episodes: "The Trolley Problem." Chidi is trying to teach Michael ethics, but Michael—never one to miss an opportunity for gratuitous and clever torture—turns the tables and has Chidi actually live through multiple iterations of the ethical thought experiment he's been describing. Carnage ensues. Placed in charge of an out-of-control trolley without brakes, Chidi must decide to do nothing and run over five workers, or switch tracks and kill one person instead. The first time around Chidi is, of course, too paralyzed to make any decision at all. The entrails of five workers spatter reproachfully.

What should we do when confronted with a situation like this? Eleanor and Tahani both think it's obvious: switch tracks so that you run over one person, instead of five. And this is what Chidi himself decides to do, on his second try. So far, so good: most people agree that this is the best choice. It's certainly what utilitarians would do, since it benefits five (and their families and friends) and harms only one (and her family and friends). And, by my best estimation, Kant too would at least find this choice permissible.

Now imagine a related scenario. There's only one track, and five people are tied to it. There are (still) no brakes on the trolley. (Why not, you ask? If Moral Philosophy professors had a good answer, maybe people would not hate them as much). You're no longer inside the trolley, but instead standing on a bridge, and in front of you is another pedestrian. In defiance of the laws of physics, you know for certain that if you throw this individual off the bridge, his body will stop the trolley and, as a result, five people will be saved. This is the only way you can save the five (you cannot jump off the bridge to stop the trolley yourself). What do you do?

Michael puts Chidi in a similar bind when he has him decide whether to kill Eleanor and harvest her organs to save five ailing patients or do nothing and let his patients die. Chidi—in one of his only moments of true decisiveness—immediately refuses to kill Eleanor.

These cases bring out the fundamental conflict between Kantians and utilitarians. For the utilitarian, there's no morally important difference between the first case and the second two. All three are cases of sacrificing one person to save five. Whenever you can do something that'll help more people than it'll hurt, you should do it. So, throw the guy off the bridge to stop the trolley, and murder Eleanor to save your patients. But Chidi clearly thinks there's a difference, and so would Kant. When Kant explains which kinds of principles would fail his test, he argues that we should never treat someone "merely as a means" to our end, but always "as an end in themselves." In other words, no matter what our goals are, we should *never just 'use' someone* to achieve them. When we do this, we fail to treat people "as ends in themselves" because we fail to recognize their inherent value as fellow persons.

If Kant's right, we cannot kill one person in order to save more. To do so would be to *just use* someone to achieve our goal. So when Chidi refuses to kill Eleanor, despite the opportunity to use her organs to save five innocents, he's being a good Kantian. By the same token, Kant would prohibit throwing the pedestrian off the bridge—we're *just using* him as a tool to save the others. But note that when Chidi switches the tracks, running over one person rather than five, he's *not* using that person as a tool to save the others. In fact, he'd prefer for that person not to be on the tracks at all! Here, Kant's view explains Chidi's decisions well. And, I think, Kant's view is quite reasonable. If TV is any guide, most of us agree we can't just sacrifice the few to save the many—witness the heroes in every superhero flick.

Good Place Architects Are Kantians

I've tried to suggest that, despite Chidi's occasionally exasperating behavior in Kant's name, Kant's own views were quite reasonable. Chidi's most unreasonable moments are explained by misunderstandings of Kant, not by Kant's actual positions. And when Chidi gets things exactly right, as in the trolley problem, or in his refusal to sacrifice Eleanor, he has Kant to thank for it. Of course, I don't pretend to be impartial. Kant is my philosophical hero just as much as he is Chidi's. But I think the story of *The Good Place* just wouldn't make any *sense* to us if we didn't all accept one of Kant's most important insights about the moral worth of actions: intention matters.

Kant famously argued that there is a big difference between *doing the right thing* and doing something that's *morally valuable*—something that has "moral worth." The only thing that is genuinely morally good, according to Kant, is the *good will*: a will that does the right thing because it's right. This idea is exploited in many *Good Place* episodes. When Tahani was organizing fundraisers, she collected a staggering sixty billion dollars for non-profits. Clearly, she was doing 'the right thing.' But she got no afterlife credit for it and ended up in the Bad Place!

From a basic utilitarian perspective, this doesn't make a whole lot of sense. Her behavior certainly benefited a lot more people than it harmed. And yet it makes sense to most of us, because we see that Tahani wasn't doing any of her good deeds for the right reasons. It doesn't seem as if she cared much about any of the people she was helping. She wanted to raise money so she could outshine her (admittedly *rotten*) sister and achieve fame, neither of which are morally praiseworthy goals. And because she wasn't doing it for the right reasons, Kant would say her behavior had no 'moral worth'. It had no moral value because her *will* wasn't morally good. Consequently, her behavior wasn't worth *any* Good Place points.

The same thing goes for Eleanor when she's desperately trying to earn more points at the end of Season One ("What's My Motivation?"). She does her best to be nice to everyone, performs good deeds, hosts a party, and so on. Yet her score does not improve. This isn't because she wasn't doing 'the right thing'—she was—but because her behavior didn't have moral worth. She was just acting to save herself, and that doesn't give us any reason to think she's become a better person. Even the truly evil will help others if it's necessary to save their own skin.

A world of difference away are Eleanor's admission of guilt when Michael announces his horrific 'retirement', and her later willingness to go to the Bad Place ("The Eternal Shriek"). Here she finally does the right thing *because she knows it's right*, not just because it'll help her out. That's something a selfish person just wouldn't do. It's a sign of *real* moral improvement—a sign of genuine moral worth—and that's why it's so shocking to the demons in charge, who didn't think she'd be capable of that.

By the way, the same principle is used to illustrate the incredible character-development of everyone's favorite demon, Michael. In "The Trolley Problem" he's still trying to torture Chidi—and suggesting ways to use the trolley to kill all six people. (JANET: Fun Fact! This strategy is known as 'multi-track drifting' and has had a cult-following online long before Michael adopted it.)

Michael is co-operating with the humans—sure, the right thing to do—but hasn't improved much morally. He's doing it to save himself. That's why it's so moving when, just a couple of episodes later, he risks his own (eternal!) existence multiple times to save his new friends, and even offers to sacrifice himself to save Eleanor as they travel through the portal to the Judge's chambers ("Rhonda, Diana, Jake, and Trent"). These acts have moral worth, because they're done for the right reasons. Now we know he's *really* on their side.

Kant thinks that, if we're to be morally good people, we'll need to do the right thing for the right reasons. The writers of *The Good Place* clearly agree: their decisions just wouldn't make much sense otherwise, and neither would our favorite show.

So Why Does Everyone Hate Moral Philosophy Professors?

Well, it'll be clear by now that if you ask me, Kant is *not* the reason everybody hates Moral Philosophy professors. If I'm right about this, it leaves us with our initial questions unanswered. Why is Chidi so bad at ethics in practice? Why hasn't his philosophy made him into a better person? And why *does* everyone in *The Good Place* hate Moral Philosophy professors?

Perhaps we really don't have as much reason to be surprised that an ethicist isn't great at ethics in practice as we might have thought. Would you expect an expert on bicycle construction to be a great cyclist? An expert nutritionist to be a great cook? We don't usually expect mastery of a theory to lead directly to mastery of the associated practice. Why should our expectations be any different in ethics? The Greek philosopher Aristotle made this point effectively more than two thousand years ago when he noted that, if you want to be a good flute-player you should practice flute-playing, and if you want to be a good human being, you need to *practice* being ethical, not just study it.

When—like Chidi—you spend much of your time thinking through very hard problems in a specific area of your discipline, you run the risk of losing sight of the big picture. Most of us wouldn't think twice to break a promise if our mother were undergoing surgery, but for Chidi it becomes another of those hard problems. In his worst moments, Chidi becomes obsessed with moral rules and lets them close him off from other people. When he does this, he fails to recognize other people's inherent value (in Kant's words, he fails to treat them *as ends in themselves*). Compare Tahani, who (at least in the beginning) uses even the people she helps as mere means to gain approval. In their *best* moments, all of our *Good Place* friends embody Kant's principle that we must *never* treat others as mere means: think of Eleanor and Michael's self-sacrifice, or Chidi's refusal to kill Eleanor.

In fairness to Chidi, fixating on the trees can make any of us—Kantians and otherwise—forget that there's a whole forest out there. Perhaps one of the greatest things about *The Good Place* is its ability to raise difficult problems *and* keep constant sight of the forest. For that, its writers surely deserve a place in the *real* Good Place.

15
Chidi's Indecision

Seth Vannatta

> Indecision caused you so much agony in your life.
>
> —Michael to Chidi, "Chidi's Choice"

Agony in life? Chidi's indecision so tortured his friends, family, and colleagues that it sent him to Hell in the afterlife! As Chidi admits to Michael, "Choices are hard for me, especially when I'm under pressure" ("Chidi's Choice").

That's quite the understatement given that Chidi once had a panic attack playing rock-paper-scissors because there were "just too many variables" ("Chidi's Choice"). He can't pick a soccer team during recess (he "filibustered recess"); he tenses up in distress when asked to choose between a dry erase board and a pen and paper. And he can't write down the pros and cons of each because that would necessitate him actually choosing one with which to do so! His indecisiveness even gets him fired from being his friend's best man in his wedding, and in the end it got him killed.

Is Chidi's inability to make a decision just a funny way to caricature a philosophy professor as an over-thinker, or is it woven into the nature of the discipline he studies—moral philosophy? (We know it's not a "brain thing"). Moral philosophy is all about what we ought to do, so you'd think he'd be an expert at making decisions. But moral philosophy also investigates the rules that guide our decision-making.

If there were moral importance to choosing between rock, paper, and scissors, then moral philosophy might involve the general rule that could guide the decision in any given game. (For example: Choose the same as your opponent's last throw). But there might be many rules vying for our attention in a given match. (Never throw the same thing three times in a row). There might even be rules that contradict each other. So if there are many rules vying for our attention when we are deciding what we ought to do in a situation that has moral import, (and if we're thoroughly well versed in all of them), deciding might be more difficult *because* of moral philosophy.

Any rule-based ethics ought to eliminate all uncertainty in moral decision-making. Just apply the rule and move on. But each system thinks it's the right one. Each of what I call the Big Three in ethics—the Right, the Good, and the Virtuous— thinks it provides the right rule of action. And entire schools of moral philosophy form around the Big Three. Philosophers call these Deontology, Consequentialism, and (unoriginally) Virtue Ethics. And while Chidi claims to be a deontologist, worshipping at the feet of the Prussian, Immanuel Kant, I don't think he's sold. I even think *The Good Place* promotes a brand of ethics that is never mentioned on the show: Care Ethics.

The Right

Chidi likes Kant's ethics probably because they're strict and binding. Kant's ethics are called deontological, which comes from the Greek word, *deon*, meaning a duty which is binding. Chidi refuses to lie, even in an attempt to get through The Bad Place to be judged. He tells Eleanor, "Principles aren't principles when you pick and choose when to follow them" ("Best Self"). He tortures himself while alive because he falsely told a colleague that he liked his ridiculous red cowboy boots ("The Eternal Shriek"). (The real problem with them is that the colleague tucked his jeans into them. That should earn him minus points on the moral scoreboard).

Kant thought that the consequences of your actions do not matter. Only your intentions do, and the characters learn a lot by reflecting on their motivations. Eleanor learns in "What's My Motivation" that she cannot increase her point total of good deeds because she's doing all of the good acts for the sake of self-preservation, and she deems this a corrupt motivation.

For Kant, the *only* good in itself is a good will, and a good person acts from a good will. A good will acts out of a duty imposed by a command it gives itself. It doesn't count if you're just doing as your mother told you to. You have to do as you tell yourself to. But don't get lazy. This doesn't mean you can command anything of yourself. The imperative must apply to all people and to all situations. Otherwise, rules would change based off of your conditions, such as *if you see shrimp, grab as many as possible!*

The true Kantian asks, 'Could I create a rule based on my action and then make it a rule for everybody that can understand rules?' Duty and intent are what matter, and the only consequence that enters into the moral question is whether applying the rule to everyone ends in a logical contradiction. Kant loved logic, which meant that he hated contradictions. For Kant you must not merely act in accordance with duty, but *out of* duty. Tahani shows us the difference.

Tahani acted in accordance with duty, but not out of duty, as her intent in her over-the-top charitable fund-raising activities was to outshine her famous sister Camilla, not to treat the recipients of her charity as ends in themselves. For her, they were mere means for her reputation as a good person. Kant thought we should never treat each other as mere means, or tools for our own purposes. Rather, people themselves are purposes, or ends.

The Good

The second of the Big Three moral theories, Consequentialism, focuses on the *outcome* of our actions. Chidi teaches this approach to his friends, and Eleanor is attracted to it by its simplicity. She says, "I like this one. Uh. It's simple. Screw all the other complicated theories. Why did you not start with this one?" ("Category 55 Emergency Doomsday Crisis").

As Eleanor puts it when defending her decision to kill Janet, "we're doing one small murder thing for a bigger, better reason. The ends justify the means" ("The Eternal Shriek"). Jason illustrates this moral measure by providing an example. He framed one black-market alligator dealer with a pierced jawbone to save his sixty-person break dance crew. I think his example was in line with Jeremy Bentham's version of ethics.

Bentham thought that to be moral, we only need to asked one question: does the action increase happiness or decrease pain? The increase in happiness or reduction in pain he called utility, and his moral theory is called utilitarianism. Its goal is to achieve the greatest happiness for the greatest number. Bentham's student, John Stuart Mill, amended his teacher's approach arguing that there are differences in types of pleasures. For Mill, reading a smart book on *The Good Place* was qualitatively more pleasurable than just eating frozen yogurt.

In Season One we learn that those who have earned a spot in The Good Place have been judged quantitatively on the sum of their good deeds minus the deficit of their moral missteps. When Michael is charged with writing an essay on the ethics of *Les Misérables* in Season Two, we learn that stealing a loaf of bread is –17 and –20 if it is a baguette (because it makes you more French) ("Existential Crisis"). The measure used to determine good from bad appears to be other-centered actions, such as working as a lawyer fighting against the death penalty and doing human rights missions in the Ukraine.

The episode which illustrates the differences between the first two of the Big Three approaches to moral and ethical decision making is "The Trolley Problem." The famous hypothetical dilemma of whether to choose to kill one person to save five is meant to unveil our moral intuitions or which of the Big Three guides our conduct.

The utilitarian deploys the pleasure-calculation and saves the five people, while the Kantian refuses to use the one victim as a mere means and lets the reign and sway of cause and effect in nature run their course. Michael puts the professor in charge of a simulation, where his inaction causes him to crush five innocent workers whose guts end up in his face-hole and whose pain is actually experienced. Chidi's indecision is made manifest again. So is his half-hearted faith in Kant. So are the shortcomings of the first two of the Big Three.

If Kant or the utilitarians were right, and Chidi knew who was right, he would not panic at all. He would apply the right rule come what may. But that's not how moral dilemmas are experienced, and *experience* matters. The poverty of these approaches is their rationalism, the idea that moral conduct is a function of reason and not at all one of feeling. Michael tries to get Chidi to realize this at the end of Season One, when Chidi has to choose his true soul mate. When Michael offers him an option, he tells Chidi that he instinctively knows whether it *felt* right, stating "no more thinking, Chidi, just do something" ("Chidi's Choice").

The Virtuous, the Last of the Big Three

Measuring the morality according to virtue looks different than according to duty or outcomes. The virtuous person would consider the way her character over time is formed by her habits. The sum total of, for instance, scheming to avoid taking her turn at being the designated driver, over time form Eleanor's character, whose decisions are seen as means to living the good life of flourishing or happiness. (Chidi's version of the good life involves rowing out on a lake with a good bottle of wine and reading French poetry). A person's character includes their disposition to exemplify virtuous character traits.

Aristotle out-does the first of the Big Three because he realizes that virtues often conflict with one another. But you still *reason* your way toward the answer, and this is the common flaw in the Big Three. The virtuous person deploying practical reason finds the proper mean between excess and deficiency. The courageous person, for instance, avoids Jason's rashness, throwing Molotov cocktails at docked boats, as an excess and avoids Chidi's cowardly fear to make any decision as a deficiency. So each particular virtue is itself an average of sorts between too much and too little of something.

Chidi's Indecision

The poverty of the first two of the Big Three and the reason Chidi ends up in the bad place are interrelated. The deficiency of Kant's approach is that it does not start with an honest description of how moral problems are experienced. Chidi's experience of terror on the trolley car simulation and in the face of the family members of patients whose lives he has chosen not to save show this. Kant derived duties that bind universally and necessarily, but those duties are less likely to serve as a resolution to the problems felt by Chidi as morally uncertain.

The deficiency of the utilitarian approach is that it is less likely to distinguish a good and a bad person. Jason's not the most ethical guy, but he scores utilitarian points by saving his break-dancing crew and selling out the black-market alligator dealer. Deontology can distinguish good and bad people by their intentions, as in the case of Tahani, whose actions increased the happiness of the recipients of her charity, but whose intent was not from a good will.

Neither the deontological and utilitarian approaches, by prescribing universal, albeit different, principles to be applied regardless of the situation treat situations as uncertain. But uncertainty is a big part of moral action, as Chidi understands too well. If their divergent principles, when applied, never fail to yield moral action, then there would be no such thing as a genuine moral problem. But as Michael's all too real simulation evinces, Chidi experiences the situation as precarious and uncertain.

The conflicts which emerge from either deontology or utilitarianism are treated as only *apparent* conflicts. Conflict is not an inherent part of the obligatory or the good. So if Chidi tries to reason his way toward the right decision using only one of the Big Three, the feeling he has of the conflict between his duties and good outcomes is imaginary and unreal. He experiences situations as morally problematic, so we should offer a better, more accurate description of how moral inquiry works.

John Dewey points out the flaws in relying on only one of the Big Three when trying to resolve a real-life moral problem. The main problem with each is that they are not true to our experience of moral conflict because they eliminate the element of uncertainty in those situations. But uncertainty and conflict (if not a category 55 emergency doomsday crisis) are inherent in morals ("Three Independant Factors in Morals," p. 280). Consequentialism makes the Right derivative, such that the rights of the one onlooker sacrificed to save the five workers on the trolley track are ranked lower because of the end goal of increased utility. One's duty then is only a means to achieve the Good, which is primary. According to the Right, the reverse is the case.

Law just tells us what is obligatory. Acting to satisfy natural inclinations for facials and yoga is mere desire, nature working through Tahani, but does not point to any moral good. For Kant, moral is just whatever agrees with the universal command ("Three Independant Factors in Morals," p. 281). So each of the Big Three thinks the other two are dependent and derivative. But if these conflicting moral factors derive from different sources, neither can be reduced to the other, so they are each independent factors. And what morality is made up of is the ability to judge the claims of the Big Three (of desire for the good, of duty to law, and of gaining public praise and avoiding blame), as they call for our attention in our lived experiences.

Dewey's approach takes seriously that varying desires—such as Jason's for jalapeño poppers, Eleanor's for shrimp, or Tahani's for praise—are real, not merely apparent, factors in their decision-making processes. They are quite possibly natural inclinations, and others, such as desires to do well in Chidi's ethics class are merely responses to the teacher's commands. But each character can foresee both beneficial and detrimental consequences of fulfilling these desires through various means.

Dewey says that Virtue is a function of someone's actions deserving praise or blame from the members of their community. Different communities might praise or blame different actions, but such communal praise or blame is what determines the virtue or the vice of the conduct. Tahani seems to be most attuned to Dewey's idiosyncratic interpretation of virtue ethics, as she spent her life trying to gain praise, albeit only in order to compete with her sister.

Dewey thinks the Good has to do with one's desires and purposes, the Right with socially authorized demands, and Virtue with widespread social approval. These factors come into conflict as some desires are goods that the community thinks are wrong. Public opinion may approve of the type of action that doesn't allow Jason or Eleanor to get what they want. But anyone genuinely concerned with the experience of moral uncertainty wants to reconcile the legally forbidden with the socially allowed or encouraged. This is a more difficult task that simply applying a rule.

Eleanor appears most Deweyan as she is constantly searching for an overlooked middle ground in a problematic situation, where her teacher, Chidi, sees only binaries and dilemmas. He tells her: "You have two options: you can confess and save Michael or continue to lie and condemn him to an eternity of unimaginable pain." Eleanor chooses a third way: "Or option C, continue to lie about myself and find a way to save Michael" ("The Eternal Shriek").

She's trying to reconcile the good and her natural desire, albeit at the expense of the Kantian principle not to lie. Eleanor even seeks to avoid the good place–bad place dilemma, arguing that there should be a medium place, which, as we find out, there is. Ordinarily, Chidi, seeing only dilemmas with the clarity of a philosophy professor, is shackled in the uncertainty that pervades actual moral decision-making.

The Implicit Moral Theory of
The Good Place

Care ethics, the one theory *not* taught by Chidi, (or referenced on the show), is the best candidate for the moral reality of *The Good Place*. Care ethics is not based on rules. It's based on the feeling that accompanies the memory of being cared for and attempting to care for others. Rule-based ethics thinks you can logically reason your way to the right decision in a moral dilemma by ranking some goods, protecting a friend from the bad place, over others, such as not lying. But *The Good Place* does not seem to praise those who have the ability to rank goods. Rather, it seems to commend friendship and the maintenance of relationships.

We get a clue that care ethics might rule the day on *The Good Place*, even if it does not constitute the moral reality of "The Good Place," in "What We Owe to Each Other." Eleanor, having been asked to help Michael find the problem in "The

Good Place," realizes that if she helps him, she will be confessing that she is the problem, and if she does not, she will be breaking a promise and the chaos she thinks she has caused will continue. But when she decides to both help and not help Michael (her solution to the dilemma), he tells her he has been studying the human concept of friends.

This theme (and what friends owe to each other) persists through the first two seasons. Later in the same episode, Chidi claims that he and Tahani are "soul friends." The episode ends with Eleanor telling Michael, "I promised to help you, and I will however I can," and we get the sense that this constitutes moral growth for Eleanor. Under a lie-detector test, Eleanor tells Michael that she will not disclose who murdered Janet, and for that, Michael admires her for protecting her friend ("Most Improved Player").

When Eleanor is sentenced to The Bad Place, she realizes that Tahani and Jason came to see her off because they are her friends. Chidi's friendship is so strong that he confesses to murdering Janet to save Eleanor. Eleanor's growth, from her character while living to her character in her afterlife is that she wants to be a part of a group, a team, and foster the relationships that constitute one important end of care ethics. Michael also refuses to kill Janet in Season Two because they're friends. Michael's best line of the first two seasons, "You guys, I was so scared for you!" perfectly illustrates the moral growth of a demon! He *cares* for his friends ("Leap to Faith").

Care ethics is related to feminist ethics. Some philosophers who advanced an ethics of care noticed that girls and women often responded to moral dilemmas differently than boys and men, but their thinking had been dismissed by philosophers as deficient because they were not applying universal rules to the dilemma and reasoning their way to the right action. Some women, in various moral experiments involving dilemmas similar to the Trolley Problem, conceived of the moral goal differently, and so they thought of alternative strategies outside the parameters of the dilemma. Their goal was often the maintenance of relationships, not the search for justice.

These women also had a different conception of the self than their male counterparts. The respondents' different answers were a function of an alternative conception of self, a self not independent from others, but relational, in process, and dependent on a community. Eleanor's social isolation during her life exemplified the independent self, while Eleanor's friendships that develop in "The Good Place" and her decision to join Team Cockroach illustrate the relational one.

But care ethics is not only feminist ethics. And many feminist philosophers had problems with its early formulation. They thought that care ethics was trying to say something about the essence of womanhood, that all women were natural caregivers. But this was not the intention. And *The Good Place* shows us the importance of friendship and care for others without reference to gender. The goal of care ethics is the maintenance of relationships by caring for others and for oneself. Jason gives Tahani a lesson in this latter end: "Be nicer to yourself" ("Team Cockroach").

Rule-based ethics often values impartiality. And there is value in being impartial. Chidi acts out of principle in agreeing to help Eleanor. He is not initially enamored of her, as she insults him, repeatedly forgets Janet's name, and cops to so many moral missteps in her life. Care ethics, on the other hand, thinks that some partiality is good. We should give some moral priority to those we're emotionally close to.

Eleanor morally progresses to care for Chidi because of her affection for him, but she is willing to throw Tahani under a bigger bus. Tahani's constant belittling of Eleanor was not likely to foster emotional connections between the two. But care ethics is not about harming your enemies and helping your friends. It just means that care is situational, where personal and cultural differences will result in different versions of care. There's no universal rule of care, no recipe for action. Care ethics looks to the human condition of birth, physical and emotional needs, and the desire to be cared for.

We learn to care by the experience of being cared for. Perhaps this is why Eleanor was so antisocial and uncaring during her life. She lacked that crucial experience of being cared for by her dissolute parents. But when she experiences Chidi's care, she shows moral progress. And care ethics takes moral education seriously. While *The Good Place* shows Chidi teaching Eleanor ethics in a formal chalkboard way, her real education is the experience of him caring for her. He models care, he doesn't lecture on it.

The absurdity of a rationalist approach to ethics—the idea that we can reason our way to the right moral decision without emotion—the common shortcoming of the Big Three, is illustrated when Michael, Chidi, Tahani, and the "real" Eleanor describe her moral improvement without any sign of feeling on their faces to Judge Sean, who only allows cold hard facts to be presented in a case. (Farts are also inadmissible).

The lesson is clear; they do care about Eleanor. In fact, care for oneself and care for others might motivate someone to learn about moral philosophy, to think deeply about the Big Three, those factors which vie for our attention when we're in a moral conundrum. Care for oneself and for one's family and friends is the necessary condition for taking moral philosophy seriously, and so we see that care ethics is the show's hidden moral theory.

V

No Exit?

16
Is Hell Other People?

KIKI BERK

The Good Place is unmistakably reminiscent of Jean-Paul Sartre's famous play *No Exit* (1944). The resemblance is no accident, for Michael Schur admits that Sartre's play is one of the inspirations for his show.

In both works, a small number of people (three in *No Exit*, four in *The Good Place*) find themselves in what turns out to be Hell. But Hell isn't what we would expect: lakes of unquenchable fire, horned devils with pitchforks, souls of the damned screaming out in pain. Rather, in each case, Hell is surprisingly similar to life on Earth: a stuffy drawing room in *No Exit*, and a small town of 322 people (318 of whom are disguised demons) in *The Good Place*.

But isn't Hell supposed to be *bad*—a place of suffering and torment for those who end up there? Of course, it is! But the central idea in both *No Exit* and *The Good Place* is that the inhabitants of Hell are intended to *torture each other*. Hence, the famous line from Sartre's play: "Hell is other people!"

Despite this major plot similarity, *No Exit* and *The Good Place* take the idea that "Hell is other people" in very different directions. Whereas the characters in *No Exit* succeed in torturing each other, the characters in *The Good Place* end up helping and even improving each other. In fact, we get the impression that *The Good Place* is meant to be a modern-day reworking of *No Exit* in which the latter's pessimistic message about relationships is turned on its head. Far from being "Hell," other people in *The Good Place* are a source of redemption and, perhaps, even salvation.

Despite the initial plausibility of seeing *The Good Place* as an optimistic challenge to Sartre's pessimism about relationships, a closer look at Sartre's philosophy reveals his view of

145

relationships to be far less negative than is usually supposed. Indeed, the famous line from Sartre's play ("Hell is other people!") has been consistently misunderstood. As we'll see, the messages about relationships in *No Exit* and *The Good Place* are, upon closer examination, actually *compatible* with each other.

Relationships in *The Good Place*

The episode of *The Good Place* that finally reveals its Sartrean nature is the last of Season One, "Michael's Gambit." Up to this point, the four main characters, as well as the audience, have been led to believe that "The Good Place" really is The Good Place. We learn in this episode that the architect of the "The Good Place," Michael, is actually a demon whose bosses (also demons) have allowed him to try out an experiment: in the spirit of Sartre's *No Exit*, Michael's "neighborhood" contains no torture chambers or hot irons, but just four flawed people (Eleanor, Chidi, Tahani, and Jason) who are supposed to make each other miserable.

Before Michael's Sartrean experiment comes crashing down on him, how exactly was it supposed to work? In addition to many small irritations—such as a lack of cell phones and an overabundance of frozen yogurt shops—Michael's design involves more agonizing issues. Eleanor's house is decorated with clowns, which she abhors; and Tahani's house is smaller than her neighbors', which makes her jealous. Eleanor can't stand how tall and beautiful Tahani is, and Tahani can't bear that Eleanor gets to wear the "best person" sash at their neighborhood welcome party.

Such annoyances pale in comparison to the obvious mismatch of "soul mates." Soon after their arrival in the afterlife, the four characters are informed by Michael that they've been partnered with soul mates with whom they'll live forever, happily ever after. Eleanor and Chidi are a match, as are Tahani and Jason. The incompatibilities in these partnerships are all too obvious. Chidi cares so much about doing the right thing that he often fails to act at all, whereas Eleanor is just the opposite: impulsive and uninterested in anything but her own personal gain. For someone who cares so much about appearances, Tahani is extremely unhappy with Jason, who isn't just shorter than she is but doesn't even talk to her on account of his vow of silence. And all Jason wants to do is play video games, which he's forced to keep secret from Tahani.

Judging from their barely concealed reactions, Michael's plan seems to be working. Indeed, the only thing that prevents the characters from realizing immediately they aren't in The Good Place is the fact that two of them (Eleanor and Jason) believe they're there by accident, which explains the soul mate mismatches and the unpleasantness they bring.

Despite some friction between the four main characters, however, they don't really torture each other. Michael constantly has to intervene in order to cause conflict. In fact, the worse the situation becomes, the more the characters actually get along with each other. Eleanor and Chidi team up after she confesses to him that she isn't supposed to be in The Good Place, Eleanor and Tahani become friends despite their mutual jealousy, and Eleanor and Jason form an unlikely bond when each realizes that the other isn't what they pretend to be. Instead of torturing each other, the four develop surprising friendships and display unexpected loyalty toward each other. As Eleanor says to Michael when she finally figures out that "The Good Place" isn't The Good Place:

> Holy motherforking shirtballs! . . . This is The Bad Place! . . . You saw us all on Earth: a selfish ass, an idiot DJ, a tortured academic, a hot, rich fraud with legs for days. . . . You thought we would torture each other, and we did for a little, but we also took care of each other. We improved each other, and the four of us became a team. So, the only thing you succeeded in doing was bringing us all together. ("Michael's Gambit")

Perhaps most surprising of all is the fact that the characters actually make each other better. Chidi teaches Eleanor how to become a more ethical person, and Eleanor in turn helps Chidi learn how to make decisions. Tahani discovers that the world doesn't end when you wear cargo pants, and Jason, unimpressed by Tahani's pretentious name-dropping, turns out to be a caring and loyal friend. The developments of Season One are a testament to friendship as well as to the redemptive power of relationships. As Michael remarks: "In the afterlife, they all got better because they helped each other" ("Everything Is Bonzer!").

Season Two builds on this theme. Michael decides that, despite its initial failure, his plan still has potential. After erasing the characters' memories of the afterlife, he attempts a "reboot." One major change, however, is that he separates the characters in order to prevent them from supporting each other. As he puts it, "my big mistake was bringing you all together, having you be soul mates living next to each other" ("Everything Is Great!"). But despite Michael's new strategy, which he tries no fewer than 802 times, the four characters always end up finding and helping each other. Indeed, in one reboot, Eleanor and Chidi fall in love, and in another Tahani and Jason share a passionate relationship. The fact that there isn't a single "successful" reboot in which the four characters manage to make each other miserable sends an unambiguously positive message about the nature and power of relationships.

Even Michael isn't immune to the positive influence of relationships. Throughout the second season, he's forced to hide from his bosses the fact that he's rebooted the neighborhood so many times. The long series of unsuccessful reboots, together with the ongoing deception they require, eventually turns Michael's neighborhood—ironically—into Hell for *him*. For help, he turns to the four humans, and the five of them together try to find a way to The Good Place.

Once again, relationships prove to be a source of salvation rather than suffering. Michael is even amenable to the moral improvement that personal relationships can bring. "I met new friends who helped me become a better person," he says in Season Three ("Everything Is Bonzer!"). Indeed, the more he cares about his new group of human friends, the better of a person he becomes. At one point, Michael is genuinely sorry for offending Chidi, and in a heart-to-heart conversation with Eleanor, he learns what it's like to be human.

The climax of Michael's moral transformation comes near the end of Season Two, when he gives Eleanor his own badge so she can escape The Bad Place, thereby showing his willingness to sacrifice his own life for hers.

At the end of the second season, Michael says to Eleanor: "The real question, Eleanor, is: What do we owe to each other?" ("Somewhere Else"). The answer comes in the form of a three-hour YouTube lecture by Chidi, in which he states that "we choose to be good because of our bonds with other people. . . . Simply put, we are not in this alone." In the end, love, loyalty, and friendship are what save all five characters. Even flawed people in bad circumstances can find salvation in, and through, each other. This is the core message about relationships in *The Good Place*.

Relationships in *No Exit*

While *The Good Place* is, by Schur's own admission, inspired by Sartre's *No Exit*, the latter seems to contain a very different message about relationships. *No Exit*, the first play to be performed in Paris after World War II, opens with one of the three main characters, Garcin, being led into a sparsely furnished drawing room. There he's joined by the two other characters, Inez and Estelle. Garcin, a journalist, confesses that he humiliated his wife by bringing young women into their home in order to sleep with them, and he later admits to having fled the war (presumably World War II) under the pretense of being a pacifist, thereby branding himself both a deserter and a coward. Inez is a self-proclaimed sadist who seduced her cousin's wife and then convinced the latter that she was to blame for the death of her husband (Inez's cousin), who committed suicide after he found out about their affair. Estelle is a pretty, superficial, and cruel woman who had a baby with an extramarital lover and then killed it in front of him, while he was powerless to stop her.

Garcin, Inez, and Estelle don't know each other, but they do realize that they've died and are now in Hell. Hell isn't what any of them expected, however. Where are the racks and hot pincers? The lakes of fire? The horned devils with pitchforks? Inez is the first to realize the truth about their situation:

> INEZ: It's obvious what they're after—an economy of manpower—or devil-power, if you prefer. The same idea as in the cafeteria, where customers serve themselves.
>
> ESTELLE: What ever do you mean?
>
> INEZ: I mean that each of us will act as torturer of the two others. (p. 17)

After this discovery, the three characters make a few half-hearted attempts to avoid harming each other, but they invariably fail. In the end, they really do make each other miserable. As Garcin famously remarks:

> So this is hell. I'd never have believed it. You remember all we were told about the torture-chambers, the fire and brimstone, the "burning marl." Old wives' tales! There's no need for red-hot pokers. Hell is— other people! (p. 45)

Given that Garcin, Inez, and Estelle don't know each other and so apparently have no good reason to hurt each other, why do they end up torturing each other? Let's focus on just one character: Garcin. Garcin, recall, is a journalist who fled the war, he says, on account of his pacifism. But he worries that the real reason he fled is because he's a coward. He wants very badly for someone—anyone—to assure him that this isn't true. He tries initially to get this assurance from Estelle, who's happy to give it to him in exchange for his affection, which she wants very badly. But Garcin soon realizes that Estelle's opinion of him is worthless, for, as Inez points out, she would say anything, whether she means it or not, for the love of a man. Garcin next pins his hopes on Inez, who isn't interested in men and so won't affirm him just to gain his affection. However, Inez is jealous of Estelle's desire for Garcin, and this, together with her sadistic nature, moves her to absolutely refuse Garcin's request to be dubbed a hero. So, Garcin is trapped: Estelle is willing to tell him what he wants to hear, but without any real meaning behind it; Inez could mean what she says, but she refuses to play along. Thus, Garcin is effectively tortured by the other two, apparently with no way to escape.

In light of the foregoing, it should come as no surprise that *No Exit* is commonly interpreted as a metaphor for the suffering caused by our relationships with other people. This interpretation is seemingly justified further by Sartre's pessimistic discussion of relationships in his difficult (some would say *obscure*) philosophical work, *Being and Nothingness* (1943). Here, Sartre paints a bleak picture of human relationships, which, he says, involve a constant struggle over freedom, for we either treat other people as objects (which undermines their freedom), or we allow ourselves to be treated as objects by them (which undermines ours). Sartre considers a variety of attitudes towards each other which we can adopt in order to resolve this tension—such as love, hate, and indifference—but none of them succeed. People can't be both fully subject and fully object, so encountering another person necessarily results in a struggle for dominance. Thus, Sartre's pessimistic view of relationships isn't accidental but rather grounded in his theory about the very nature of our existence.

While *Being and Nothingness* seems to support the standard interpretation of *No Exit*, according to which relationships are always bad, this interpretation faces a serious challenge. In an oral preface he gave for a 1964 recording of the play, Sartre claims that his statement that "Hell is other people" has always been misunderstood. As he explains in *Sartre on Theater*:

> It has been thought that what I meant by that was that our relations with other people are always poisoned, that they are invariably hellish relations. But what I really mean is something totally different. I mean that if relations with someone else are twisted, vitiated, then that other person can only be Hell. (p. 199)

In other words, according to Sartre, the statement that "Hell is other people" is implicitly conditional: other people are Hell for us *if* our relationships with them are bad. Sartre explains further:

> . . . if my relations are bad, I am situating myself in a total dependence on someone else. And then I am indeed in hell. And there are a vast number of people in the world who are in hell because they are too dependent on the judgment of other people. But that does not at all mean that one cannot have relations with other people. It simply brings out the capital importance of all other people for each one of us. (*Sartre on Theater*, pp. 199–200)

According to Sartre, other people's judgments invariably enter into our thoughts and feelings about ourselves. This isn't bad in itself, for without these judgments we couldn't truly know ourselves. What's bad is when we allow ourselves to become overly dependent on the opinions of other people, especially those with whom we have unhealthy relationships (think about Tahani in Season One). But again, although other people *can* be hell, as they are for the three characters in *No Exit*, they *needn't* be so, as Sartre makes clear. We must conclude, therefore, against the standard interpretation of *No Exit*, that Sartre's claim that "Hell is other people" is a conditional claim, not a categorical one.

How does this conditional reading of "Hell is other people" fit with Sartre's pessimistic account of relationships in *Being and Nothingness*? The key to answering this question is found in a footnote at the very end of his discussion of the various attitudes that one can take toward others in order to (unsuccessfully) avoid conflict with them:

> These considerations do not exclude the possibility of an ethics of deliverance and salvation. But this can be achieved only after a radical conversion which we can not discuss here. (*Being and Nothingness*, p. 412)

It's clear from other parts of the book that the "radical conversion" to which Sartre alludes is a transformation from "bad faith" to authenticity. People are in bad faith, according to Sartre, when they deceive themselves into thinking they aren't ultimately free and responsible for their actions but rather a product of their culture, genetics, or character. Making excuses, lying to yourself, playing a role and hiding behind it (all of which would be familiar to early Season One Eleanor)—these are all ways of being in bad faith. This suggests that the various attitudes he's just considered—the ones that try but ultimately fail to resolve our conflicts with others—are all attitudes of bad faith, not of authenticity. In other words, relationships between people who are in bad faith are bound to fail; relationships between people who are authentic, on the other hand, might succeed.

Unfortunately, Sartre never tells us in *Being and Nothingness* what it takes to undergo this "radical conversion" from bad faith to authenticity. All he tells us is that he'll tackle this problem in a later work, which he began but never finished. But he did continue to think about it. In *Talking with Sartre: Conversations and Debates*, when asked about his statement that "Hell is other people," Sartre responds:

> But that's only that side of the coin. The other side, which no one seems to mention, is also "Heaven is each other." . . . Hell is separateness, uncommunicability, self-centeredness, lust for power, for riches, for fame. Heaven, on the other hand, is very simple—and very hard: caring about your fellow beings. And that's possible on a sustained basis only in collectivity. (p. 130)

So, even later in his life, long after he abandons his project of trying to explain how one can move from bad faith to authenticity, Sartre still thinks that relationships can succeed.

Comparison

There are many noteworthy differences between *No Exit* and *The Good Place*. The characters in *No Exit* are in Hell for far more serious reasons (betrayal, sadism, murder) than the characters in *The Good Place* (self-centeredness, indecisiveness, vanity, impulsiveness). Moreover, the characters in *No Exit* know they're in Hell, whereas the characters in *The Good Place* don't—at least not at first. But let's set these differences aside in order to focus on how differently these two philosophical works of art treat relationships. Taking *The Good Place* to be a modern-day reworking of *No Exit*, to what degree has the former changed the latter's core message about relationships?

As we've seen, Sartre's claim in *No Exit* that "Hell is other people" is conditional: other people are Hell for us *if* we're in bad faith and depend too much on their opinions of us. Other people *needn't* be Hell, however. According to Sartre, healthy and authentic relationships are *possible*.

Relationships in *The Good Place*, by contrast, turn out very well even though they were designed to fail and bring misery. According to the show, love and friendship can prevail even in the most difficult and unlikely of circumstances. That being said, there's no reason to think this is meant to be a categorical truth. Yes, relationships *can* be re-demptive in the toughest of situations, but this takes nothing away from the fact that people really do sometimes make each other's lives miserable. Surely nobody would deny *that*.

In the final analysis, then, it seems that the messages about relationships in *No Exit* and *The Good Place* are actually compatible. Relationships can be Hell, even with the best intentions, but they needn't be Hell, even in the worst circumstances. To be sure, Schur's *The Good Place* offers us a far more optimistic vision of relationships than does Sartre's *No Exit* (or *Being and Nothingness*, for that matter), but the difference between them is far less extreme than a superficial understanding of Sartre's philosophy might lead us to believe.

---

[1] Thanks to Craig Vasey for organizing a panel on *No Exit* and *The Good Place* at the 2018 meeting of the North American Sartre Society, hosted at the University of Mary Washington. Thanks especially to members of the audience—including Michael Schur—for their extremely helpful feedback on a presentation of this chapter. Thanks also to Steven A. Benko, Andrew Pavelich, and Joshua Tepley for reading and commenting on an earlier draft.

17
The Forking Bullshirt of Being Alone Together in The Good Place

LACI HUBBARD-MATTIX

According to *The Good Place*, each and every one of our actions throughout our lives is assigned a point value, with the sum total determining whether or not we go to The Good Place or The Bad Place.

Staying loyal to the Cleveland Browns earns you 53.83 points while rooting for the Yankees means that you lose 99.15 points. The higher your net score upon death the more likely you are to earn yourself a spot in The Good Place. Each one of us individually earns points for the actions that we take in our lives.

The four human members of Neighborhood 12358W all failed to receive enough points to secure them a place in The Good Place. Each of them (although in very different and important ways) failed in some way throughout their lives to be deserving because of the individual choices they made. However, the show does not merely stress the importance of individual autonomy and action but stresses the ways in which individual action are influenced and formed by relationships. It presents the following paradox:

1. **Each person is responsible for the choices that she makes.**

2. **Each person's identity and choices are constrained by those with whom she has a relationship.**

The discussion of individual accountability and social dependence is not new in the tradition of philosophy and roughly represents two distinct philosophical traditions: existentialism and relational autonomy.

Existentialism, as exemplified by Jean-Paul Sartre, is demonstrated throughout the show. The point system itself highlights Sartre's claim that "man is condemned to be free. Condemned, because he did not create himself, yet in other respects is free; because, once thrown into the world, he is responsible for everything he does" (*Essays in Existentialism*, p. 41). Literally every action a person takes is tallied and then that person is held accountable for the net total of her life.

The question is not whether the members of the Neighborhood deserve to be in The Bad Place upon their deaths but if they should continue to be punished once they learn from their experiences in the afterlife through building relationships with one another. *The Good Place* asks us to consider whether we can reconcile the fact that ultimately each person is and should be accountable for her actions with the fact that those actions are often constrained by those she encounters in her life. Each of the six main character's storylines presents a different view of this tension and provides a different insight for us to consider, all of which ultimately work to inform us about the importance of those with whom we form our own team cockroach.

Team Cockroach!

Each character's story arc in The Good Place describes the tension between these two themes of philosophy. Each character is ultimately held accountable for the way she chose to respond to the relationships in her life, and yet once they get to the afterlife the importance of depending on one another and the social nature of choice is highlighted. However, the show does not offer a single complete solution to the dilemma, instead it offers several complications for us to consider.

Every one of the human members' lives and deaths, in the Neighborhood represent a different way of approaching the ethical paradox between individual accountability and social dependency. Eleanor and Chidi's storylines delve into problems with individual accountability while Tahani's and Jason's explore issues with social dependency.

Eleanor's character represents the ultimate futility of rejecting our social dependency, Chidi embodies the fact that ultimately, we as individuals must be accountable for our choices, Tahani represents our dependency on others, and finally, Jason reflects the importance of social relationships for personal identity. Ironically, each of these failures is what led to their untimely death in the afterlife. Together the story arcs present a complicated but important depiction of the paradox that offers the audience a way of resolving the paradox if we are determined to develop the correct sort of relationships.

Eleanor

Eleanor's life was a rejection of her social nature and warns us of the futility of such rejections. All the flashbacks to her life on Earth indicate this aspect of her personality. She (reasonably) emancipated herself from her parents as a birthday present to herself ("Mindy St. Claire"). She loudly proclaimed from a high school cafeteria table that she would not be joining any cliques or making any new friends (". . . Someone Like Me as a Member"). She goes so far as to bring her own birthday cake to work so that she isn't entered into the social contract of birthday exchanges ("Mindy St. Claire"). She turns down a permanent and lucrative job offer because she is incapable of seeing herself as part of a team (". . . Someone Like Me as a Member"). And perhaps in the most telling flashback of all she is kicked out of after-work drinking group (which she repeatedly benefited from) because of her inability to play be the rules and be the designated driver even once ("Flying").

Yet, even though Eleanor constantly rejects this aspect of her nature it is clear that she was influenced by her relationships. For example, she is constantly pressured into bad behavior by her superficial and vapid roommates in one case going to a Rihanna concert in Vegas instead of fulfilling her obligation to dog-sit which ends up destroying another relationship ("What We Owe to Each Other"). Her very insistence that she does not need other people is an indication of how reliant she is on them. Eventually she is forced to acknowledge that her rejection of these relationships and refusal to acknowledge her need of others is a reaction to her parent's failures. She even dies because she stops to yell at a whale-humper who has judged her continued mean treatment of him and tells her that she always hurts his feelings. Her need to reject her social obligations ends her life.

She is only able to acknowledge this as problematic once she enters into the afterlife where she is able to build positive relationships and begin her journey of self-growth. These relationships, begun as a way to protect herself from exposure, led to self-actualization and acknowledgment of her past failures, that she is a human trash-bag for instance, indicates that she is able to grow through the development of stronger relationships. During the 802 reboots of "The Good Place", one thing becomes clear: through her relationships with the rest of Team Cockroach she is able to become a better person. This is especially true of her relationship with Chidi. Though they originally entered the relationship at Michael's behest as "soul mates" and she begins by using him to avoid detection, they develop a strong and complex relationship that enables her to learn and grow.

The ethics lessons act as more than ethical training, they provide her with an outlet to acknowledge the important ways in which her actions impact others and more importantly to care about that impact. This growth continues to frustrate Michael in the various reboots as she constantly foils his plans and realizes that "The Good Place" is actually The Bad Place. In the first iteration of "The Good Place" Eleanor shocks Michael by admitting publicly that she does not belong in The Good Place ("Eternal Shriek"). Her motivation is that she is causing Chidi pain and because of her experience in "The Good Place," for the first time in her life, she does not want to be the cause of another's pain. She has learned to care for others.

As the main heroine of the story she offers only the beginnings of a solution to the paradox: be sure to surround yourself with people who provide you with the opportunity to become better. Michael, while trying to find the perfect people to torment each other for a thousand years, actually created the perfect opportunity for relationships that ironically encouraged the individual growth of all the people involved. Ultimately, Eleanor is the character who has the most growth, as she is the only one who passes the Judge's test to determine if the team belongs in The Good Place.

She ends up acknowledging her feelings for her companions because even though she is offered the selfish solution (that the Eleanor of Earth would have unquestionably taken) she refuses, deciding to remain in The Bad Place with her friends, most especially Chidi her mentor and love, rather than advance to The Good Place. This is our lesson in dealing with the paradox: take care of whom we embrace in our lives.

Chidi

On Earth, Chidi's experiences also focus on the importance of individual action but in an importantly different way than Eleanor's. His life is ultimately a rejection of choice because he is too concerned with how his actions will impact those around him. By focusing on ethics and a fear of hurting others he ends up being constantly frozen by indecision which ends with him hurting all of those who are close to him. He is responsible for the choices, or lack thereof, that he made and so is responsible for the pain that he causes. Ironically, the existentialist term for refusing to be accountable for one's choices is 'bad faith' and this leads to Chidi being sent to The Bad Place.

His indecision leads to never-ending stomachaches for him and pain for those around him. For instance, he agonizes for three years about his decision to lie to a colleague about whether he not he liked his outlandishly embellished and bright red cowboy boots ("The Eternal Shriek"). Eventually, Chidi decides that he is ethically required to tell the truth about the scenario and ends up hurting his colleague even more. (This turn of events is made even more ironic as his indecisiveness leads to his inadvertently killing this colleague in one of the many iterations of the Trolley Problem.)

Chidi is unable to complete his thesis, which would allow him to help more people. He destroys his relationship, continuously strained due to his indecision, with his best friend. In the playground he takes so long to choose his team that no one gets to play. Trying to fulfill his obligations as best man leads to a failed bachelor party, no speech, and no ring being selected for the ceremony. As his best friend unleashes his frustration due to his inability to decide, an air conditioner falls onto Chidi's head, killing him. He too dies because of his failure to appropriately acknowledge his own accountability.

His life on Earth indicates the problems inherent in rejecting the responsibility of his choices and actions; however, his experience in the Bad Place demonstrates that under the right circumstances with the right relationships, growth is possible. Eleanor's growth through the ethics lessons offers an opportunity for Chidi to also learn and grow. He learns that sometimes his rigid ethics lessons must be ignored. When Eleanor outs herself and admits that she does not belong in "The Good Place," Chidi lies for her and defends her to Michael and Shawn. He learns flexibility through his relationships with Eleanor and Michael which leads to him being able to at some pivotal moments take responsibility for his actions. Michael especially forces him to acknowledge the issues that can come from taking ethical thought experiments too literally in the Trolley Problem: he is forced to choose between one Shakespeare and five Santa Clauses, an entirely unrealistic and non-useful hypothetical scenario which demonstrates that sometimes the answers are not in thinking but in acting.

Even though he ultimately fails the Judge's test of choosing either a brown or grey hat there is a lesson for us in his failure as well. It is that we need to learn from our mistakes and to learn from our positive relations from others. Chidi had been given all of the experiences he needed in the bad place to learn from his mistakes and to walk away from bad faith but he did not. This is the lesson that we are take away from his storyline and his failure of the test. Sometimes each of us must choose and bear the responsibility for that choice.

Tahani

In many ways Tahani acts as a foil to Eleanor. She has the social grace, wealth, physical attractiveness, and most importantly a complete dependence on others that Eleanor generally lacks. However, there is one important similarity: their childhoods. Both Tahani and Eleanor had childhoods where they were mistreated and unloved by their parents. Tahani was entirely ignored in favor of her sister.

Tahani's story, as opposed to Eleanor's, focuses on the importance of not allowing others to entirely define yourself. Rather than rejecting any sort of social dependency Tahani allows others to define her, which is just as problematic (although in different ways) as refusing any sort of relationships with others. Her dependency on others motivates all her actions which means that she does not receive any of the points her otherwise good acts would have earned her because her motivation is flawed.

Tahani's life is framed by her parent's constant rejection of her through the relentless upholding and support of her sister Kamilah. This starts a cycle where she constantly tries to do more and to do better to win not only her parent's support and acknowledgment but also the world's. She raises sixty billion dollars for charity, not because she cares about those who are suffering but to gain attention and accolades. Whatever approval she gets is empty because she allows herself to be defined by it. She too ends up dying because of this flaw. At her sister's award celebration, she is crushed to death attempting to pull down a statue of her sister indicating how being defined by others ends in one's destruction of oneself.

Like Eleanor and Chidi, her story does not end with her life and she is granted the opportunity to learn from her mistakes. She, herself, comes to the realization of what caused her to have earned her place in The Bad Place which is the fact that she had the wrong motivation. Once Vicky has taken over The Bad Place in reboot 802, Tahani is still capable of being tortured by social ostracism. Even though she knows that Vicky has an elaborate plan to torture her through having an elaborate party that will not be attended, she is still tortured when no one shows up and the alternative party is unquestionably better. However, she learns to be less concerned with other people as she embraces her relationship with Jason and is even at one point able to acknowledge that cargo pants are comfortable.

The Judge's test of Tahani focuses on how the approval of others has been the dominant motive throughout her life. Her results demonstrate that she has learned from her time in The Bad Place even though she also fails. She is able to pass many doors where people are talking directly about her (including Princes Henry and William) but finds herself incapable of passing the room where her parents are supposed to be talking about her. While in the room she realizes that it doesn't matter because she cannot control what others think of her.

She tells her parents "In a test where everyone is supposed to be talking about me, you are still talking about Kamilah. Which is exactly the point. I was never going to be enough for you, never going to earn your respect" ("The Burrito"). In this moment she realizes (even though it's too late) her happiest moments are when she has not cared about what others think about her, for instance, when she is shagging a Floridian or eating a Cheeto. We are to take from this that we must avoid allowing others to define us and that ultimately what value we have we must find for ourselves.

Jason

Jason's storyline, like Tahani's, focuses on issues that arise whenever we're overly dependent on our relationships. Unlike Tahani, Jason is not at all self-aware in his need of approval, but he too is limited by the social circumstances of his life. What separates Jason is that his arc is less about individual accountability and more about being limited by his social relationships. Jason is constrained by those he encounters throughout his life.

He demonstrates personal traits that are largely desirable, like loyalty and devotion, but his application of these characteristics is problematic because of his choice of the persons he has relationships with. His devotion to his dance crew and specifically Pillboi and Donkey Doug directed him to situations that led to an overall loss of points and his assignment to The Bad Place and even ultimately his death. He could not trust those he had relationships with to encourage him to have better behavior or even to prevent his untimely demise.

In the afterlife, Jason is also given the opportunity to learn a healthier balance between independence and social reliance. His beginning days in the Bad Place force him to begin down this path as he is compelled into silence due to fear of discovery that he does not belong in "The Good Place." He is incapable of relying on anyone as he is incapable of communicating with anyone. He begins to question his relationships as his with Tahani develops. When he enters couples therapy with Janet (which Tahani only does upon Jason's insistence) he realizes that something is wrong with their relationship. He tells Tahani, "Here's the thing. I'm nice to you and you are mean to me. There's something wrong about that but I can't put my finger on what it is" ("The Trolley Problem").

In "The Good Place" Jason learns to value himself. As Tahani describes him he is thoughtful and not self-aware (even Eleanor acknowledges that he is the nicest of the four neighbors) which means it is of the utmost importance that he be surrounded by people who nurture these characteristics and do not take advantage of him.

Jason ends up failing the Judge's test demonstrating that he too did not fully embrace the lessons he learned from his experiences in the afterlife. The Judge tests whether he has learned to question his circumstances and to not be blindly loyal which in his life led to copious use of Molotov cocktails. He, however, has not learned to question whether he is required to do what his circumstances lead him to. The same attitude that led him to attempt to rob a fast-food restaurant and blindly support the Jacksonville Jaguars led him to leave the parameters of the test unexamined. He is incapable of playing against his favorite team, but he didn't realize that he could have asked whether he could refuse to play at all. His acceptance of his circumstances provides another lesson which is not to blindly accept the circumstances you find yourself in.

An Ethical Clusterfork

Each of the story arcs in *The Good Place* demonstrates to us the seeming paradox that is the reality with which each person must live her daily life. Each person must be held accountable for her own actions, but those actions are are indeed formed by the others we encounter in our lives. However, these kinds of paradoxes are not new to philosophy or to our own realities. Our decisions are framed by others, but we are still accountable for the choices that we make. We must be careful to question the circumstances that we find ourselves in and in choosing those with whom we enter relationships.

Ultimately, the answer to the paradox is to embrace both sides. We are individually accountable and yet dependent on others just like our friends in the Neighborhood.

VI

The Leap to Faith

18
Heaven Is Other People

JOEL MAYWARD

God isn't in *The Good Place*, at least not in the typical ways we might imagine a deity would be depicted in a TV show about the afterlife.

Still, *The Good Place* is a theological sitcom, directly asking questions about what we're talking about when we talk about God. In a society where religious programing is usually only for a select audience, why is a show about Heaven and Hell so popular? To find out, we must recognize that *The Good Place* is about both philosophy *and* theology, both ethics and eschatology.

So, what's eschatology? Short answer: it's the theological study of "future" or "final things." It encompasses stuff like death, judgment, the end of the world, as well as conceptions of the afterlife—Heaven and Hell (and sometimes Purgatory). As we look at how *The Good Place*'s ethics and eschatology are connected, we need to evaluate the show's form as well. Paraphrasing movie critic Roger Ebert, we should appreciate not just *what* the show is about, but *how* the show is about it.

The Good Place's Eschatology

Using the genre of "magical realism" and the motif of an afterlife bureaucracy (cubicles, forms, and diabolical middle management), *The Good Place*'s aesthetic is at once inviting and inciting—it draws us in and keeps us engaged via its sharp wit, even as it deconstructs popular beliefs about goodness, badness, and the afterlife.

Formally, *The Good Place* has an eschatological narrative structure, framed as "Chapters" as opposed to episodes. The formal use of chapters suggests that the show is a story headed *somewhere*, giving the audience the sense of an ending. While many TV sitcoms are usually episodic and season-by-season, the use of chapter titles for each episode of *The Good Place* implies that, much like eschatology, the ending has already been written.

Even as it aims for a pluralistic, a-religious spirituality— Michael tells Eleanor that every religion got it about five percent right, and the show's creator Michael Schur has described the show as "spiritual and ethical" instead of religious—it reveals a Western Judeo-Christian influence: this afterlife is explicitly named by characters (and Schur) as "Heaven" and "Hell."

Chapter 31 confirms this when Chidi uses those Christian terms and Michael only semi-corrects him: "Again, it's not the *classic* Christian Hell, but . . . that's the gist, yes" ("Jeremy Bearimy"). Though the writing conspicuously avoids the name "Jesus Christ" (both in its theological and expletive senses—it'd probably be "Cheese and Rice" in this censored world), in Chapter 7, "The Eternal Shriek," the title of Chidi's sparkly-boot-wearing colleague's course on the classroom blackboard is "Eschatology and Notions of the Apocalypse," with books by prominent Christian theologians clearly listed as assigned reading.

The four books on the classroom chalkboard are: Brian E. Daley, *The Hope of the Early Church: A Handbook of Patristic Eschatology* (1991); Alan F. Segal, *Life After Death: A History of the Afterlife in Western Religion* (2004); Jürgen Moltmann, *The Coming of God: Christian Eschatology* (2000); and Jeffrey Burton Russell, *Paradise Mislaid: How We Lost Heaven—And How We Can Regain It* (2006). This is probably the first American sitcom ever to cite German theologian Jürgen Moltmann, evidence that the show's writers have done their eschatological homework.

Despite this apparent Christian influence, the afterlife in *The Good Place* also seems informed by popular misconceptions of Christian eschatology. In historical Western Christian theology, Heaven is, simply put, "God's space." But the future Heaven is not the one commonly assumed in pop culture and prevailing Greek philosophical thought: a disembodied static spiritual existence somewhere "out there" as immortal souls in angelic white robes, perhaps equipped with halos and harps. In this popular culture perspective, we *have* a body as an instrument or tool, a husk to be discarded when we enter into the ideal heavenly realms as our true selves: our souls.

In contrast, historical Christian eschatology and anthropology affirms bodily resurrection. Humans don't *have* bodies, they *are* bodies, created and affirmed by God. As the Nicene

Creed puts it, "We look for the resurrection of the dead, and the life of the world to come." This "life of the world to come" is a material renewal of body *and* soul, with the eternal outcome determined not by your individual conduct, but by God's grace and a person's faith in and faithfulness to Christ.

There are varying views in orthodox Christian tradition about where the dead are *now* during "life after death," but what's agreed upon is that "life *after* life after death" in Heaven is bodily. Instead of an "out there" static spiritual realm, Heaven is a dynamic this-world material reality imbued with God's good presence. As theologian N.T. Wright says in his book on Heaven, *Surprised By Hope*, "the central Christian affirmation is that what the creator God has done in Jesus Christ, and supremely in his resurrection, is what he intends to do for the whole world—meaning, by *world*, the entire cosmos with all its history" (p. 91).

Thus, in Christian eschatology the grand finale is not about going away to a disembodied Heaven, but about Heaven (God's space) coming to Earth (our space) to renew and restore our world in love as resurrected, material existence. So, the eschatology depicted in *The Good Place*—and thus the eschatology it aims to critique—is worth questioning.

Questionable Judgment

So far, the closest to God we've seen in *The Good Place* is the "all-knowing" judge Gen, located in a Neutral Zone between The Bad Place and The Good Place. But Gen is not divine; she's "born" or created, and seems limited in her knowledge and power (for instance, in Season Three, Michael and Janet sneak onto Earth without Gen's awareness).

In this post-mortem realm, a person's eternal destiny is judged not by an all-knowing eternal deity, but rather an impersonal algorithm enforced by a burrito-eating judiciary demigod and endless cubicles of accountants. Similarly, Janet initially appears omnipotent, but her powers change and evolve unexpectedly, making her (and us) unsure of what's possible.

Which raises a metaphysical question: What is the nature of reality itself in *The Good Place*? It appears to be an afterlife of soulish immortality rather than bodily resurrection, though there are hints of corporeality, like Jason pricking his finger on a cactus and drawing blood in Chapter 8 ("Most Improved Player"), or Chidi's pet owl goring his arm in Chapter 34, "The Worst Possible Use of Free Will" (and, of course, consuming food like frozen yogurt).

People have "essences" instead of souls, and human bodies can dematerialize, at least within Janet's Void. This afterlife is not a place of eternality or infinity, but is time-bound; Chapter 31, "Jeremy Bearimy" describes its nonlinear Jeremy Bearimy-shaped timeline. The only known realms are the "Good Place," the Bad Place, the Medium Place—a unique afterlife location created especially for one cocaine-loving supporting character, Mindy St. Claire—the Neutral Zone, the Door to Earth, Accounting, IHOP, and Janet's Void. So far, despite the team's infiltration of a celestial correspondence center in Chapter 37, "The Book of Dougs," we've never truly experienced the *real* "Good Place" (and even if we did, we'd likely still be suspicious).

Indeed, what is perceived as "real" within the show is repeatedly shown to be uncertain and unknown. Although Michael argues throughout for the unchangeable mechanics of this realm—particularly the points-based algorithm which determines everyone's fate—none of the eternal beings are omniscient or omnipotent, limiting their knowledge of what is possible. That time and memory can be instantly manipulated fosters further suspicion for both characters and the audience. With so many unexpected twists, everything is called into question, especially this realm's form of judgment.

The afterlife's system of salvation is repeatedly decried as flawed, beginning with Eleanor in the pilot episode and most clearly articulated in Season Two's finale as Michael advocates for the humans before Gen:

> The premise of our system is that a person's score during her time on Earth is final and inarguable. But these four humans got better after they died; that's not supposed to be possible . . . If I'm right, then the system by which we judge humans, the very method we use to deem them good or bad, is so fundamentally flawed and unreasonable that hundreds of millions of people have been wrongly condemned to an eternity of torture. ("Somewhere Else")

Michael's suspicions are confirmed in Chapter 36, "Janet(s)," as it's revealed that no human has made it into the "Good Place" in over five hundred years. Michael's argument appears to be a direct criticism of the Christian conception of Hell as *eternal conscious torment,* the notion that God's righteous wrath is eternally poured out upon the damned, those whose actions were unjust and whose faith was unsound.

A classic example is American pastor-theologian Jonathan Edwards's sermon *Sinners in the Hands of an Angry God.* Such a critique of Hell is not without precedent; a recent example is evangelical-pastor-turned-motivational-speaker Rob Bell's 2011 book *Love Wins*, which openly questions eternal conscious torment and strongly suggests Christian universalism—the theory that no one ends up in Hell.

Eternal conscious torment is only one of a variety of Christian understandings of Hell. Roman Catholic, Protestant, and Eastern Orthodox traditions differ, not to mention individual theologians and philosophers throughout Christian history. Views include, but aren't limited to: eternal conscious torment; Christian universalism (all are eventually saved from Hell via Christ); annihilationism (a.k.a. "conditional immortality," where persons in Hell will eventually cease to exist); and the Eastern Orthodox view that Heaven and Hell are linked to individuals' experience in the direct presence of God's love and justice (believers find God's presence wonderful, while non-believers . . . don't). Hell may be defined less as a physical location and more an existential state of being or identity. A third place, Purgatory, also has its variants, with its existence, purpose, and metaphysics differing depending on the Christian tradition or theologian.

Still, like Heaven, much of our popular imagination about Hell (and Purgatory) has been shaped more by Dante, Bosch, and horror films than by creeds or doctrines. Thus, the conceived afterlife in *The Good Place* is, again, worthy of such critiques—the show is inviting us to rethink our common (possibly mistaken) conceptions of Heaven and Hell, even as it bases its criticisms on a mistaken view of the Christian afterlife. Just like Eleanor, it's as if the show unknowingly stumbled into its eschatology, accidentally getting some key things right along the way.

To see what it gets right, we can turn to two ethicists who have not yet been mentioned in *The Good Place* to help us better understand the sitcom's (and our own) eschatology and ethics.

The Face of the Other

The Good Place depicts the Other as the *means* of transcendence in the vein of Jewish philosopher Emmanuel Levinas, who developed these ideas in *Alterity and Transcendence* (1995), *Totality and Infinity* (1961), and *Otherwise than Being* (1974). For Levinas, ethics is based in responsibility engendered by an encounter with the face of the Other, where "ethics is a spiritual optics" with intersubjectivity as a view toward the divine.

Writing in the aftermath of the Holocaust, Levinas sought an ethical framework which went deeper than the ethicists who had come before him. He proposed that ethics *precedes* ontology, that we are responsible for others even before we're conscious of existence. As Levinas puts it in *Totality and Infinity*, alterity (otherness) and transcendence (beyondness) are somehow united in the human face-to-face interaction, beginning with our birth and seeing the face of our mother, then in every subsequent human encounter throughout our lives. We must not reduce the Other to the Same, but respect the alterity of the Other in this "curvature of space," the relation between human beings, what Levinas calls "the very presence of God" (p. 291).

In other words, we're inherently responsible to and for *every* person we see and meet, and they in turn are intersubjectively responsible to and for us. This family member, that neighbor, the stranger walking down the street or sitting next to us on the subway—human beings, all of 'em, and each a call towards ethical responsibility and care.

Moreover, as Levinas declares that any eternal or divine judgment of our goodness cannot consist "in hearing a verdict set forth impersonally and implacably out of universal principles" but rather goodness and truth can exist "only if a subjectivity is called upon to tell it . . . The call to infinite responsibility confirms the subjectivity in its apologetic position" (pp. 244–45). So, *The Good Place*'s questionable algorithmic judgment wouldn't cut it for Levinas—true justice is intersubjective, not impersonal.

While Levinas was very skeptical of artistic representations of this ethical alterity and opposed to incarnations of God, I wonder if *The Good Place* is more Levinasian than its creators may realize. Even as the *visage* for Levinas is not just a literal human countenance, the face-to-face encounter is formally depicted throughout *The Good Place*, which often forgoes the traditional shot-reverse shot or over-the-shoulder shot to place two or more characters *within* the frame together, either looking directly into each other's faces or facing a situation side-by-side.

This formal decision also strengthens the audience's empathetic connection to the characters—we are *with* them and *for* them in this afterlife conundrum. The very way the show depicts them helps us care that these six strangers-turned-soul-mates are ethically responsible for each other's mortal future. Morality and existence become intertwined; as Levinas puts it, "the fact that in existing for another I exist otherwise than in existing for me is morality itself" (p. 261).

Per Levinas, every face-to-face human encounter is a site for transcendence and ethical transformation, and thus a potential encounter with God. These for-the-Other ethical decisions often come prior to full comprehension; in a Levinasian manner, characters will *do* good, then *understand* the good they do.

We can see this in Eleanor, who often will make a good ethical decision spontaneously, almost by accident. The evidence of having learned something from Chidi's ethics courses comes not from essays or memorized answers, but in the actual conflicts and situations emerging from the narrative. Instead of Eleanor treating people as obstacles or tools—what Levinas calls violence, making the Other into the Same—she begins to view others as subjective Others instead of annoying objects. We can also see Levinas in Chidi's repeated acceptance of Eleanor as his ethics student in the 800+ reboots. Despite his indecisiveness, he nevertheless makes a decision *for* Eleanor every time. Perhaps this is motivated by his Kantian categorical imperative, but it's more likely due to the face of the Other before him, something he can only recognize after he has already chosen for her wellbeing. Genuine transformation means our habits and attitudes are wholly reborn.

Religionless Christianity

Such radical transformation leads us to the ethics of Dietrich Bonhoeffer. Levinas and Bonhoeffer were both born in 1906; Levinas was a Jewish philosopher and a POW survivor of World War II, while Bonhoeffer was a Christian theologian and pastor who was executed by the Nazis in 1945 for participating in a plot to assassinate Hitler. Though they differ in their ethics, I think both of these guys are worthy of The Good Place.

In his magnum opus, *Ethics*, Bonhoeffer states that the reality of the world and the reality of God are reconciled via the reality of Christ—God's space (Heaven) and human space (World) are united through Jesus *now*. Thus, if reality is best understood through Christ, then to live fully in reality is to be a responsible person—someone who acts in accordance to God's will and follows Christ's example. So, what is Christ's example?

Grounded in theological virtue ethics rather than ideologies, Bonhoeffer suggests a semi-relativistic approach to moral decisions: our defining guides are not categorical imperatives nor utilitarian frameworks, but simply to "Love your neighbor as yourself" in the manner and model of Jesus Christ. We can't fully know whether we're doing the right or wrong thing in a given situation, yet we can look at Christ's character and teachings, then act accordingly, trusting that divine grace covers any mistakes. Bonhoeffer says (in language similar to

Levinas) that even as we may be unsure of a right action, we are still responsible to and for one another as responsible agents.

Responding to the German Church's capitulation to Nazi ideology, in his *Letters and Papers from Prison* Bonhoeffer describes a "religionless Christianity" stripped of the traditional adornments of institutional religion, where Christ becomes not a dead object of worship but a living-and-present subject active within reality and moving us to gratitude. Bonhoeffer writes that "gratitude is what enriches life. One easily overestimates the importance of one's own acts and deeds, compared with what we become only through other people" (p. 154). Following Bonhoeffer, in the "religionless" world of *The Good Place*, responsible agents like Eleanor love (and thus transform) their neighbors through sacrificial action—God via Christ is present in such grace, even if unrecognized. In Season Three, as the "soul squad" accepts their eternal fate in the Bad Place, they choose to practice Bonhoeffer-like love towards others, not to save themselves, but to transform and potentially save others.

In Christian theology ethical transformation occurs via an intersubjective exchange of confession and repentance. For example, when Eleanor publicly reveals that she's actually bad at the end of "The Eternal Shriek," Michael later tells her in "Michael's Gambit," that it was this confession which ruined his plan: "My big mistake was bringing you all together. Next time I'll spread you out," he quips. But after 800-plus iterations, the four humans keep finding and improving each other through face-to-face encounters, admitting their flaws and extending grace.

Similarly, the Levinasian face-to-face professions of love Eleanor tells Chidi in "The Eternal Shriek," "What's My Motivation," "Dance Dance Resolution," and "The Worst Possible Use of Free Will" are transformative moments for both characters, whose selfishness (Eleanor) and indecision (Chidi) are challenged and rectified in the face of the Other.

This notion of repentance—a holistic 180-degree turnaround of one's entire life—is clearly depicted in Eleanor's arc. For instance, in "Jason Mendoza," she slaps a video game controller from Jason's hand and tells him he needs to be in Chidi's ethics class, "because you suck!" "You suck!" Jason retorts. Eleanor immediately responds, "I *know*! That's what I'm trying to tell you—we *both* suck."

"I just want to be myself," Jason laments. "That's a very, very bad idea. Do not be yourself—you need to be a better version of yourself, and I do too," declares Eleanor. This is not a feel-good message of "just believe in yourself." It's one of radical life-altering reversal, and it's via this repentance that transformation (and transcendence) can occur. We see another vivid example of repentance in "A Fractured Inheritance," when Eleanor goes to confront her mother Donna, only to realize that Donna has repented of her previous selfish life. How did this transformation occur? Through confession and honesty, both to her new husband and to herself.

In the same Chapter, Tahani also repents of the self-destructive grudge she held against her sister Kamilah, again via honest confession and a Levinasian face-to-face encounter with Kamilah, culminating in an embrace.

Michael is transformed by repentance and Bonhoeffer-like sacrificial action over the course of Season Two, converting from a demonic antagonist to a friend, even savior. As the group navigates the Bad Place headquarters to escape through a trans-dimensional portal to Gen the judge, they are short one pin which will allow them through the portal. Realizing this, and having taken Chidi's ethics course alongside the humans, Michael turns to Eleanor as he places the pin on her lapel: "I just solved the Trolley Problem. You sacrifice yourself," he tells her before pushing her through to safety ("Rhonda, Diana, Jake, and Trent").

There is an incarnational resonance when Michael earlier states, "Architects aren't supposed to live with humans in the place they design, *but I love you so much*" ("The Eternal Shriek"). By Season Three, it's Michael who risks his welfare and intentionally goes to Earth to save the four humans from death. He gives each a "nudge," prompting them to find and help each other, then continues to linger on Earth as their guide (along with Janet's help).

Michael's actions here remind me of the Christian doctrine of the incarnation, which claims that Jesus Christ is fully human and fully God, God's space (Heaven!) embodied in human history. Pastor-theologian Eugene Peterson's paraphrase of John 1:14 resonates with Michael's confession of neighborly love: "The Word [Jesus] became flesh and blood, and *moved into the neighborhood*." In an unorthodox paradox, a demon character in *The Good Place* is also a Christ figure.

Practicing Heaven

Jürgen Moltmann (the German theologian from Chapter 7) once wrote, "Whenever we ask about 'life after death' we are really asking about a meaningful, livable, and beloved 'life before death'." (p. 3). This is the significance of *The Good Place*, a show so full of hope and joy (even in the midst of Hell itself) which invites us to practice hope and joy in our present-day Hells.

The Good Place reminds me of Jesus's parable in Luke 16 of Lazarus and the rich man, where two men experience role reversals as the poor Lazarus, who suffered while on Earth, ends up in Heaven while the rich man suffers in Hell. The function of a parable is not as an allegory or a moral illustration; rather, to paraphrase philosopher Paul Ricoeur, parables bring reorientation via disorientation, challenging our deep-rooted beliefs and myths through surprise and subversion.

Jesus's parable (like *The Good Place*) is not intended to bring comfort about the afterlife or describe an eschatological system, but to confront and provoke the audience's theological and moral imagination, to make them rethink how they're treating other people *today* in light of eternity. In our contemporary world filled with political turmoil and vitriol, where systemic injustice runs rampant via impersonal systems, *The Good Place* reminds us that our theology and philosophy must be practiced—our orthodoxy (right belief) is only as good as our orthopraxy (right action). We can practice the presence of Heaven in the here and now, acting as responsible agents in caring for the Other. Regardless of our personal religious persuasion, Jesus's command to "love your neighbor as yourself" is a moral philosophy worth considering.

Ultimately, salvation in *The Good Place* is attained not by individualistic merit nor impersonal bureaucratic algorithm, but by an intersubjective grace-infused repentance in which each person is transformed by encounters with other human beings. In the Levinasian face of the Other and Bonhoeffer's religionless Christianity, God may be present in *The Good Place* after all.

Whereas Sartre declared that "Hell is other people," *The Good Place*, with its subversive eschatology and ethics, suggests that *Heaven* is other people.

19

Hinduism Gets More than Five Percent Right

KAMALPREET KAUR AND
MEENU AGGARWAL GUPTA

In the first episode, Michael tells Eleanor that most religions—including Hinduism—got some part of the afterlife right. Each got about five percent. But as the show unfolds, it seems that for Hinduism it was actually much more.

The *Bhagavad Gita* (the name means "Message of the Master," or the "Lord's Song") shows up as one of the examples on Chidi's chalkboard ("Jason Mendoza"). It's one of the most philosophical, religious, and at the same time, secular texts in Hinduism and in Indian culture.

The story it tells takes place amidst a great war, with Prince Arjuna talking to Lord Krishna about Arjuna's doubt over the impending battle. It ends with Arjuna ready to follow the righteous path of Duty or *dharma*. But it's more than just a story of a man who comes to do his duty. Scholars believe that the *Bhagavad Gita* imparts a different lesson to everyone based on their 'plane of unfoldment'. These planes represents the various levels of perception our minds are open to which further depends on the level of knowledge achieved by us.

Karma Is Like Gravity, It's So Basic

In Hindu tradition, *karmic* theory holds that the fruits of your actions are decided by the nature of your actions. If you do good deeds, good results are inevitable and if you do bad deeds then you should be ready to face the consequences. "The Good Place," too, has a system in place which decides the final score of each person based on their deeds, in consonance with the *karmic* theory.

As Michael explains in the orientation day clip, a person commits good and bad deeds over the period of his existence on

Earth and upon the person's death all the positive and negative points are added. Based on the combined total, the cream of the crop gets a chance to enter The Good Place.

The *Bhagavad Gita* talks about three kinds of Action or *Karma*: Right Action, Inaction, and Wrong Action. Inaction is actually a misnomer, since it does not mean that there is no action involved, but (as Lord Krishna explains in the *Bhagavad Gita*) it involves the conscious effort at action for the non-performance of another action. Put another way, inaction is not doing nothing; inaction is doing something else, or, choosing and doing otherwise. Hence, in essence it is an Action.

On the other hand, we have Wrong Action which leads to negative points as highlighted in *The Good Place*. It is a result of what we call desire, which is the root cause of all evil in Hindu belief.

Right Action is not just doing the right thing, but also involves overcoming desires. This leads to the concept of *nishkāma karman* or 'desire-less action', an extension of the *karmic* theory. As the name suggests, 'desire-less action' propounds that you should perform an action without any desire for its results. Once desire becomes the motivation for your actions, they lose significance and become worthless or take the shape of wrong action.

Eleanor exemplifies this concept of desire-less action at the end of Season One. At first she tries to achieve her place in "The Good Place" by doing good deeds like holding the door open and greeting every resident of the neighborhood. Despite her best efforts, she realizes that her motivation is selfish and that is why she is not earning any points towards remaining in "The Good Place" (in reality, Michael is still evil and he's forking with her, but the karmic principle still applies).

She ultimately realizes that it is the motivation behind her actions which determines their worth. Once this realization sets in, she decides to leave "The Good Place" for The Bad Place without informing any of her friends about her plan. As a result of her desire-less action, she helps convince Michael that humans are worthy of another chance and are in need of just a push in the right direction.

Of All Things Indian

Another Hindu doctrine which is highlighted in the *Bhagavad Gita* is the cyclical way of life consisting of birth-death-rebirth. Death is not considered to be the final stop, rather it is a brief hiatus before we re-enter the same space from another side.

The reason for this belief is that the ultimate aim of human life is the union with the Supreme Being (in the *Bhagavad Gita* represented by Lord Krishna).

The only way to achieve this union is through self-realization, an idea explored in the episode "Best Self." Janet announces that The Balloon will transport to The Good Place "only those who have attained self-realization." Even though the Golden Balloon is, in fact, a lie, the underlying theme of the statement is quite important. These words, though based in deceit, force Eleanor and Chidi to question whether the current version of themselves is their best version.

Their previous eight hundred versions represent their rebirths in the afterlife. We call it a rebirth because they do not possess any memories of the previous versions, which is one of the pre-requisites of rebirth in Hindu belief. Desires have to be overcome each time and memories form an obstacle to the temptations of the world. However, the knowledge gained previously is not forgotten as such, but is deep within the mind and can be accessed with a bit of effort; just like Janet re-gains her knowledge after every reboot.

The *Bhagavad Gita* considers our soul to be the Real Self or *ātman* and refers to our body as the physical self. *The Bhagavad Gita* puts forth the theory that the main cause of suffering in this world is the ineffectiveness of the Real Self to differentiate between itself and the physical body, desire being one of the reasons. Desires lead to attachments in this world— attachment to our precious life, to feelings of pleasure and pain, to our friends and family. The *Bhagavad Gita* teaches that all these desires need to be overcome if Self-realization is to be achieved. Lord Krishna uses this as one of his arguments to convince Prince Arjuna to resume the fight against his friends and family.

The only way to overcome desires, and become our best selves, is through Knowledge. In the *Bhagavad Gita*, Lord Krishna says that knowledge is most important as it will help the individual to arrive at Right Thinking which is important for Right Action. Hinduism posits that the most common way to achieve knowledge is through logic.

This is the logic of Eleanor, and not so much of Chidi. While Chidi uses his knowledge to arrive at a conclusion logically, Eleanor always uses logic to reach a knowledgeable conclusion. Chidi's way leads to his indecisiveness which is the cause of his torture but Eleanor's way helps her in uncovering the true nature of their so-called utopian afterlife. The Indian system of logic, known as Nyaya, talks in detail about the categories involved in logically reaching a conclusion, but let's stick to the basics as highlighted in the *Bhagavad Gita*.

Let's Unfold those 'Planes'

Coming back to the 'plane of unfoldment' mentioned before, the characters in *The Good Place* present themselves as perfect examples for understanding this concept. We can divide the major characters into three categories: Humans, Eternal Beings, and Janet. Now let's consider the different planes of unfoldment achieved by a person as steps on the ladder to self-realization. Hindu philosophy states that our attachment to desires is what makes us human and far away from self-realization.

Eleanor represents the bottom step as she is most controlled by her desires. Her incomplete desires present themselves as her anger which she vents on everyone around her, her friends, her co-workers, supermarket employees, or environmental activists. She commits Wrong Action knowingly and willingly.

Above her, we find Jason who is even more engrossed in his desires than Eleanor. His only saving grace and the reason why he is higher than Eleanor is that he commits all the bad actions unknowingly, which represents Inaction in many ways. Jason firmly believes that he is not performing any type of action as there is no thinking involved beforehand. Yet he commits deeds which are branded as 'bad'. As a result, he ends up causing pain to himself and others but without the knowledge of the effects of his Inaction.

Above Jason is Tahani who does good deeds with a corrupt motivation. Her desires do control her emotions but she is not constantly in the grip of anger. It's only when her parents refuse to give her due share that she is overtaken by anger. She does perform the Right Action but with the wrong Thinking motivating it. This places her third to last which is one above her fake neighborhood rankings.

Above Tahani is Chidi, the most advanced human in terms of 'plane of unfoldment'. He has acquired vast knowledge by logically pursuing his life goals and overcoming his desires which has resulted in his three-thousand-plus pages of manuscript. His knowledge of morals and ethics show that he possesses all the tools required for Right Thinking before performing Right Action. His only drawback is his inability to decide whether his thinking is right or not. Chidi's inability to use his vast knowledge to reach a definite conclusion is the cause of his torture as well as that of his near and dear ones.

Next come the Eternal beings like Michael and his boss Shawn, who are above the humans on the ladder to self-realization, at least in the beginning. No doubt, Michael lies about everything to sell his experiment to the four humans, yet he does attest to the truth in a number of ways. As Michael tells Eleanor in "The Trolley Problem," "I am an eternal being who can see in nine dimensions. I can see from your aura that you are about to fart quietly and then lie about it."

Both Michael and Shawn have overcome their attachment to the feelings of pleasure and pain to a large extent when compared to the four humans. A very good example showcasing this is when Shawn visits "The Good Place" as a judge. Michael tells the humans that the judge will recede into his cocoon if he even gets a whiff of emotion. Though it is all based on a lie, the cocoon represents one of the planes of unfoldment talked about in Hindu philosophy. It stands for a conscious attempt at detachment from desires in the form of feelings.

Michael also follows in the footsteps of Shawn and is shown to have overcome most of his desires as well. As a result, he is able to perform his *dharma* perfectly. Even though his *dharma* revolves around torturing humans for eternity it is his Duty and needs to be followed. Lord Krishna in the *Bhagavad Gita* says to Prince Arjuna that you should perform your *dharma* to the best of your abilities. You are not to take up the *dharma* of others even if it seems to be nobler than your own—the reason being that you have been given your *dharma* for a specific reason which is to test you based on your abilities and to prove that you can overcome your shortcomings.

Michael eventually strays from the path of his *dharma* and joins Team Cockroach. His actions are completely wrong, since Right Action has as its basis Right Thinking which is further dependent on performance of one's *dharma*, which Michael doesn't fulfill. The main reason behind his deviating from his *dharma* is his proximity to the humans while adorning a human suit.

Lord Krishna says that desires and temptations are always present around us: for someone on a diet it comes in the form of chocolates, fries, ice-creams; for Michael it came in the form of building a perfect neighbourhood to torture humans for years to come. It is his desire for success which causes him to reboot the neighbourhood more than eight hundred times. It is the temptation for something better on the 'next attempt' that forces him to sway from the path of his *dharma*. The frustration of incomplete desires cause him to join Team Cockroach where Michael confesses that he is helping the humans to give himself a fighting chance of entering The Good Place as well. It might have been a lie as well. But then, he repeatedly convinces Janet to help him in his plans beginning with the frozen yogurt to the very end, viz., escaping The Bad Place. As his motives behind helping the humans are also not pure, his actions cannot be termed *nishkāma karman* or 'desire-less actions'. And so, he is above the humans on the ladder to Self-realization but below Janet.

The highest 'plane of unfoldment' reached by anyone in the series is represented through the character of Janet. Janet is shown to be completely free of attachment, at least in the very first attempt. She further exemplifies, quite perfectly, the Hindu cycle of birth-death-rebirth. Michael reboots the neighbourhood more than eight hundred times and each time Janet is rebooted as well. The act of pressing the red button leads to Janet's death while the rebooted version represents her rebirth. This goes on for more than eight hundred times which means she has had eight hundred rebirths.

The reason we use the word 'rebirth' is because Janet doesn't possess any memories of her previous life. After each reboot, the first order of things for Janet is to regain the Knowledge of the universe which involves all her previous Knowledge as well as the new things she had experienced before being rebooted, but without the memories. This helps Janet to evolve into a better version of herself each time, which forms the stepping stones for climbing above the rest of the characters on the proverbial ladder and achieving self-realization.

In the *Bhagavad Gita* Lord Krishna stresses the point that self-realization is a must in order to overcome the cycle of birth-death-rebirth. We are not saying that Janet has achieved Self-realization; what we are saying is that she is better placed compared to the rest. Just like when Michael tells Chidi that he was the closest to getting into The Good Place, just not that close. Why do we say this? Well, Janet does not eat or drink which shows that in the realm presented in the series, she is free from the most basic desire of every living being which is food. She doesn't sleep and calls her living space a "boundless, limitless void" which is similar to how the Hindu thought system describes the Universe or *Brahman*.

Hinduism defines the Universe as a boundless and limitless space from which everything begins and in which everything ends. "Everything" here means the world as we know it with all its life forms, everything which is known to us and that which is still unknown. Hinduism says that once we attain self-realization, we will be able to uncover all the secrets of the

Universe and then nothing will seem impossible. Just like how Janet creates Derek (her boyfriend) in the void and later on puts him back in the void.

Janet is the only one who can access the void and this makes her a representative of the highest order among the characters on the path to self-realization. But her major drawback is that she starts to have feelings for Jason. After each reboot, these feelings keep on growing to the extent that she starts to malfunction. Her malfunctioning represents her going from the peak to near the bottom. How is that possible? At first, she was the perfect specimen who was not affected by the temptations around her and as such she had no desires. But she gives into the temptation (her feelings for Jason) when she is the most vulnerable, instantly after being rebooted, in her 'infancy'.

The reason we said "near the bottom" and not 'bottom' is because even though Janet gives in to her desires, her knowledge does not leave her. It's true that she starts to malfunction because she is unable to remain detached from her feelings. But then again she does have control over her desires and this is where her *dharma* comes in. The only purpose of Janet is to assist the humans in the afterlife. As Eleanor, Chidi, Jason and Tahani are the only humans in "The Good Place," she is duty bound to help them in whatever way possible. When seen from this aspect, Janet still retains her position above the rest on the so-called proverbial ladder to Self-realization.

It is her *dharma* to make the humans' stay as comfortable as possible which results in her being emotionally attached to Jason. It is her *dharma* to assist them in every way possible which is why she helps Michael in planning their escape from The Bad Place. She follows her duty even after the humans are given another chance at increasing their points by continuously monitoring them and helping Michael in bringing them together on Earth. When seen from the angle of the *Bhagavad Gita*, Janet follows her *dharma* which leads to Right Thinking based on logic and ends in Right Action.

This is just the tip of the iceberg when it comes to the teachings of the *Bhagavad Gita* as well as Hindu philosophy. It has taken scholars years of hard work to decipher what Hinduism's religious and philosophical texts actually mean and there is still a long way to go as the answers are still dependent on the 'plane of unfoldment' achieved by each individual.

So instead of sinking deep into it like the Titanic and losing our way, let's part ways here by following in the footsteps of Michael in the mid-life crisis episode and politely saying, *Namaste!*

VII

What's My Motivation?

20
Moral Health Warning

JONATHAN DANCY

Don't believe what they tell you.

What they tell you in *The Good Place* is that studying moral philosophy can make you a better person. I'm not sure that this is ever made explicit, but it's certainly the reason why Chidi is teaching Eleanor about the works of Kant and Scanlon and introducing her to the intricacies of the Trolley Problem.

It's not just that he enjoyed teaching these things when alive, and that he has managed to persuade Eleanor to give him an opportunity to carry on doing it in "The Good Place" when everyone else there is spending their time eating frozen yogurt. Chidi is a good person and he is trying to help Eleanor convert herself, out of a concern for her good.

The trouble with this is that few moral philosophers would claim that reading their work has much chance of making you a better person.

What's involved in becoming a better person? The main change must be a change in your motivation. The people who earn entry to the Good Place are people who have done considerable good in their lives. But even though doing good may be required for entry to the Good Place, entry also depends on *why* they did those good things.

If, for instance, they spent a lot of time helping others just because that gave them the best chance of a cushy billet in the afterlife, they are not as good as those who help others for some other reason—for instance, that those others need help, or that you ought to do your best to help those in need.

This is a matter of motivation. You're a good person if your motivation is of a certain sort. And reading moral philosophy isn't very likely to change your motivation. In fact, if it did succeed in changing your motivation, the first difference it would make is that it would stop you reading moral philosophy, because doing that isn't very likely to result in your doing more good. It looks more like self-indulgence, since you're spending time learning about Kant and Scanlon when you could have been doing a lot more good in other ways.

I don't mean to say that it's absolutely impossible that studying the works of moral theorists will indirectly lead to an improvement in character—in motivation, that is. If the distinction between right and wrong is in the forefront of your attention, and you have spent long hours wondering whether it's permissible to kill one person in order to save five others, or to prevent someone else from killing two, it may be that your efforts will indirectly lead to a greater sensitivity to, and interest in, the distinction between right and wrong. A theoretical interest can become a practical interest. But no moral philosopher that I know of would claim that most students leave their moral philosophy classes as better people as a result of what they have studied. How nice that would be! But don't forget that we're studying the wrong as well as the right. So why should those studies lead you to prefer the right to the wrong? They *presume* that the right is preferable to the wrong, but can hardly claim to show that this is so.

So there are two reasons for doubting this basic premise of *The Good Place*. The first is that intellectual studies do not affect motivation, except indirectly.

The second reason is that if such studies did affect motivation, there is no reason to expect them to make us more motivated to do the right rather than to do the wrong.

But isn't everyone already more interested in doing the right than in doing the wrong? Maybe. But even if they are, this isn't enough to get them all into The Good Place. It is more selective than that, alas. What's more, if what you are doing is good, you don't have to think of it as a duty, as morally right, in order to get the credit of doing it. In fact, helping others because it is the right thing to do may be less estimable as a motivation than doing it just because they need help.

In this sense, explicitly moral motivation is not required for you to get the moral credit for your efforts. A sympathetic engagement with the concerns and needs of others should be enough to get you into The Good Place. Douglas Wynegar brought roses to his grandmother ("Book of Dougs"). There's no reason to think that he did this out of a sense of duty, believing that he ought to do it. If he just did it for her sake, out of love for her, that's the sort of thing that should get him into The

Good Place.

Kant thought otherwise (though I hope he was wrong). He thought that you don't get moral credit for your actions unless you do them out of a sense of duty. You might get some credit for actions done our of concern for others, true, since we will love you for them, but that won't be moral credit. We will love you for doing those things but morality requires more. An action gains you no moral credit unless it is done from a sense of duty. It seems to follow that getting into The Good Place requires a specifically moral motivation. And Chidi hasn't chosen a very effective way of instilling that into Eleanor.

21

You Gotta Be Bad if You Wanna Be Good

REBECCA SHEARER

Everyone wants to think they're a good person, right? That's why we've all been drawn to *The Good Place*. We're also fascinated by the idea that not everyone is as good as they think they are.

The little bit of Eleanor Shellstrop in each of us likes the idea that everybody else is not as good as they think they are. We think, "I'm pretty good, right? I'm not one of those confused people who doesn't understand what their mistakes are. I, of course, know that I'm not perfect, but I'm pretty good."

We, like Eleanor, think we at least deserve a spot in The Medium Place. We aren't out killing people or burgling houses, so we must be okay, right? If *The Good Place* is any indication, we may all have huge flaws we aren't even aware of, and any of us could find ourselves in The Bad Place. So if we're all worse than we think, how can we be better? Why is it so hard for all of us to notice our own flaws? Why is it so easy for us to forgive ourselves and our friends while the rest of the world drives us crazy?

If it's so hard to know whether we're doing good, or if we're a good person, then how can anyone have any confidence that they are living a life that will gain them entry into the Good Place? The simplest answer to this is that no one can make any progress towards being good if they aren't able to admit that they are (at least a little bit) bad.

Good, Bad, and Medium

There's a very clear dichotomy playing out in *The Good Place*: the black and white distinction between The Good Place and

The Bad Place. They are fully separate and distinct, and there is no overlap between the two. This is not a new idea by any means. Most religions, dating all the way back into ancient history, have a concept of the afterlife that includes a version of Heaven and Hell.

Just like in the show, where you end up after you die is determined by how you live on Earth. *The Good Place* reveals the problem with this idea that can't quite be addressed in real life. Namely, does any of it work?

The idea of Heaven and Hell hinges on a belief that good and bad are mutually exclusive. Depending on which religion's ideas you look at, there are a variety of ways for separating out the good from the bad but the majority settle on the belief that an individual earns their place in Heaven or Hell through individual actions. Do enough good and you find yourself in The Good Place; do enough harm, and you're stuck in The Bad Place.

The absolute difference between right and wrong, good and evil, Good Place and Bad Place, is the origin of so much polarization in our society. The idea that one side is wholly good and the other side is wholly bad is the kind of thinking that allows for racism, sexism, ageism, or any other kind of ism. Thinking in terms of two things that are mutually exclusive causes all kinds of "us" and "them" or "others" type thoughts, and it is called ethical dualism.

The dualism in *The Good Place* is a mix of both of these ideas. You earn your place by your actions, but there are actions that are worth enough negative points that it would be basically impossible to overcome the deficit they cause. But that doesn't mean that someone didn't try! The Medium Place exists because Mindy St. Claire found a fault in the dualistic system. She was pretty terrible but figured out a way to help thousands of people. She did not easily fit into a category of good and bad that was based on objective points alone. Nor would it make sense to look at only the good or only the bad that she had done. Doing so would not give a full picture of the person, and wouldn't result in a fair outcome.

This is the flaw in the dualism of The Good Place and the Bad Place that Eleanor laments from the start and Michael eventually discovers as he gets to know the humans. He learns that no one is simply the sum total of their visible actions and that anyone can surprise you. Anyone can learn, grow, and evolve. Seasons One and Two are all about whether or not learning to be good is worthwhile and possible.

We're All Like Little Chili Babies

The first hurdle that Eleanor and Chidi have to overcome in their clandestine lessons is whether or not it is even possible to learn to be good. Some say it's not, but *The Good Place* adopts a perspective more in line with Aristotle's ideas of virtue ethics. Learning to be good is no different than learning to read or learning an instrument. Neither of these are things we're born being able to do, but they are all things we are all born with the ability to learn, though some might have an easier time with a particular subject than others. Just like some people are good at math and others good at piano, some people have an easier time being good.

Some may be more empathetic as Michael proves to be, while others are more receptive to guilt and consequences, much like Chidi. Some may be oblivious to all of this, such as Jason. Not only is everyone predisposed to one leaning or the other, everyone learns from what they observe. Someone growing up with a piano being played in the background is more likely to be musically inclined, just like someone who grows up seeing kindness and good deeds are more likely to emulate those actions, whether they are understood or not.

If you have to learn to be a good person, then there's no reason why Team Cockroach can't succeed in their goal of learning to be good, even in the afterlife. Of course, just like learning to read or play an instrument, the more life you live not being good or trying to learn to be better, the harder it is to improve. It's no longer a matter of learning from scratch. It's now a matter of unlearning old ways *before* even beginning to learn new ways. This is clear from the number of times that all of our characters fail, even after they have been taught what they should do.

If We Have to Learn, How Do We Have to Start?

Being a good person is a choice, and learning to be a good person requires a decision to start changing. In order to make a significant change, the person changing has to see some benefit that will make a new skill worth the effort necessary to learn it. This usually means that the person has discovered a weakness or problem that they want to remedy. For our friends in "The Good Place," the deficiency they discover is that they are actually bad people and have been making the wrong decisions. The realization that they have been wrong is what prompted them all to change, though it happened differently for each.

This idea, like most of the ones Chidi tries to teach Eleanor, comes from an old guy. In his book *The Apology*, Plato recorded Socrates reflecting on the virtue and value of constructive self-awareness and knowing one's limitations.

> I am wiser than this man; it is likely that neither of us knows anything worthwhile, but he thinks he knows something when he does not, whereas when I don't know, neither do I think I know; so I am likely to be wiser to this small extent, that I do not think I know what I do not know. (*Apology*, lines 21–27)

Socrates, in a fancy old guru sort of way, is asserting that the key to wisdom, which would include ethical wisdom and maturity, is admitting what you do not know, and therefore admitting that you can be wrong and are likely to be wrong. Ignorance of when you are wrong is just like any other kind of ignorance. It will make it that much harder for you to gain wisdom because a big part of wisdom is the absence or overcoming of some sort of ignorance.

Now that all of that background information is out of the way, here is how each character realized how wrong they were, learned how to be good, and rejected the dualism around them.

Eleanor

Eleanor, having come to the conclusion, all on her own, that she was wrong, had an easier time adjusting. She also recognized the problems with a purely dualistic reality. As she began to understand her own shortcomings, she also began to understand her growth. As she experienced this growth, the finality of the dualism between The Bad Place and The Good Place, which did not leave room for growth, did not make much sense. So, she stops respecting the system and seeks a better solution.

Personal moral growth requires both the ability to grow as an individual by admitting you're wrong and a belief that it's possible to move out of a cultural box of being "bad." Eleanor quickly convinced herself of both, and this makes her successful in her attempts to be good while the rest of Team Cockroach struggles or remains oblivious. Though Chidi and Tahani are able to make progress as well, they have a harder time because they did not discover on their own the need to start the process. They have to be told that they are bad instead of having the self-awareness to realize it for themselves. Until they're told the truth, they can continue to live in their dualistic mindset of "good people" and "bad people." The most growth comes from being able to realize your faults without having to be told.

In Season One, we find that each breakthrough Eleanor has is a result of something going horribly wrong. Each time, she has to be prompted to see the need for a change. For instance, in Chapter 2, "Flying," Eleanor struggles to combat her selfishness. She is unable to do so until she fails and makes the selfish mistake of trying to hide trash that she was supposed to be cleaning. This, of course, starts the trash storm that injures the flyers and results in flying being banned. After Eleanor is faced with this clear consequence of her selfish actions and the way that they affect her and those around her, she is able to do a truly selfless act to correct her actions. This is her first major breakthrough, and as Chidi points out, without making a choice to stop being selfish, Eleanor could never have learned the ethical lessons that were to come.

The choices that follow all come after clear mistakes, and they enable her to arrive at the realization that her wrongdoing, even if it's a secret, can cause negative things to happen to people she cares about. She learns to respect Chidi's needs after first pushing him away and almost getting caught ("Category 55 Emergency Doomsday Crisis"). She confesses her true identity when she learns that her being a "bad person" in the wrong place could cause Michael's horrendous retirement ("The Eternal Shriek").

This action is the ultimate selfless act, proving how much she has learned by this point. She is essentially offering to substitute her life for that of someone she cares about. She is willing to be tortured for eternity in order for Michael to live. This is a fascinating issue with the dualism of the afterlife because had she done this on Earth, it would have earned her a place in The Good Place, but the way she did it in the afterlife appeared to earn her a spot in The Bad Place. As Michael admits, this illogical turn of events is what ultimately ruins his evil plan and starts to unravel the dichotomy of this version of the afterlife.

Tahani

Tahani represents a subtlety in the study of ethics that suggests our motives are just as important as our actions. Though Tahani raised tremendous amounts of money for the poor, she did not care as much about the poor as she cared about the attention she got from her efforts. Just like Eleanor, she realizes this after a failure. When she fails to throw the best party even though she knew she could not succeed, she finally realizes that all she has ever wanted was to receive attention and approval for herself ("Existential Crisis"). Once she realizes this, she is able to understand how unfulfilled this has actually made her. She is then able to look up from herself and see that the people around her give her the kind of attention that she has always desired, regardless of how popular or unpopular her party was. This helps her understand just how wrong she had been her whole life, even if she appeared to have done exponential good. Though she fails the final test by going into the room that her parents are sitting in, the fact that she is able to tell them that their unfair opinions of her don't control her anymore shows the progress she has been able to make in her short time attempting to become better. After her confrontation with her parents, she's a better person than when she went in that room ("The Burrito"). Again, this change comes from the realization that it was a mistake to go into that room and seek her parents' approval. She realizes this mistake, makes a change, and improves.

Tahani is an example of a character doubting the dualism present both on Earth and in the afterlife. She fights against that doubt as an extension of fighting against her insecurities. Even while she believes that she is in The Good Place, she's constantly trying to prove how good she is. Because of her insecurities regarding being unloved and unnoticed, she is not able to trust the system and believe that if she has made it into The Good Place, she does not have to do any work to keep her place there. Through her constant efforts to be the best of the "good people," she shows that she does not truly believe in a dualism that allows for one group of people to be irrefutably good while another group can never be good. Otherwise she would not be trying so hard to be good on Earth after being constantly told that she was never good enough. Nor would she be trying to "out-good" everyone in The Good Place to prove that her goodness should not be discredited.

Chidi

Chidi is in a unique situation because he is so aware of how to be right theoretically, that he hasn't spent enough time thinking about how it all plays out practically. He also doesn't spend quite enough time thinking about his real weaknesses and the things that hold him back, even though they are obvious to all of us watching. Chidi's predicament represents an aspect of learning to be good that anyone trying to do so needs to remember. It's not enough to know how to be good in the abstract. You also have to understand what you specifically need to change in order to meet the standards of the abstract idea of "good." Knowing stuff doesn't fix your problems unless you know how to put the problem and the solution together.

By living in a theoretical world, Chidi sees the world in black and white much more than the average person. He lives fully in the dualism of people who follow the rules vs. people who don't. This blinds him to his own faults because as we see in the episode "Rhonda, Diana, Jake, and Trent," following the rules precisely doesn't mean you are actually doing the best thing practically. The grey area requires you to consider what will have the best outcome for those around you, even if it's hard to fit it into the dualism that comes from following the rules. Chidi eventually learns this and it slowly begins to affect how he makes a decision. He had to learn to reject a specific kind of dualism before he could tackle his biggest flaw.

What about Jason?

Jason Mendoza poses a unique philosophical question. Jason seems to be so oblivious to the concepts of right and wrong that it's clear that he is not intentionally trying to do either. Things he does that are considered wrong seem essentially the same to him as those that would be considered right. Having had no real moral training, and not being the most ambitious person, Jason does not actually seem to have the type of moral compass that would allow him to actually make bad choices on purpose. He is a strange kind of neutral, seeking only to get through life.

Since he lacks the moral compass to make morally grounded decisions, he also lacks the self-awareness necessary for a fulfilling life. This is why he continues to make such reckless and dangerous choices. A rush of adrenaline can substitute for purpose. With the same motivation for good acts such as artistic performance and bad acts such as robbery, it's hard to categorize Jason as anything more specific than neutral. His motivations are not selfish, though they come across as self-satisfying.

If he is morally neutral, he also reveals a blind spot in the framework of ethical dualism. If there are only good and bad, right and wrong, what should we do with someone who is naively neutral? He's not quite the same as Mindy St. Claire, because she was both willfully good and willfully bad. Jason is willfully nothing while on Earth, and therefore hasn't quite earned himself a fair place in either The Good Place or The Bad Place prior to his death. The fact that he exists the way that he does means that the idea of total separation of The Good Place and Bad Place does not make sense, to begin with.

His growth away from neutrality is further proof that the duality of the afterlife is ineffective when it comes to determining his fate. After Jason has been exposed to ethics while in The Good Place and has learned about the kinds of actions that are considered right and wrong, as well as the consequences of those actions, he is able to understand how he has been wrong in the past. While this makes him ultimately able to learn, it also makes him more accountable for his actions. This is why he passes the balloon test believably (despite the fact that this is ultimately proven worthless) but fails the Judge's test. His ridiculousness when it comes to the test is more annoying than his past actions because as soon as he is able to understand what is right and what is wrong, every careless action appears more significant.

Do the Same Rules Apply to Demons?

What about Michael? Aristotle and Socrates discuss how a human can become better, but what about a demon? So far there are no established rules for that sort of thing. However, *The Good Place* pushes the question of who can learn to be good by asking this very question. Can Michael also learn to be good by admitting that he is wrong?

If everyone starts with the same lack of understanding of morality and ethics, why wouldn't Michael be able to learn it? If he has the capacity to learn, should it matter that he's not a human? Logically it shouldn't. If he can admit that he is wrong, he can learn what is right. If he can regret an action, he can learn to perform a better action in the future. If he can understand pain, he can understand a harmful consequence. Throughout the course of Season Two, these are precisely the things that Michael learns, some more easily than others.

Before and after joining Team Cockroach, Michael challenges the viewer's perception of the dualism between The Good Place and The Bad Place. He is a demon trying to go above and beyond at work. Not only that, but he appears to want to do something well for the sake of doing it well more than for the joy of torturing the humans. Excellence is often considered a morally good quality. So, Michael is bringing aspects of The Good Place into The Bad Place and thus contesting the validity of the separation between the two before he rejects it completely by proving that a demon can learn to be good. Additionally, Michael realizes that once he got to know the humans, he came to love them and could not continue to seek their downfall. One of the biggest problems with dualism is that it requires no interaction between the two sides because it much harder to dehumanize someone who is your friend.

Ultimately, Michael and Eleanor prove to be the most selfless. Michael sacrifices his own well-being for the sake of the others multiple times. This is often considered to be the ultimate good deed. Eleanor also does this when she tells the others she fails her test to get into The Good Place, as well as when she confesses to Michael in Season One that she does not belong in The Good Place. In fact, her whole test was whether or not she would sacrifice her friends or herself. If this is the test to get into The Good Place, it must be pretty important. Also important is the fact that the two characters performing this ultimate good deed started out as objectively the worst.

Michael and Eleanor were the worst in the beginning because they were intentionally looking out for their own interests, knowing they were harming others in doing so. However, they were also the ones who were able to realize and admit their faults on their own, without someone else telling them they were wrong. Because they admitted their wrongdoing on their own and saw the depths of consequences and pain they had caused, they made the most progress in the time they had. While they had to fight with their habits, they did not have to fight with their own way of life because they had already admitted its failure and weaknesses.

While all of Team Cockroach made progress and admitted their mistakes, Michael and Eleanor made the most progress. Eleanor was the only one to pass the Judge's test. While Michael is not put to the same test, his test is convincing the Judge to help him, and he passes. Because Michael and Eleanor were the worst, they were able to become the best in the end.

22
Professor Stomachache Needs Neurocience

ROBIN L. ZEBROWSKI

> I am in a perfect utopia and I'm getting a stomachache.
>
> —CHIDI ANAGONYE, "Flying"

> I had all the arguments, philosophical and theological, one could imagine. I had all of the moral education I could handle. I had moral ideals aplenty. I had all of the moral laws I could use, and then some. And I couldn't decide what was "right."
>
> —MARK JOHNSON, *Moral Imagination*, p. 186

For all of his thoughtfulness and rationality, Chidi Anagonye was never the one to figure out that they were really in the Bad Place. But from the beginning, Chidi should've known something was wrong in paradise. In a sense, he did know, in his gut. He felt it: every time he was faced with a tough decision, with every stomachache.

And if we'd known a bit about neuroscientist Antonio Damasio's Somatic Marker Hypothesis, perhaps we would've been in on the trick from day one, too. Because that feeling we get in our gut that tells us something is wrong is not an accident, but an important, evolved mechanism that helps us navigate tricky social and, importantly, moral situations. That gut feeling is an alarm, a call to help highlight intuitively better pathways or steer us away from danger without forcing us to deliberate through every possible option for a given action.

Stomachaches and Rationality

Chidi's stomachaches frame the entire first episode of *The Good Place*. When Eleanor first reveals that she doesn't belong, she asks Chidi to keep her secret:

199

ELEANOR: Come on, I'm just asking you to fudge a little bit. You must've told a few white lies in your life. I mean, what was your job?

CHIDI: I was a professor of ethics and moral philosophy.

ELEANOR: Motherforker!

CHIDI: I'm getting a stomachache. I'm in a perfect utopia, and I have a stomachache. ("Flying")

And the final scene in that same first episode, when she reiterates her plea for help:

ELEANOR: My soul is in your hands, soul mate. What's it gonna be?

CHIDI: Ohhhh, stomachache.

We tend to think of emotion as the thing that clouds our pure rationality. We're advised not to make big decisions when we're angry, and it has long been argued that someone who is in any way invested in some outcome cannot possibly be objective about it; that their emotionality will interfere with their ability to step back and reason objectively.

In fact, a great deal of moral theory rests on some version of this story. Take Utilitarianism, for example. (This is the view that Chidi highlights with his discussion of the Trolley Problem in "The Trolley Problem"). It's understood that each person is meant to count for exactly one unit in the moral calculation, regardless of who they are (including yourself). Utilitarianism in some ways is explicit about this: it all comes down to the math, not about how much you may love or hate someone on the track that the trolley is hurtling toward.

We know that Chidi is familiar with every ethical theory on offer, and discusses each at different times (without ever committing to one, because he's Chidi.) But there's one particular theory that plays a big role in the show: Scanlon's version of Contractualism. You may recall that in the Season One finale, "Michael's Gambit," Eleanor tears a page from a book and scribbles a note for Chidi. The book is T.M. Scanlon's *What We Owe to Each Other*, and Chidi immediately trusts her when he sees that the note is on a page of this book. Season Two also ends with a lecture by Chidi on Scanlon. Scanlon's claim, in a nutshell, is that it is in and through other people that our moral choices become both clear and correct, and this will be a guiding principle in understanding Chidi's stomachaches.

What We Owe to Each Other

The history of ethics has largely revolved around a number of dominant theories, all of which are at least briefly mentioned in Chidi's lessons.

- We see Aristotle's Virtue Ethics, where you are able to be a good person insofar as you are in the habit of performing good actions.

- We see Bentham's Utilitarianism, where the morally good action is whatever produces the largest amount of good for the largest number of people (making Jason's anecdote about framing an alligator smuggler to save a sixty-person dance troupe relevant and morally praiseworthy).

- We see Kantian Deontology, where there are certain actions (like lying) that can never be undertaken because they are always wrong, based on certain duties we have toward the rationality of others.

- And finally, we see Scanlon's Contractualism, where the morally good action is one that other people would not reasonably reject if given the chance ("Like if your Uber driver talks to you, the ride should be free," Eleanor says, understanding ("What We Owe to Each Other").

You might have noticed that all of these views (except probably contractualism) rely on a split between rationality and emotion or feeling; between body and mind. But contractualism is different. Within contractualism our relationships to other people matter in important ways. And what seems special about this bold new torture that Michael has devised? Other people.

You may have heard the saying "Hell is other people" before; in the case of *The Good Place*, that is literally true. But the surprising twist turns out to be that morality is other people, too.

Embodiment

The traditional split between reasoning and emotion is at the heart of how we should understand Chidi. You've all heard some version of it during your life: being told that you're "too emotional," or that certain conditions of your experiences make you incapable of passing broader judgment ("You're too close to be objective").

It's also a harsh critique of moral philosophy in general, in that our model moral theories tend to preserve that split between emotion and reasoning as though it were real, as though the brain does all the computing and the body just gets in the way. Whereas in reality, we are living beings who don't merely happen to have squishy meat bodies, but we *are* squishy meat bodies, and emotions are not accidental.

To understand Chidi, we ought to look to contemporary cognitive science, a discipline that takes as its goal an exploration of the nature of the mind, of thought itself. There has recently been a revolution among the disciplines of the cognitive sciences: it took a few millennia, but we have finally acknowledged that *people have bodies*. And, even more surprisingly, those bodies matter tremendously to how we think and reason about things, including moral things.

Reasoning itself is deeply dependent upon the kind of bodies we have. Consider: our concept of an argument as something that can be won or lost like a war is not universal. There are other ways of conceptualizing an argument as, for example, a dance, where the beauty and elegance of the display are what matters, not who has scored the most points in battle (I assure you, there is another essay here to be written about Dance Dance Resolution).

Philosopher Mark Johnson tells a story of when his draft number came up in 1970 as he was finishing college, and how he recognized that he was about to face the most intense moral decision of his life (pp. 185–87). He recounts the conflicting moral demands he felt pulling him both to serve his country and also to protest the grave moral mistakes of the Vietnam War.

He accepts that all his knowledge of the moral, theological, and practical laws and motivations in play made him acutely aware that he could've justified *any* decision, and so it wasn't just a case of having access to moral laws that might matter. Instead, he emphasizes that an understanding of how our minds engage with information, including and especially moral information, provides insight, criticism, and the possibility of radical moral transformation. He says, "I had all of the moral laws I could use and then some. *And I couldn't decide what was 'right'.*" Our bodies are what enable that engagement with moral information in very particular ways.

Our lived bodily experiences play an important role in how we proceed in making moral decisions. And when we think about *The Good Place*, this notion of moral imagination gives us a starting point for making sense of how Chidi could fail so terribly to be moral in his life, and how his interactions with Eleanor and the others offer the possibility of redemption: when Eleanor asks for help, *he chooses to help*.

Some Science

One researcher who has taken the body-mind split to task is neuroscientist and physician Antonio Damasio. He argues for what he has called the Somatic Marker Hypothesis, offering neural and body-based evidence that shows how our bodies, in interaction with other people, in a cultural, social, and physical environment, build up shortcuts that codify social and moral rules to help us navigate these situations without drowning in reasoning.

Damasio's claims are based on clinical work he has done with patients who have a specific kind of damage to a specific area of their brains (the ventromedial prefrontal cortex). These individuals show serious deficits in their ability to perform certain kinds of reasoning tasks, but only under particular real-life, time-pressured conditions. Kind of like Chidi, who can analyze all sorts of interesting ethical quandaries in the classroom, but collapses in the face of real moral decisions.

Think about how excited Chidi is to teach the Trolley Problem, and how unenthused he is to live it. In other words, rather than causing poor reasoning, emotional experiences appear to be vital to good reasoning. How could anyone make a decision if they weren't able to weigh their values against possible outcomes? Those emotions play a vital role in decision-making.

The Somatic Marker Hypothesis

The Somatic Marker Hypothesis is a claim built on clinical and neuroscientific evidence about social reasoning. Damasio argues that there's no such thing as pure rationality in the sense that both philosophers and psychologists have imagined, set up against emotion that allegedly clouds our best judgments. Instead, rationality itself is deeply bound up (both conceptually and neuroscientifically) with emotionality and sociality.

The Somatic Marker Hypothesis claims, in particular, that our biological systems build up a kind of "gut reaction" or a bodily alarm that, while not performing deductive reasoning for us, cuts down on the options we need to consider in a real-time decision-making scenario. Imagine playing a card game where the rules have not been explicitly explained up front, but where, after playing for a while, you have some sense that certain moves invoke a greater penalty than others and you learn to respond appropriately.

The somatic marker is the gut feeling drawing you to some moves rather than others, even before you can explain why.

And it has been built over your lifetime of social interactions with others, on top of the biological machinery that we come into the world with to process emotions. And, according to Damasio, it is deeply bound up with our social obligations and morality. And morality is itself a social obligation.

The details of how the somatic marker system works involve understanding a bit about how our bodies experience feelings and emotions. Damasio, following William James (one of the pioneers of the field of psychology), shows how we come into the world as babies equipped with a very primitive system for responding to a handful of universal emotions such as sadness, happiness, anger, and the like.

Over our lifetimes, we build a more complex system on top of this one that gives nuance to these and allows us to experience and distinguish between things like joy and glee and euphoria rather than simply "happiness." As Damasio points out, "somatic markers are thus acquired by experience, under the control of an internal preference system and under the influence of an external set of circumstances which include not only entities and events with which the organism must interact, but also social conventions and ethical rules" (*Descartes' Error*, p. 179). So it takes a rich (and healthy) culture and social world to build up healthy ethical somatic markers, which again, do not deliberate for us in moments of moral decision making, but bias us toward some set of options by cutting out many possible actions that are undesirable based on a lifetime of experiences.

Damasio offers an illustration of what reasoning looks like in the absence of somatic markers. He describes a patient of his who was tasked with choosing the date of a follow-up appointment, given two options. He says:

> For the better part of a half-hour, the patient enumerated reasons for and against each of the two dates: previous engagements, proximity to other engagements, possible meteorological conditions, virtually anything that one could reasonably think about concerning a simple date . . . he was walking us through a tiresome cost-benefit analysis, an endless outlining and fruitless comparison of options and possible consequences. It took enormous discipline to listen to all of this without pounding on the table and telling him to stop, but we finally did tell him, quietly, that he should come on the second of the alternative dates. His response was equally calm and prompt. He simply said, "That's fine." (pp. 193–94)

Don't get me wrong! I am not implying that Chidi suffers from brain damage, or even damage to his somatic marker system (we would be having a *very* different conversation about ethics in that case). He very definitely gets these (in his case, overt) alarms that are trying to steer him toward one course of action and away from another, but he fails to heed them. He just doesn't trust his own ethical system, built up over a lifetime of interaction with others, that tries to warn him via stomachaches, and instead insists that such decisions can be made purely rationally, through critical analysis and weighing of options.

Unfortunately for Chidi, we are not machines performing mindless ethical calculus in the void: we are people, with social relationships, bodies, environments, and messy ethical situations that require flexibility, social intelligence, and the ability to sometimes trust our gut. Recall that telling moment when Chidi is being tortured into believing he has to choose his own soul mate out of two options, one which seems an obvious match for him and one which makes no sense. He acknowledges his somatic marker, almost finally making an important decision, when he says, "If I had to say who I sort of immediately bonded to, on a *gut* level . . ." ("Everything Is Great! [Part 1]").

Of course, Michael stops him and implies the decision would've been wrong. We see an echo of this a few moments later when he tries to decide between red and white wine. He's told by Pevita, "Oh, deep down in your heart of hearts, you probably already know which one you want," prompting him to immediately ask Janet to show him to the bar so he can avoid the choice as presented to him and opt for the relatable choice of hard liquor instead.

Chidi is what happens when we mistakenly believe our ethics to be a matter of following strict laws rather than acknowledging the way our social experiences build up over time, becoming a literal part of our bodies and brains, that are designed over vast evolutionary timescales to help us be the social and ethical beings we are.

What Scanlon Thinks We Owe to Each Other

We know that T.M. Scanlon's work is important to Chidi (and to the show) because of how often this view shows up in contrast with the other moral views he introduces. (Season Two even closes with Eleanor being inspired by Chidi's three-hour YouTube lecture on Scanlon's book). We hear surprisingly little about the theory itself explicitly, but it seems to be the undercurrent running through every big moment, every big reveal.

Unlike deontology or utilitarianism, where there is exactly one correct answer for every moral question, Scanlon's contractualism claims that moral decisions necessarily involve negotiation with others. It comes down to other people. When Eleanor demands emancipation from her mother, she says, "That way, I'll be alone. You won't owe me anything; I won't owe you anything". In the Season One finale, Michael realizes his mistake was bringing them all together, just as in the Season Two finale he realizes he can only save them by bringing them together again. *The Good Place* is well aware that ethics relies on embodied social life.

The Afterlife

All of this tells a compelling story of how cognitive science and embodiment theories offer a lens through which we might make sense, biologically, socially, and morally, of Chidi's actions (and stomachaches). The Somatic Marker Hypothesis seems to add a piece of the puzzle that explains how real people are bound up in a complicated dance with our bodies, other people, and our cultural expectations around social and ethical actions. But what are we to make of the fact that at least Eleanor (and, one hopes, Chidi, and Tahani, and Jason) have continued to develop moral sensibilities after death? That is trickier.

Here's where moral imagination and the somatic marker hypothesis come together to begin to form an answer. John Dewey argues that "we are committed to noting that morality is a continuing process not a fixed achievement . . . in the largest sense of the word, morals is education. It is learning the meaning of what we are about and employing that meaning in action" (*Human Nature and Conduct*, p. 194).

Damasio argues that "the critical, formative set of stimuli to somatic pairings is, no doubt, acquired in childhood and adolescence. But the accrual of somatically marked stimuli ceases only when life ceases, and thus it is appropriate to describe that accrual as a process of continuous learning" (*Descartes' Error*, p. 179).

If we combine these insights from Dewey and Damasio, we can see what might be happening at the end of Season Two: Eleanor and Chidi and the others never stop having bodies when they die in this universe. They are still engaged in the process of morality and growth that cultivates a strong moral instinct and imagination, and it is their engagement with one another, their commitment to one another as social beings, as other subjects, that makes this growth possible.

So, should we trust our somatic markers? According to Damasio, yes, but only if we assume the brain is not damaged and the culture in which the mechanism has been tuned is healthy. The healthy culture is key: there cannot be wisdom in repugnance (for example) when the social world around those markers has warped or dehumanizing views. And of course, Damasio reminds us repeatedly that these biological alarms do not deliberate for us: they do not give us a right or wrong answer, but they bias us toward a narrower set of options and help exclude the obviously wrong or problematic solutions.

Unfortunately, we all live in broken cultures, but the very fact that we can recognize that fact gives us some hope that our somatic markers are continuously tuning to aim us toward the best possible future. We must keep learning and improving. Morals is education. That sinking feeling in your gut when you make a mistake is helping to recalibrate your actions so that in the future, you'll have an easier time making the right choice.

Of course, the exact opposite might be true.[1]

---

[1] This chapter was written after Season Two aired, but before Season Three had begun. The stomachache I'd been nursing between submitting this work and awaiting Season Three finally subsided as they put Chidi in an MRI machine and started tossing around references to the ventromedial prefrontal cortex.

23
Like Boxing Gloves of Sadness

Steven A. Benko

This above all: to thine own self be true,
And it must follow, as the night the day,
Thou canst not then be false to any man.
Farewell, my blessing season this in thee!

— *Hamlet*, Act 1, Scene III

Fans will be forgiven if they think that the Trolley Problem is the most important traffic-related philosophical problem in *The Good Place*. But actually the most important traffic-related event in *Good Place* history occurred long before the show started filming. Creator Mike Schur told *The A.V. Club* that the origin for the show was at a traffic light that left him pondering the social dimensions of driving:

There's an intersection that I pass through a lot where I have to turn left and it's a left-hand arrow and it's like three seconds. It's one of the really fast ones. And when it gets to be a yellow light, people turn left around you, right? And my feeling was, we have all made an agreement, a tacit agreement, that two cars are allowed to do that. And whenever there was a third car, I would be like, "I'm going to give you the benefit of the doubt because you might need to race home and see your sick kid or something. I'm going to give you the benefit of the doubt even though you're slowing us all up." When there's a fourth car, I lose my mind. I started thinking, "If someone's keeping score, that's like negative twenty points. I just know it is." Because you're saying, "My need to go left trumps everyone else's need to either go right or straight." It's selfish behavior and I think it's wrong. (Erik Adams interview)

When he gave that interview Schur had already immersed himself in the philosophy that would serve as the foundation for *The Good Place*; that is why you can hear echoes of T.M. Scanlon's social contractualism in Schur's description of the social nature of driving. If we all agree to play by the same rules, we can navigate intersections in a fair and just manner. Schur even allows for the possibility of grace, admitting that some people are going to have interests and goals that require them to break the social contract and slightly disadvantage others. Those with legitimate reasons can be forgiven while those who are acting selfishly deserve some punishment (in this life or the next).

Fans will also be forgiven if they think that *The Good Place* is about ethics. It is about ethics, but before it's about ethics, *The Good Place* is an argument against selfishness and an argument for the importance of being authentic for others. Here, authenticity is defined as being true to yourself and sincere in your relationships with other people. Relationships with other people are authentic if they allow people to realize their most authentic selves.

The authentic person has three main characteristics. First, she knows who she is and explores and performs that self via a project of self discovery and improvement. Charles Guignon writes in *On Authenticity* that becoming authentic means moving away from your "unevolved" self towards "an image of what you can become if you become all that you can be, that is, if you realize your full potential" (*On Being Authentic*, p. 4).

Second, there is a coherence between your idea of yourself and your behaviors. To be authentic is to be honest with yourself and others about who you are. Authentic people can be relied upon because they say what they mean and mean what they say. Third, the authentic person, at least in the vision constructed by Schur and the writers, lives for others.

The ethical vision of authenticity on *The Good Place* is that characters help others live their most authentic lives. As a result, being ethical is not just about doing what's right and good, but doing both so that others can be their most authentic selves. *The Good Place* shows that the social dimension of authenticity is inherently ethical: authenticity requires more than living with others. Authenticity requires living for others.

Selfish Authenticity as Narcissism

Schur labels the driver of the fourth car "selfish." But what does it mean to be selfish? To be selfish is to put the needs and interests of the self before others (who also have needs and interests). The selfishness that Schur and the writers of *The Good Place* find so problematic is not the selfishness that is taking more for yourself than you deserve; it is not possessiveness or hoarding. Schur and the writers believe that the type of behavior that earns a person an eternity in the Bad Place (being tormented by bees with teeth) is behavior that stems from an over-investment in your sense of self (that is the selfish part) with the added feature that you are unaware of, or not being honest with yourself about, the origin and intentions behind that behavior.

This type of person, and their actions, are rightly labeled "inauthentic." Where an authentic person understands and maintains a connection between their idea of themselves and their behavior, the inauthentic person is unaware of who they are or those actions that do not cohere with their professed values. This means that when each of the characters performs themselves—makes a conscious effort to publicly act out their inner thoughts and sense of self—the motivations, values, and interests they act from are not who they really are.

Each of the four humans in *The Good Place* have in common that their selfishness makes them unaware of their motivations. This leaves them unaware of the effect that their behaviors have on others and ultimately undermines everyone's pursuit of what they value and the expression of their own most authentic selves. Seeing selfishness as the cardinal sin explains why Tahani is in the Bad Place: the good she did raising $60 billion for charity was offset by the harm she did to herself and others by doing it for selfish reasons. Tahani is an example of someone who is inauthentic: she thinks she knows who she is and what her motivations are, but she does not.

Tahani's lack of self-knowledge means that she's pretending to be sincere and authentic. Instead, she's an example of a selfish inauthenticity defined as an over-investment in her own sense of self to the exclusion of those around her. Tahani is always attempting to establish her worth by association with celebrities and world leaders. She finds a way to make everything about her (or who she knows and is friends with) to cover up what she does not want to admit about herself: that she is deeply insecure and feels compelled to prove herself worthy of the attention she seeks for herself. Tahani's insecurity leads her to over-share about her relationships with famous people. Were Tahani here to confront this evaluation of her self-worth, she might become upset, like the time her "good friend Taylor" was rudely upstaged by her other friend Kanye, who was defending her "best friend, Beyoncé" ("Most Improved Player").

Eleanor, on the other hand, is selfish in more overt and obvious ways. Unlike Tahani, Eleanor is not a phony; she knows exactly who she is and when she acts out against others it's a performance of self. Eleanor's unique form of selfishness is that she can only be herself—her true self—if she isolates herself from others. Eleanor knows that she's pursuing her own interests and is unapologetic for her desires and ability to pursue her own interests as she defines them. Eleanor feels most like herself when she puts her needs and her own idea of herself ahead of the needs and interests of others, sometimes at the expense of other people, and one time at the expense of a bulldog she had agreed to take care of ("What We Owe to Each Other").

An example of Eleanor performing her image of herself in a way that alienates those around her is in "Someone Like Me as a Member," when Eleanor stands up on the lunch table and declares that she's uninterested in becoming friends with anyone: "I'm Eleanor, I'm new here, and as a blanket statement for everyone: I don't wanna be a part of whatever little group you've formed because they're all equally lame. Everybody cool? Great."

In both instances, Eleanor justifies her anti-social behavior by claiming that this is who she is. As she grows into a more complex and moral person, she maintains that honesty, but admits that she is a bad person (or, as she puts it, "a trash-bag from Arizona") who needs to be better.

Chidi's selfish inauthenticity is similar to Tahani's: he doesn't know who he is and the impact his behavior has on others, but he should know better. In "Chidi's Choice" we see that Chidi's death is preceded by his friend, Uzo, pretending it is his wedding day to see if Chidi could handle all the best man responsibilities (alas, there was no bachelor party because Chidi could not settle on a place or time). Chidi could have known that his actions were harming other people because he does not seem emotionally damaged like Tahani or Eleanor, and he's definitely smarter than Jason.

Here, being Kantian harms Chidi's interactions with others: it's a principle of Kantian ethics that you act from duty and, therefore, outcomes and consequences do not carry moral weight. As a Kantian, Chidi is so overwhelmed with the responsibility he has taken on to always do his duty that he cannot see the outcomes of his actions. Conversely, Doug

Forcett is so concerned with outcomes that he's unable or unwilling to consider whether or not he ought to perform a particular action (like reducing his carbon footprint by recycling his own urine for drinking water). Chidi needs to learn, as do the other characters, that our duties to ourselves include duties to others.

Jason is authentic: he does know who he is (even if he doesn't display a very deep understanding of self). Like Chidi his actions do have a negative impact on others, but his self-involvement obscures that from him. Jason's brief career as a DJ in "Jason Mendoza" perfectly demonstrates how selfish authenticity harms others. What Jason lacks in talent he makes up for in being the same size and weight as his EDM DJ idol Acidcat. Jason is offered the iPod and costume that will let him pretend to be Acidcat while he attends the amateur porn awards in Reno. Pretending to be someone he is not leaves Jason frustrated and disappointed:

PILLBOI: They love you, dude.

JASON: They don't love me, man. They love Acidcat. These cheers are fake. They hit my ears like boxing gloves of sadness.

PILLBOI: Whoa, that's some poetic thoughts, B.

JASON: I got to be myself. [*crowd cheering*] Attention, Jacksonville. I'm not Acidcat. I'm Mr. Music, the DJ. And this is a Mr. Music, the DJ original.

With that, Jason puts on his own music and begins to dance in front of the crowd. They quickly turn on him by booing and throwing glowsticks and drinks at him. The viewer is right to feel ambivalent about this scene: Jason's desire to be himself and perform his identity is an admirable attempt to be his authentic self. How can he be faulted for wanting to be true to himself and express that truth to others?

Of course, the exact opposite might be true. The crowd had paid to hear Acidcat and they were getting what they paid for until Jason took off the helmet and started playing his own mix. Jason's need to be his authentic self was at the expense of everyone in the audience. In that way, it was selfish. But because we value authenticity we are more likely to take Jason's side and feel bad for him. Two things need to be improved: Jason's DJ skills and a definition of authenticity that focuses on discovering or performing the self at the expense of others.

Authenticity and Other People

The criticism of selfish authenticity is that even though the person may be honest with themselves and others about who they are, they pursue their authenticity in a way that harms others. These harms can range from treating people instrumentally—that is, using another person to advance your own interests or sense of self—to frustrating other people's opportunities for self-expression so that they do not get to live out their values, priorities, or interests.

Chidi tried to live an ethical life by following Kantian dictums to their logical—or illogical—conclusions. He never realized how his moral filibustering and indecision made it impossible for others to get close to him (and is the reason why everyone hates moral philosophy professors) or what he prevented other people from doing (playing soccer at recess) while he could not make up his mind. In Kantian language, the main characters cannot treat themselves as ends because their intent is obscured from them. The result is that other people are treated instrumentally, as a means to an end.

Charles Guignon sums up this point nicely:

> If the social realm is inherently inhuman, the way to humanize it is to be sincere in our dealings with others: we need to say what we mean and mean what we say. And the best way to be sincere . . . is to follow Polonius's advice and be true to ourselves. If you are true to yourself, you cannot then be false to any man. (*On Being Authentic*, p. 35)

The characters on *The Good Place* think they are learning what they ought to do. Before they can learn what they ought to do they need to accept and understand who they are.

Though we later learn that she is a demon intent on undermining Eleanor by exploiting her insecurities, Real Eleanor (Vicky), does more to help Eleanor understand both who she is and why she is the way that she is. In ". . . Someone Like Me as a Member" Eleanor is explaining how her parents divorce when she was eight undermined her and ultimately led her to withdrawing from other people. Real Eleanor one-ups her with this tale of her upbringing:

> They put me in an empty fish tank and abandoned me at a train station in Bangladesh. Luckily, I was found and adopted by a very nice couple, the Shellstrops . . . But then they died when I was four . . . bird flu . . . Anyway, orphanage burned down, yadda yadda yadda, made my way to America, yadda yadda yadda, learned English from watching *Seinfeld*, put myself through law school, and here I am.

This scene becomes relevant later in "Michael's Gambit" when Eleanor explains to Jason why she sought legal emancipation from her parents. She ends her story by telling Jason that she now realizes how she has to take responsibility for her actions: "I've been using their crappy parenting as an excuse for my selfish behavior all my life. No more. We know what's right here. We have to go back."

Eleanor's realization that the best version of herself involves other people is an important moment in her moral growth. It happens in stages: in ". . . Someone Like Me as a Member" she admits that she may not be the type of person who belongs in the Good Place, but that is the type of person she wants to become. Eleanor's transition from selfish authenticity to something approximating an authenticity for others reaches its conclusion in the episode "Team Cockroach." When Michael tells her that Chidi always agreed to help her, Eleanor realizes that Chidi is the key to overcoming her selfishness and that it would be selfish not to stay and help the others realize their best selves:

> ELEANOR: How many times in all the reboots did I ask Chidi for help, he refused to help me and then I had to get better on my own?
>
> MICHAEL: Never. He always helped you.
>
> ELEANOR: God. Really?
>
> MICHAEL: Yep. No matter how I set it up, you found him, confessed you didn't belong, asked him for help, and he said yes. Now his agreeing to help was part of my plan. What wasn't part of my plan was it actually working. Drove me nuts. Pesky little nerd. Stuck with you and always helped you overcome your biggest problem.
>
> ELEANOR: Assuming that's my selfishness.
>
> MICHAEL: No. No, no, no. It's that you never found a haircut that framed your face properly. Yes, your selfishness.
>
> ELEANOR: I'm not that selfish.
>
> JANET: Eleanor, your cocaine and escape train are ready.

What Eleanor realizes is that Chidi's most consistent character trait, displayed over 802 reboots, is his commitment to other people. It's not just that Chidi feels obligated to keep his promises, it's that keeping his promises is who Chidi is. Put another way, Chidi is his most authentic self when he is helping others become better versions of themselves.

Ethical Authenticity

The Good Place dramatizes the transition from selfish authenticity to social authenticity by having each of the characters become better versions of themselves by realizing how their self-expressive behavior negatively impacted other people. Time and again viewers see Eleanor defending her dismissal of the sacrifices required for the common good as 'who she is'. Eleanor's moral journey is less about her learning to be a better person than her learning to accept who she is. The final episode of Season One, "Michael's Gambit," opens with Eleanor dreaming about the day of her death. Both the dialogue and the song playing in the background ("My Way" by Frank Sinatra") testify to Eleanor's need to be herself by going it alone:

> JOE: You know, I see you here all the time, and you're always mean to me, and it really hurts my feelings.
>
> ELEANOR: It does? Because the minute you're out of my line of sight, I literally forget you exist. Watch. You exist. You don't exist. You're bothering me. Don't care if you die. See?
>
> JOE: Why are you like this?
>
> ELEANOR: Excuse me? Why am I like this? You don't know me, dude. You don't know what I'm like. Look what you made me do, jag-off.

Realizing the consequences for being how they are (Heaven or Hell, eternal frozen yogurt or eternal torture) is how the show makes self-knowledge the precondition for moral behavior. *The Good Place* makes the social dimensions and demands of authenticity ethical because Schur and the writers have grounded ethics in our obligations to other people.

Eleanor's realization in "Team Cockroach" is that she needs Chidi, Tahani, Jason, Michael, Janet, in order to be the best version of herself. The message of the show is that, first, we cannot be ourselves without other people, second, that other people—rightly—limit and burden us, but that, third, we ought to embrace those burdens and limitations as they set the horizon for our own meaningful actions.

The difference between Team Cockroach and the Soul Squad is the sense of responsibility each member feels for those outside the core group. Here, Michael's moral growth is illustrative of the transition from authenticity that is preoccupied with the self to an authenticity that puts the possibility of meaningful authentic actions by others front and center. The arc of Michael's moral growth begins with his strategic alliance with Team Cockroach and culminates at the end of "Rhonda, Diana, Jake, and Trent" when he tells Eleanor that the solution to the Trolley Problem is that you sacrifice yourself to save others. In Season Three, Michael's concern for the four humans is expanded to include all humans. His belief that if the world knew about Doug Forcett then all humans could be saved from the Bad Place. It's for this reason that he becomes frustrated with how the representatives from the Good Place want to investigate if the points system has been corrupted.

Of course, the exact opposite might be true. It can be argued that Michael's obsession with helping the humans in "Snowplow" is so desperate that he has over-invested in that part of his identity. This would explain why he shuts down at the worst possible moment. Michael has found himself becoming more concerned about other people, so much so, that in the Season Three finale "Pandemonium" he becomes paralyzed by the thought that some form of him (in this case, Vicky impersonating him) could be used to harm his friends.

At this moment Michael's sense of self is tied to his being able to save his friends. Confronted with the possibility of that failure and letting them down, he shuts down. To the extent that Michael needed to be the hero is his own story, his authenticity was selfish. It is left, then, to Eleanor, to demonstrate what an other-oriented authenticity looks like. Eleanor can only give up what she values most (Chidi) because she has become someone fundamentally different from the Eleanor who sold "Dress Bitch" T-shirts. Instead of seeing the loss of Chidi as a threat to herself, she knows that the only way that she can get Chidi back is to be the best version of herself: a person who protects and promotes opportunities for others to be their most authentic selves.

At its core, authenticity is simple: consistently perform actions that cohere with your expressed moral vision of the world. The challenge of becoming authentic is finding a reason. Though we're used to thinking about authenticity as a good all by itself, the moral vision of *The Good Place* is that other people are the reason for becoming authentic. The best people that we can be are people committed to living with and for others.

While the Eleanor who would spit olive pits onto the floor of the grocery store, and then go back and grab more while people were distracted and helping someone who had just slipped and fell on an olive pit, would argue that other people—their needs, interests, and priorities—are a direct threat to her being her most authentic self, the Eleanor who opens the door at the end of "Pandemonium" and invites into "The Good Place" the lover who no longer remembers her is someone who sees her own authenticity necessarily linked to someone else's.

Here the logic becomes circular: if people are going to live an authentic life, then they have to treat others respectfully, and treating others respectfully is the precondition for living an authentic life. Without prioritizing other people our authenticity is selfish and our relationships with others is instrumental. Authenticity, then, is the first step to becoming ethical because only by caring about yourself in a way that compels care for others can you even begin to have conversations about right, wrong, and what we owe to each other.

References

Adams, Erik. 2016. Michael Schur Knows Where *The Good Place* Is Going, Thanks to *Lost*. *AV TV Club* (September 19th). <https://tv.avclub.com/michael-schur-knows-where-the-good-place-is-going-than-1798252040>.

Aquinas, Thomas. 1948. *Summa Theologica*. New York: Random House.

Arendt, Hannah. 1969. A Special Supplement: Reflections on Violence. *New York Review of Books* (Februaey 27th).

Averroës. 1996. On the Harmony of Religion and Philosophy. In Andrew B. Schoedinger, ed., *Readings in Medieval Philosophy*. New York: Oxford University Press.

Berkowitz, Joe. 2017. *The Good Place* Creator Mike Schur on Pulling Off That Huge Twist. <fastcompany.com/40472937/the-good-place-creator-mike-schur-on-pulling-off-that-huge-twist>.

Bergson, Henri. 1900. *Laughter: An Essay on the Meaning of the Comic*.

Boethius. 2010. *The Consolation of Philosophy*. New York: Norton.

Bonhoeffer, Dietrich. 2015. *Letters and Papers from Prison*. Minneapolis: Fortress Press.

Burley, Mikel. 2009. Immortality and Meaning: Reflections on the Makropulos Debate. *Philosophy* 84:330.

Chaney, Jen. 2017. *The Good Place* Creator Michael Schur on Season Two, Food Puns, and Why You Shouldn't Expect Another Finale Twist. <vulture.com/2017/09/the-good-place-michael-schur-season-2-premiere-interview.html.Contat>.

Damasio, Antonio. 1994. *Descartes' Error: Emotion, Reason, and the Human Brain*. New York: Quill/Harper Collins, 1994.

Dewey, John. 1988. Human Nature and Conduct. In Jo Ann Boydston, ed., *The Middle Works of John Dewey 1899–1924*. Carbondale: Southern Illinois University Press.

Dewey, John. 1967–1990. Three Independent Factors in Morals. In Jo Ann Boydston, ed., *The Later Works of John Dewey*. Volume 5. Carbondale: Southern Illinois University Press.

Egner, Michael. 2017. Michael Schur on *The Good Place*, Ted Danson, and Kantian Ethics. *New York Times* (January 18th) <www.nytimes.com/2017/01/18/arts/television/michael-schur-on-the-good-place-ted-danson-and-kantian-ethics.html>.

Fischer, John Martin. 1994. Why Immortality Is Not So Bad. *International Journal of Philosophical Studies* 2.

———. 2005. Free Will, Death, and Immortality: The Role of Narrative. *Philosophical Papers* 34.

Foot, Philippa. 1978. The Problem of Abortion and the Doctrine of the Double Effect. In *Virtues and Vices and Other Essays in Moral Philosophy*. Berkeley: University of California Press.

Gerassi, John. 2009. *Talking with Sartre: Conversations and Debates*. New Haven: Yale University Press.

Guignon, Charles. 2004. *On Being Authentic*. New York: Routledge.

Hobbes, Thomas. 1994. *Leviathan*. Indianapolis: Hackett.

Jackson, Frank. 1986. What Mary Didn't Know. *Journal of Philosophy* 83:5 (May).

James, William. 1975. *The Will to Believe*. Cambridge: Harvard University Press

———. 1981. *The Principles of Psychology*. Cambridge: Harvard University Press

———. 1983. *Essays in Psychology*. Cambridge: Harvard University Press

———. 1983. *Pragmatism*. Cambridge: Harvard University Press

Johnson, Mark. 1993. *Moral Imagination: Implications of Cognitive Science for Ethics*. Chicago: University of Chicago Press.

Levinas, Emmanuel. 1969. *Totality and Infinity: An Essay on Exteriority*. Translated by Alphonso Lingis. Pittsburgh: Duquesne University Press.

Lewis. C.S. 2001 [1946]. *The Great Divorce: A Dream*. New York: HarperCollins.

Loux, Michael J. 1998. *Metaphysics: A Contemporary Introduction*. New York: Routledge.

May, Todd. 2014 [2009]. *Death*. New York: Routledge.

Moltmann, Jürgen.1998. *Is There Life After Death?* Marquette University Press.

Nietzsche, Friedrich. 1974. *The Gay Science*. New York: Vintage.

———. 2009. *Human, All Too Human: A Book for free Spirits*. Amherst: Prometheus.

Patton, Laurie L., 2008. *The Bhagavad Gita*. Penguin.

Plato. 2017. *Apology*. Alpha Editions.

Rousseau, Jean-Jacques. 1984. *A Discourse on Inequality*. Harmondsworth: Penguin.

Rybalka, Michael and Michel Rybalka, eds. 1976. *Sartre on Theater.* London: Quartet Books.

Sartre, Jean-Paul. 1958. *Being and Nothingness*. London: Routledge.

———. 1989. *No Exit and Three Other Plays*. New York: Vintage.

———. 1993. *Essays in Existentialism*. New York: Citadel Press.

———. 2007. *Existentialism Is a Humanism*. New Haven: Yale University Press.

Scanlon, T.M. 2000. *What We Owe to Each Other*. Cambridge, Massachusetts: Harvard University Press.

Wierenga, Edward R. 1989. *The Nature of God.* Ithaca: Cornell University Press.

Williams, Bernard. 1973. A Critique of Utilitarianism. In J.C.C. Smart and Bernard Williams, eds., *Utilitarianism: For and Against*. Cambridge: Cambridge University Press

Wright, N.T. 2008. *Surprised by Hope: Rethinking Heaven, the Resurrection, and the Mission of the Church*. HarperOne

Zagzebski, Linda. 2008. Omnisubjectivity. In Jon Kvanvig, ed., *Oxford Studies in Philosophy of Religion*. New York: Oxford University Press.

Residents of Neighborhood 12358W

MEENU AGGARWAL is Assistant Professor in the Department of Cultural Studies, Panjab University, Chandigarh. She has three books to her credit and a manuscript ready for publication on "Mapping the Ethical Turn through the Indian Tales." She has research interests in the areas of Children's Literature, Literary Theory, Salman Rushdie, and comparisons between the French philosopher Gilles Deleuze and Indian Philosophy.

JOHN ALTMANN is an independent scholar in philosophy who works primarily in producing philosophical content for public consumption. He once published an essay titled "Why The Bad Place Does Not Exist" and it ended up costing him 2,000,000 Good Place points.

STEVEN A. BENKO is Professor of Religious and Ethical Studies at Meredith College. He received his MA and PhD from Syracuse University. He has published and presented on the intersection of comedy, ethics, and religion; posthumanism and ethics; and critical thinking pedagogy. He is a frequent presenter at meetings of the Popular Culture Association. His favorite *Good Place* frozen yogurt flavor is 'Empty Email Inbox'.

KIKI BERK is an Associate Professor of Philosophy at Southern New Hampshire University and currently holds the Papoutsy Chair in Ethics and Social Responsibility. She received her PhD in Philosophy from the VU University Amsterdam in 2010. Her current research interests include value theory (especially happiness), analytic existentialism (especially the meaning of life), and the philosophy of death. She worries that she'll lose points in the afterlife for failing to end this bio on a witty note.

KYLE BROMHALL is Professor of Philosophy at Sheridan College in Oakville, Ontario. He received his PhD from The University of Guelph in 2015. He writes mostly about how our beliefs cause us to act in certain ways, and how our actions cause us to believe certain things. He hopes his chili recipe is enough to get him into The Good Place, even if it doesn't include marshmallow peeps or peanut M&M's.

JONATHAN DANCY is Professor of Philosophy at the University of Texas at Austin. He was trained at Oxford University in England and taught at various universities in the UK before moving to Texas in 2005. He is best known for his defense of particularism in ethics; you can find an introductory account of particularism at <http://plato_stanford_edu/enties/moral-particularism/>. Jonathan is not particular, morally speaking, about his yogurt flavors; it depends on the situation.

GUUS DUINDAM is a JD/PhD Candidate in Philosophy and Law at the University of Michigan. He has published and presented on various areas of Kant's philosophy and is primarily interested in Ethics and the Philosophy of Law. His dissertation will interpret and defend Kant's moral philosophy. When in the company of utilitarians, Guus carefully avoids trolleys.

JUSTIN FETTERMAN is a writer, editor, philosopher, and stage director in southern Vermont, with degrees from Ohio Wesleyan University and Emerson College. His philosophical work focuses on language and consciousness and he has previously contributed to Popular Culture and Philosophy volumes on *Westworld*, *The X-Files*, and *The Princess Bride*. His favorite flavor of frozen yogurt is curling up with a blanket, a fresh pot of tea, and a new book.

DANIEL GROSZ is a PhD Candidate in Philosophy at the University of Oklahoma. His research interests include epistemology and philosophy of religion. His dissertation focuses on a view about epistemic justification called evidentialism. He's had his share of epistemological nightmares and sometimes creates them for others.

LACI HUBBARD-MATTIX is a philosophy instructor at Washington State University. She studies feminist theory and ethics. Her current career aspirations include convincing somebody, anybody would do really, that the phrase "and this is why nobody likes moral philosophy professors" is a blatant disregard of the truth.

KAMALPREET KAUR is a Doctoral Research Scholar in the Department of English and Cultural Studies, Panjab University, Chandigarh, India. The attractions of literature, popular culture, philosophy, and theology led her to her present research. Having lived a life in a religious milieu deeply entrenched in the Karmic theory, she is curious to know how this chapter will alter her final points tally. Although not a huge fan of Michael's little experiment, she wouldn't mind a spot in it till the time she gets the last corner piece of the cake.

DANIEL P. MALLOY teaches philosophy at Aims Community College in Greeley, Colorado. He has published numerous chapters on the intersections of philosophy and popular culture, including chapters on *Family Guy*, *Arrested Development*, *Monk*, *The Big Lebowski*, *The Princess Bride*, and Terry Pratchett's Discworld. As a moral philosophy professor, he has a stomachache.

JOEL MAYWARD is a pastor-theologian and movie critic. He is the author of *Jesus Goes to the Movies* (2015) and *Leading Up* (2012). A PhD candidate researching theology, philosophy, and cinema at the Institute for Theology, Imagination and the Arts (ITIA) at the University of St Andrews; he is an associate editor for ITIA's online journal, *Transpositions*. He is a member of the Online Film Critics Society and Inter-Film, and a Rotten Tomatoes "Tomatometer-Approved" critic, you can read Joel's film reviews and essays at <www.cinemayward.com>.

MATTHEW MONTOYA is an Adjunct Professor of Philosophy and Ethics at Old Dominion University and Tidewater Community College. His work often includes ethics, nihilism, existentialism, and digital technology. He hopes that The Good Place has rain, coffee, and angst, like all good existentialist philosophers wish for.

ANDREW PAVELICH is an Associate Professor of Philosophy at the University of Houston-Downtown, with an MA and a PhD from Tulane University. He has written on a wide range of subjects, including God's relationship to time, and cat health care ethics. He imagines that The Good Place smells like a pile of completely graded Intro Philosophy essays on a cool Saturday morning.

MAX ROMANOWSKI received his MA in Communication from Baylor University. His research interests include the sitcom, developments of new media, and science fiction in the twenty-first century. His personal Good Place probably includes lots of crossword puzzles, unlimited Coca-Cola, and being able to watch *The Sixth Sense* without already knowing the twist ending.

ELIZABETH SCHILTZ is an Associate Professor of Philosophy at the College of Wooster in Wooster, Ohio, where she teaches courses on

Ancient Greek, Comparative, and Indian Philosophy, as well as seminars on the Meaning of Life, the Philosophy of Sports, and Ontology. She will know she is in The Good Place if and when she finds herself watching *Friday Night Lights* and eating burritos with Janet and Judge Gen.

REBECCA SHEARER is an independent scholar of culture, philosophy, and literature. She writes about pop culture, and how it affects the religion, ethics, and social awareness of the world it lives in. She hopes that she has rescued enough kittens to offset the almond milk she continues to drink, despite its effect on the environment.

ZACHARY SHELDON is a doctoral student in the Department of Communication at Texas A&M University, where he is studying the intersection of religion, media ecology, and popular culture. He's a little bit worried that his love for fountain pens, admiring the movies of David Lynch, and correcting people's pronunciation are just pretentious enough to land him in The Bad Place.

JOSHUA TEPLEY is an Associate Professor of Philosophy at Saint Anselm College. He received his BA in philosophy from Bucknell University and his PhD in philosophy from the University of Notre Dame. His research focuses on the intersection between twentieth-century continental philosophy and analytic metaphysics, which will send him straight to The Bad Place when he dies. He hopes that Ted Danson will read his chapter and initiate an email correspondence with him about philosophy <jtepley@anselm.edu>.

SETH VANNATTA is Professor and Chair of the Department of Philosophy and Religious Studies at Morgan State University in Baltimore, Maryland. He's the author of *Conservatism and Pragmatism in Law, Politics, and Ethics* (2014), editor of *Chuck Klosterman and Philosophy: The Real and the Cereal* (2012), and co-editor of *The Wire and Philosophy: This America, Man* (2013). Shirtless, he resembles William Jackson Harper.

JOSEPH WESTFALL is Associate Professor of Philosophy at the University of Houston-Downtown. He is the editor of *Hannibal Lecter and Philosophy: The Heart of the Matter* (2016) and *The Continental Philosophy of Film Reader* (2018), as well as the author of numerous essays in academic journals and books. He's frequently engaged in the effort to make himself a better person, and his latest efforts have been directed at breaking the annoying habit of near-constant name-dropping (something Cardi B, the Dalai Lama, and Blake Bortles have all recommended he do).

ERIC YANG is Assistant Professor of Philosophy at Santa Clara University. He remains engaged in the most human thing of all: attempting to do something futile with a ton of unearned confidence.

ROBIN L. ZEBROWSKI is Associate Professor and Chair of Cognitive Science at Beloit College in Wisconsin, where she also teaches philosophy, psychology, and robotics. She writes on artificial intelligence, embodiment, and cyborg technologies. None of her near-death experiences have prompted a rethinking of her ways. She once got lost on an escalator.

Index